Selves and Others
Language, Identity, and Literature

Second Edition

GWEN KANE | **DEIRDRE BYRNE**

FIRST EDITION DEVELOPED BY:

Myles Holloway, Gwen Kane, Riana Roos,
Michael Titlestad, Finuala Dowling,
Alice Goodwin-Davey, Dennis Walder,
Deirdre Byrne, Karen Scherzinger,
and Becky Simmonds

OXFORD
UNIVERSITY PRESS
Southern Africa

OXFORD

UNIVERSITY PRESS

Southern Africa

Oxford University Press Southern Africa (Pty) Ltd

Vasco Boulevard, Goodwood, Cape Town, Republic of South Africa
P O Box 12119, N1 City, 7463, Cape Town, Republic of South Africa

Oxford University Press Southern Africa (Pty) Ltd is a subsidiary
of Oxford University Press, Great Clarendon Street, Oxford OX2 6DP.

The Press, a department of the University of Oxford, furthers the
University's objective of excellence in research, scholarship, and education
by publishing worldwide in

Oxford New York

Auckland Cape Town Dar es Salaam Hong Kong Karachi
Kuala Lumpur Madrid Melbourne Mexico City Nairobi
New Delhi Shanghai Taipei Toronto

With offices in

Argentina Austria Brazil Chile Czech Republic France Greece
Guatemala Hungary Italy Japan Poland Portugal Singapore South Korea
Switzerland Turkey Ukraine Vietnam

Oxford is a registered trade mark of Oxford University Press
in the UK and in certain other countries

Published in South Africa
by Oxford University Press Southern Africa (Pty) Ltd, Cape Town

Selves and Others: Language, Identity, and Literature
ISBN 978 0 19 578912 6

© Oxford University Press Southern Africa (Pty) Ltd 2006

The moral rights of the author have been asserted
Database right Oxford University Press Southern Africa (Pty) Ltd (maker)

First published 2006
Sixth impression 2011

Publishing Manager: Alida Terblanche
Commissioning Editor: Zarina Adhikari
Editorial team: Diane Awerbuck / Arthur Attwell / Helen Hacksley / Marisa
Montemarano / Lindy-Joy Dennis
Designer: Sharna Sammy
Illustrator: Marlise Keith
Permissions researcher: Felicity Chetwin
Cover image: Jeff Barbee/iafrika

Set in 10.5 pt on 13.5 pt Minion Pro by Simon van Gend
Printed and bound by ABC Press, Cape Town
115109

Contents

Introduction

SELVES AND OTHERS: LANGUAGE, IDENTITY AND LITERATURE is a book that approaches English studies from a slightly unusual angle. Written for those studying literature and writing in a first-level course at University, its purpose is to introduce ways of reading, thinking and writing that will provide solid foundations for academic work, but will also inspire the creative, thoughtful enjoyment of studying texts.

In preparing this, the second edition of *Selves and Others*, we have been guided by a desire to lay down useful pathways for exploring literary texts. The field of English studies is wide and varied. Approaches to literary study are equally varied, as the discipline embraces many different manners of formulating knowledge about, and through, literature. Open to new approaches, it seeks to understand and respond to literary texts by making connections between texts and the varied contexts within which they exist and to which they relate.

This book looks at some of these contexts, and traces some of these connections. It does this because we believe that, often, people who enter English courses (as well as those who simply want to read for other, informal purposes) are deeply uncertain about how to approach thinking about texts. Many have had few opportunities to read widely; others may have developed a sense that reading is about desperately seeking the 'deeper meaning' of books and poems. And that meaning, they have come to think, is annoyingly elusive, evading their capture unless others (such as teachers or lecturers) tell them what it is and where to find it.

This book looks for ways out of the idea that meaning is hidden. It traces a journey through other concepts, all of which involve thinking about how writers shape meaning and how those meanings relate to situations in which we assign significance to feelings, events and experiences in our lives.

Central to each step of the journey in this book is our fundamental interest in stories. Many of the ideas you will encounter here emerge from a wide range of differing academic pursuits (including sociology, psychology, linguistics and philosophy). Yet, this book is above all designed to stand alongside and to facilitate the study of writing. It puts into play knowledge from different sources, but its object is, always, to lead the reader towards the many aspects of literature – and of writing about literature – with which it engages.

How to use this book

It could be argued that literature is about human life. This being so, we should not be surprised to find that writing covers an apparently inexhaustible number of subjects in an apparently infinite number of ways. After all, each one of us is able to construct an infinite number of completely original sentences, which have never been said or written by anyone before, every day. Human life keeps changing and creating new situations, new relationships and even new variations on old situations. It follows, then, that writing is incredibly various. One of the most difficult choices that we faced when writing this book was what to put in and what to leave out. We tried to put in as much information and literature as we could, which meant that we were only seldom able to include texts in their entirety (although we could include entire short stories and poems). Instead, for the most part, we have given you extracts from literary works. But the extracts you encounter in this book have been specifically chosen because they can be read alone, without any further information from the works they represent. You need not feel obliged to read any of the works that are quoted here in their entirety, although in many cases they are drawn from books that we respect for their insights and literary qualities, and we would be very glad if you could read the whole texts. Indeed, we hope that your interest will be provoked to explore and read further than the bits that we have included here.

Selves and Others is designed to give you many different kinds of information about the strange creature called 'English studies'. In order to achieve this, we have included some boxes on your page. These boxes include all kinds of interesting facts and snippets about the English language: the correct way to use it; the way authors use it; and historical details about writers and the worlds they live in. For example, some boxes help with your own language, such as the correct grammatical use of words in sentences and essays. Others deal with the uses of words and phrases in literary works. Still others give you facts about literary personalities, or the views of critics on a particular piece of writing. Please read these boxes with attention, for, even though they do not deal with the most important aspects that you need to learn in this book, they will enrich your studies in English.

From time to time, as you read, you will see the heading EXERCISE. Each of these headings is followed by numbered questions. We have created these exercises in order to give you practice in writing about the theme of each chapter. Writing improves with practice, and the more you write, the better your writing will become. We cannot force you to do the exercises, but we encourage you very strongly to buy a student's journal (an A4 exercise book with a hard cover will do nicely) and to use it to answer the questions set in the exercises. English departments always assess your writing skills (how you write) as well as the content of your answers (what you write). Therefore, if you do the exercises in the book, you will give yourself valuable practice in answering the kinds of questions you are likely to find in University modules.

The structure of the book

Chapter One begins this journey by discussing the most immediate context in which we shape meaningful expressions: our own lives. In beginning here, we step back and think about the self, a concept which we often take for granted. The chapter shows that, in an important sense, the self is a creation. Ideas about selfhood vary between individuals and across different places, cultures and times. How individual people see themselves – and how they choose what to say about themselves – is intriguing, and forms the basis of the discussion in this chapter. Our particular concern, here, is with autobiography. The form of writing known as autobiography has a complex and interesting history of its own, but the chapter moves towards considering how particular writers present written portraits of themselves. The idea of identity is introduced, and explored in relation to autobiographical texts that develop a sense of how the writer would like his or her life to be seen by others. An important focus is the process of putting into words an idea of who one is. Therefore, the chapter closes with writing exercises that lead the reader to explore this form of writing by crafting a short autobiographical piece. This constitutes a significant aspect of our purpose in the book: namely, to develop skills in writing. An awareness of writing as a process is developed and put into practice. At the same time, the chapter offers a grounding in fundamental aspects of storytelling, which can be applied to other forms of narrative and literature.

Having investigated writing about the self (ourselves) in the form of autobiography in Chapter One, we move on to look at writing about other people. This opens up the area of character, which is surely one of the most interesting aspects of writing, and the subject of Chapter Two. Fictional characters, imagined by writers and described in language for readers to identify with (or not), come in all shapes and sizes. They are the lifeblood of literature. In all their complexity, they are modelled on real people in the sense that they reflect certain qualities that we find in the people that we meet every day; but they are not real people because they 'live' only on pages of writing and in the imaginations of readers and writers. Their destinies are already fixed by the writer who has created them; they cannot choose what to make of their lives. Nevertheless, they have a powerful attraction for readers. People like the writers of this book, who are addicted to reading stories, cannot seem to get enough of the fortunes and misfortunes of people who have never lived, but who exist between the covers of literary texts. In Chapter Two, we explore some of the ways in which language can be used to represent other people, and the kinds of characters we meet in literature. One of the important aspects of character in literature is the point of view from which the character is seen and described. Accordingly, Chapter Two also looks into the way point of view can direct the reader's attention and sympathies towards the characters in literary texts. We also encourage you to try the tricky art of describing another person in writing.

One of the most important foundations of our ideas of ourselves concerns sex and gender, the subject of Chapter Three. When we reflect on who we are, we are likely to think, near the beginning of our thoughts, 'I am a man' or 'I am a woman'. When we do this, we are thinking about gender and where we fit into a social system of values and beliefs. This system gives value to a certain kind of person – men – and withholds it from others – women. Lest you think we are exaggerating, you only have to think about society as we know it and the numbers of men and women in positions of power in families, companies and political or social institutions (schools, churches, universities and government organizations). It does not take much thought to discover that the leaders of our society are men and the followers are women. Chapter Three of this book explores some of the things that have been written about this state of affairs. You may not be surprised to find that some literary texts are not very kind to women, casting them in supporting or dependent roles as brides, wives or mothers, but very seldom in the role of heroes. Of course, though, in the vast diversity of literature, there are also texts that do portray women as strong, resilient and in leadership roles. One of the most famous examples is taken from Virginia Woolf's 1929 lecture, *A Room of One's Own*. While researching the topic of 'women and fiction', Woolf tells us that she read the sentence, 'Chloe liked Olivia' (Woolf, 2005: 613). She goes on to explore how unusual it is for women to be given centre stage and for their friendships to be treated as important in fiction. Chapter Three of this book attempts to do the impossible by giving you a tour of some of the areas of gendered existence that have been written about. These include: the condition of being male (masculinity); the condition of being female (femininity); growing up in a gendered society; women's and men's protest against a society where gender difference is constructed almost from infancy; and relations between men and women. Naturally, each of these aspects of gender in writing is much more complex than our discussion in the limited number of pages we have available here. Each of them is given as a starting point for you to explore further at your leisure, including (and especially) the literary texts themselves. Because sex, gender and their companion, sexuality, are so important in our understanding of ourselves and other people, it is also important that you try to write about these matters yourself, using the exercises at the end of this chapter.

Our focus widens in the fourth and final chapter, which considers the concept of culture as it relates to writing. In doing this, our purpose is to explore some aspects of how groups – of various sorts – are characterized and written about. Ideas from previous chapters are applied, such as point of view, and traced further in order to think about how ideas concerning others are expressed. Various forms of writing are discussed – including novels, poems, persuasive writing and science fiction – to see how culture becomes visible in texts. We reflect on different meanings of culture, and on how ideas about oneself, one's society, and the perceived identities of others emerge within writing. In the readings here, we think about the assumptions that find expression in xenophobia and racism, stigmatization and other forms of 'Othering'. We also discuss cultural difference and look at the shifting senses of imperialism and colonialism, particularly as they find expression in considerations of culture and in cultural expression. But our focus remains, as in the previous chapters, on writing and literary expression. We therefore look at several instances of writing in which culture emerges either as a concept which the writer invokes for particular reasons, or in which cultural assumptions shape the perceptions expressed. In closing, we move to further, practical considerations about writing. Since essays are the form in which knowledge of texts is most frequently asked for or examined, we look at this form of response, and suggest important guiding principles regarding how to formulate opinions and knowledge about literary texts. In this, we seek to draw together what we have explored about writing.

Writers and writing: a note on *Selves and Others*

The book has been extensively revised for this, the second edition. Originally designed and written nine years ago, it has been central to our teaching in the first-level module for which it was prepared. Enthusiastic responses from many students over the years have convinced us that the book plays a useful role in engaging students' interest in thinking about writing. We often think of it as a way to converse with our students – who study in the context of distance learning, often in far-flung regions and frequently with limited resources for further reading easily available to them. The process of sharing ideas, posing thoughts, challenging viewpoints and extending knowledge lies at the heart of tertiary study. In this book, we engage directly in that important process. We have carefully and deliberately developed, in the text, a conversational tone in order to bridge the distance between us and our readers. In this, we hope to show that ideas about literature – however complicated, unfamiliar or strange – need not be expressed in threatening terms or intricate jargon.

The book itself has emerged from endless hours of conversation. The writers of the first edition worked as a team, debating ideas and approaches in the best spirit of creative interchange. The primary writers were Myles Holloway, Gwen Kane, Riana Roos and Michael Titlestad. Others who made valuable contributions to the first edition were Deirdre Byrne and Karen Scherzinger.

In this, the second edition, the presence of all the first writers remains. However we, Gwen Kane and Deirdre Byrne, have re-shaped the previous book, in a careful process of editing, revising and reviewing. We have developed new approaches, and devised a large amount of new material which we believe brings the book up to date with current teaching needs and academic developments.

Our voices, and those of our colleagues, blend almost indistinguishably in this edition but we wish to acknowledge with full respect and gratitude all that they have given to the book, and on which we have built this second edition. In particular we acknowledge Myles Holloway, who now directs the John Povey Centre for English Studies in the University of South Africa; Riana Roos Paola, who currently lives, works and studies in Europe; and Michael Titlestad, who is now an Associate Professor at the University of the Witwatersrand.

We wish also to thank the many students in the Department of English Studies at the University of South Africa – past, present and future – for whom we have developed this book, and with whom we continue to learn.

GK & DB
2006

Selves and Others

1 Autobiography: Stories of the Self

IN THIS CHAPTER you will encounter a range of ideas about writing and the self. Our explorations begin here since autobiographical writing is itself intriguing – both to read and to create – and it offers much to consider in relation to the larger concerns and purposes of this book. As you read, think about yourself as an individual in the process of thinking about identity, and how people represent that identity to one another, especially in writing. Keep in mind that this book is an exploration of writing intended to lead you towards an understanding of factors central to stories, narrative and representation. Knowledge of this sort provides a good foundation for creating your own writing, whether for creative or academic, personal or formal purposes. We hope that the ideas you explore here will prove useful as you approach literature, and the writing tasks that are often required when you study literary texts.

ONE LANGUAGE, SELF AND MEANING

Identity and the self

What do we mean when we talk about the self? Although it may at first glance seem a fairly straightforward question, there are several ways to think about what a 'self' might be. Since our concern in this book is fundamentally with stories and representation – and with how ideas are crafted in words – the ideas about the self which interest us here are those to do with how people speak (and write) about the self, particularly in creative texts. We will think about some of these ways of understanding the self.

We tend to take the idea of the self somewhat for granted. However, this has not always been the case. Historians and philosophers argue that our contemporary concepts of the individual have arisen over time. During the Middle Ages in Europe, how an individual was seen related closely to the role or job performed within society. Scholars claim that at this time there was far less emphasis on the self as a uniquely-constituted individual than there generally is in contemporary society. However, from about the sixteenth century onwards, ideas of the self evolved rapidly and became more and more important within thinking, art and writing. In the Renaissance* and Enlightenment* periods in Europe, for example, social, cultural and political changes, and developments in knowledge, beliefs and philosophies, led to new ways of considering what it might mean to be human.

The 'I' became an increasingly important subject, with a renewed interest among many people in keeping diaries and journals. Reflecting on the experience of being human, and on the meaning of experiences, seemed important. Ideas about the meaning of the individual's place in the world took on new significance. In art, portrait painting – the depiction of an individual in forms that would speak meaningfully of his or her life – took on huge significance. Words such as 'identity' and 'consciousness' came into use to describe the awareness of being human and distinct from other human beings. In literature, forms such as the essay emerged. These originated as pieces of writing that showed a writer's views and ideas about significant matters. Essays allowed the 'I' to voice personal opinions and unique reflections on a wide variety of ordinary or unusual matters.

The development of ideas about individual identity has been, and remains, a process. Ideas about selfhood are affected by a wide range of beliefs and experiences. Religion, politics and law, for instance, all have a bearing on how one thinks about the self. Society places various values on human individuality. Indeed, some cultures are more individualistic than others, value independence, and emphasize individual desires or potential, whereas other groups or cultures might consider the characteristics and activities of the group as more important than those of each person.

* Renaissance: In European history, a time (during the 14th–16th centuries) of renewed interest in learning, art and literature, following the Medieval period.

* Enlightenment: Known also as the Age of Reason, an era in European history which saw the emergence of new ideas in various fields of inquiry, many of them still influential today, that frequently explored the relationship of human beings to their world and to one another.

Indeed, individuality is often understood in Western nations as uniqueness and independence. In other words, there is a tendency to think of individuality as what separates us from others. We often imagine that we exist as solitary beings and that other people have very little to do with making us who we are (or who we like to think we are!). But there are other ways of thinking about individuality, for instance in concepts such as 'ubuntu'. This term has been popularized in recent times, although its meaning is not fixed and it is applied to many diverse situations. In the thinking that arises from 'ubuntu', the individual is seen as part of a wider, human wholeness. An expression often used to explain the idea is the isiZulu saying, *Umuntu ngumuntu ngabantu*: 'A person is a person through other people'. The identity of an individual is sometimes seen as being dependent on other people and on the relationships between people. Who one is, then, depends on who one is in relation to one's fellow human beings. The individual is not seen as solitary but as someone whose identity cannot really be completely separated from the people among whom he or she lives. Compassion and being supportive towards others is often seen as a virtue of such an outlook.

How we think of ourselves is significant not only for our own sense of who we are but also for how we relate to other people and to the world around us. The idea we have of ourselves, our beliefs, and our own personality and characteristics enable us to identify who we are in relation to our environment and to other people. We develop a personal identity, which is the basis of most of our physical and emotional interactions with others.

Using ourselves as points of departure when viewing and acting in the world seems to be an inescapable part of being human. Whether we speak about things as unrelated as tall buildings and the future of marriage, or political trends and small changes in temperature, everything we say, think and do comes from a point in time that is ultimately unique to us as individuals. Even the way we speak marks us as different from one another. The small, often unnoticed individual differences in how we form standard speech sounds (even when we are speaking conventionally or 'correctly') are as unique to each of us as the fingerprints on our palms.

> The language of the self has a historical character and is not fixed. A new sense of self in the seventeenth century is a crucial part of what is distinctive, modern and Western. Modern people are preoccupied by personal feelings, personal wealth, personal fulfillment, personal health, personal privacy and much else 'personal' besides.
>
> Smith in Porter (ed.), 1997: 49

Human beings may look alike, act alike, and think alike, but in one way or another everyone is different from everyone else. People differ not only in physical characteristics such as weight, height, hair and skin coloring, and facial features, but in their abilities, personality, and behaviour as well. Even identical twins, who have identical heredities, are not exactly alike. They may appear initially like two peas in a pod, but on further acquaintance are seen to possess a number of dissimilarities. People are born different, and may become even more dissimilar as they grow older. These differences enable us to distinguish among people, thereby serving as a basis for differential treatment of friends, acquaintances and strangers.

... Although the body and mind of a given person operate according to the same natural principles or laws as those of other people, everyone is a unique whole in his or her own right. Consequently, the uniqueness or individuality, as well as the general biological and psychosocial principles that apply to all people, must be taken into account to obtain a clear understanding of why a person behaves in a certain way. (Aiken, 1999: 1–2)

EXERCISE 1.1

1. What makes you a human being?
2. How are you different from other people?
3. What makes you special as a person?
4. What, for you, is the most important aspect of who you are?
5. What is your 'true self'?
6. What value do you place on being an individual?
7. Does the society in which you live value individuality highly?

The capacity for self-knowledge and self-reflection, which you have just demonstrated in answering these questions, may very well be a defining characteristic of humanity, one that seems to make us different from other species. Indeed, an important aspect of being human, which you might have mentioned in your answers, is humankind's ability to use the tool of language. From infancy, we are adapted to the acquisition of language, and it is a crucially important factor in human lives, in many different ways. Language is one of the means by which we make sense of ourselves and our world. By naming, we order and distinguish between different elements within the vast array of what we see and encounter, giving meaning not only to things but also to experiences, thoughts and feelings.

Look, for example, at these photographs:

How easily can you describe the difference between the things in the photographs without words?

Words empower us to make sense of things, enabling individuals to communicate and to interact in forms understood by other people. Language is a symbolic code or system, in which symbols are used to express ideas. Sounds are used, according to complex rules of usage, to symbolize and refer to things or ideas. Broadly speaking, language is both expressive and receptive; that is, it conveys thoughts and is also a medium by which thought is comprehended or understood. Using a language means using specific sounds and signs according to a code that is accepted and understood by a particular community of users. In this book, the code we are using is the English language.

Read the following, which offers an unusual view on what we are so familiar with: language and one of its most complex functions, poetry.

The poem on the page

In its beginnings, with the dawn of human language, poetry was simply an oral art – an entertainment, a communicative and demonstrative game of skill based on socially recognized speech sounds. We have no idea how many thousands of years passed before people tried to record their word-sounds in some permanent form. The earliest writing we know of is from the thirtieth century BC, and this is only a kind of representational shorthand – its shapes symbolize external objects, not speech-sounds (the same is still true of certain scripts today – such as that used by the Chinese). Only much closer to our own times, around the ninth century BC, do we find the first use of symbols to represent the actual sounds of speech. The most ancient surviving written poem, the Odyssey of Homer, is a mere twenty-eight centuries old.

Roberts, 2000: 107

The idea that language is a complex set of codes may be one you have encountered before, or it may be new to you. Consider what you think about this concept, and what it might mean. People's depictions of themselves or of the world around them are sometimes highly complex, formal expressions. In the case of poetry, for instance, the poet may use symbols to refer to feelings and ideas. An example of a symbol would be using a dove to represent peace, or a rose to suggest love. The language of the poem is likely to be tightly structured and may be carefully planned to fit patterns of rhythm and rhyme. The writer may also have deliberately experimented with variations of sound through a certain choice of words (and by changes in word order) to communicate a specific message or suggest various ideas.

Words are used in unusual ways; here 'caught' is used in place of 'saw'.

Alliteration: words begin with the same sound.

Unusual terms are used to refer to things indirectly. Here the bird is first a servant and then the prince (dauphin) of the dawn.

I caught this morning morning's minion king-
　　dom of daylight's dauphin, dapple-dawn-drawn Falcon,
　　　　in his riding
Of the rolling level underneath him steady air,
　　　and striding
High there, how he rung upon the rein of a wimpling wing

Everyday language
This morning I saw a falcon flying over the hills and soaring high into the sky …

Poets bend the rules of grammar. Hopkins ignores usual word order here for effect.

Rhyme: lines end on similar sounds.

'The Windhover' by Gerard Manley Hopkins

But even less formal, everyday language can be complex. There are situations in which you would use a more formal type of language (and behaviour) than in other circumstances. For example, lectures, religious addresses, political speeches and job interviews all demand a particular kind of language use. Imagine that you are discussing your prospects for promotion with the chief executive of the company for which you work. Think about the following questions:

○ How would you dress for the interview?

○ How would you sit?

- Would you use the chief executive's first name?
- Why or why not?
- Would the chief executive call you by your first name?
- Why do you think so?
- Would you speak to the chief executive formally or informally?

Now think about how different the meeting would be if you were talking to a junior employee who works under you. You are now the boss. What would change? How?

Your discussion with the chief executive is likely to follow certain unspoken rules and conventions (for example, you probably won't swear or pick your nose during the discussion). You will adopt a specific tone and attitude, which will be indicated both by your choice of words and by the way in which they are delivered. You may even adopt a particular way of standing or sitting in order to show that you acknowledge the authority your boss has over you. Significantly, much of what you do and how you behave will be unconscious. You will probably take it for granted that speaking and behaving in this way are natural and normal, when in fact your behaviour and use of language might be learnt, in other words, they might be conditioned and socialized.

But before we look at some of the ways in which people represent themselves – in language and life, formally and informally – we need to look at ourselves as individuals. Let's begin by stating who we are and by locating ourselves in time and space. Start by completing the following:

NAME: I am …

DATE: I am working through this chapter on …

LOCATION: I am in / at …

In these statements you have taken a step towards representing yourself autobiographically: you have asserted an aspect of your identity. These statements have also established a particular relationship between you, me and this chapter. The reason for locating yourself in relation to this chapter and this book is straightforward: you are an active participant in the learning process. Just as you are at the centre of all your experiences, you are also the focus of this learning experience. As such, learning is not just about receiving knowledge. It is also about making that knowledge personally valuable. Your viewpoint is important. At each stage of this book, you will be actively involved in making your own learning meaningful to yourself.

Identity and writing

The next step in our thinking about the self is to see how a dictionary can help explain what an autobiography is.

> **autobiography** *noun* (*pl.* -ies) the story of a person's life, written by that person; this type of writing – compare BIOGRAPHY **autobiographical** *adj.*: an autobiographical novel (= one that contains many of the author's own experiences)

The word 'autobiography' comes from three Greek words, *autos*, which means 'self', *bios*, which means 'life', and *grapho*, which means 'I write'. Literally, then, an autobiography is the 'story of one's life written by oneself'. The word seems to have been invented in the eighteenth century, an era which saw widespread interest in personal histories and reflections about life. Most stories share certain characteristics. For instance, they tend to have a beginning, a middle and an end; they are set in specific places and times; and they are told from a particular point of view or perspective. When you write an autobiography, you are writing about yourself and your experiences from your perspective.

Writing about yourself without using your name involves using the personal pronouns 'I' and 'me'. These pronouns are among the simplest ways of referring to yourself. In other words, they are the primary means of self-reference. When you are the subject of your reference, you use the pronoun 'I'. However, when you refer to yourself as the object of your sentence, you use 'me'. The pronouns 'I' and 'me' indicate different relationships between you and the world. Let's look at some sentences which use the word 'I':

⊙ I am studying English.

⊙ This morning I spoke to my lecturer.

⊙ I hope to write the most important novel of the century.

In each of these sentences the word 'I' is the subject. As the subject, 'I' indicates the person who is performing an action or who is in a particular condition. In other words, the speaker is doing or experiencing the action or condition expressed in the sentence. The sentences themselves are expressions which describe or characterize the subject. If you had written the sentences above, they would tell your reader something about you.

Describe yourself in more detail by completing the following sentences.

I AM ...

I LIKE ...

AT THIS MOMENT I AM FEELING ...   BECAUSE ...

Individual identity and consciousness of the self are possible only through showing how we are different from other people. We cannot think or speak of being an 'I' unless we can separate the 'I' from someone who is not 'I'; in other words, unless we can think of a 'you'. The world population is approximately 5,3 billion. Every one of these 5,3 billion people has the right to use the pronoun 'I' (or the equivalent, if there is one, in their own language). Whenever we say 'I' we are explicitly separating ourselves from all other people. This may seem obvious, but it is a crucial point. Being aware of the concept 'I' is the first step towards establishing an individual identity.

Another way in which we separate ourselves from all the others who use the word 'I' is through the use of proper nouns or specific names.

The proper nouns in each person's name set individuals apart from one another. They distinguish them from people who have different names. They might also reveal certain aspects of information about the individual, such as gender and cultural background The information given by names is partial, and often misleading. Names are far from being full descriptions of a person. They give very little information about one's body. Similarly, a name says nothing about one's psychological identity, for it usually reveals nothing about the individual's feelings, ideas, beliefs and experiences. There is no necessary connection between a name and the physical or psychological identity of the individual who bears it.

The poet E. E. Cummings often used lower-case letters where we would usually use capitals. He especially preferred using 'i' instead of 'I' to make his readers think about the significance we attach to ourselves. He even spelled his name with lower-case letters. This is one of his poems:

who are you,little i

(five or six years old)
peering from some high

window;at the gold

of november sunset

(and feeling:that if day
has to become night

this is a beautiful way)

Cummings, 1964: 52

EXERCISE 1.2

1. Do you speak any language other than English?
2. If you do, does that language have the same kinds of pronouns as English does?
3. If the other language you speak does not have the same kinds of pronouns as English, how do the pronouns differ?

If you had been given a different name when you were born from the one you were given, how might it have influenced your life?

NAMING: NOUNS AND PRONOUNS

A word is a sign: it usually conveys meaning and can be interpreted. Whether this sign is made up of spoken noises or of written marks, the relationship between the sign and what it indicates is a human invention. Take, for example, a sign which we all know well: a red traffic light. There is no particular reason why a red light should mean 'stop' and a green light 'go'. They have these specific meanings only because a (large) group of people has chosen these signs to function in this way. We could change the signs and the meanings if we could persuade enough people to follow a new code.

Similarly, there is no magical connection between the word 'frog', for example, and the creature we call a frog. Another set of sounds or combinations of symbols could have been used just as well to indicate frog. Indeed, if you speak another language you will know this to be true. 'Frog' signifies frog because a linguistic community* 'agrees' to attach the particular meaning to a particular sound pattern. In other words, meaning is formed socially, and is not something that occurs automatically.

* linguistic community: a group of speakers of that language

If language is made socially, and if we as people establish our individual identities mainly through language – by saying 'I' or by giving ourselves specific names – to what extent are we 'made' by language and society? Is there something that can be called an essential, concrete self – an essence of individuality? Does each person have an 'inborn' identity that is not changed or shaped by their environment? Or are our identities, our positions as individual people in a certain sense produced or made up by other people or by society? These are tricky questions to answer. Their purpose, however, is simply to lead you to think about how the self might be understood. As you consider them, read the following autobiographical poem, which is about representing and reflecting on an individual life.

In the company of words
Gcina Mhlophe

It is truly marvellous, wonderful and comforting
To know that I have eyes to read
Hands that can write
And an enormous love for words
I am lucky to be speaking a few extremely beautiful languages
For I love words – language's ancestor
When I'm happy, words define my happiness
When I'm sad and confused
Words turn into clay and allow me
To mould and remould my muddled-up thoughts
Till I find inner peace in my soul

Had I to choose between weeping and reading
I'd most definitely choose reading
A good book
For I have proof, for aches and tensions
It works!
Countless times I've turned my back on pain
And found friends in characters from far-off lands
Countless times I've defied anger
And caressed my nerves with an old comic book
Countless nights I've triumphed over insomnia
And had a heart to heart talk with my pen and paper

I come to my desk in the dead of the night
I sit, without a clue as to how I wish to start
But then, before I know it, words of all types and sizes
Come rushing into my fingertips
As I feel my whole body smile
I welcome them, every single one of them
Like the good old friends they are
When they start dancing in large circles around me
Throwing teasing wordy circles on my walls
I am convinced that I was not born to be bored
For how indeed can boredom even begin to penetrate

My timeless word circle
Now you see why I'm so content
In the company of words

In this poem, the importance of language is expressed in terms that show how it has become, for the speaker, integral to how she thinks about herself. It is part, indeed, of her sense of self, her identity. The poet, Gcina Mhlophe, has this to say about her piece:

The curious thing for me, is that words have always been an important part of my life. Long before I set foot in school. Long before I ever imagined that I could even attempt to write. It was my grandmother who was the source of my love affair with words. She told me so many stories, sang me songs that taught my imagination to fly very early in my life. That was lucky for me!

The poem … is really the story of who I am, told in the shortest possible way. When I perform it to a live audience, it feels like I am introducing myself as honestly as can be. (Mhlophe, 2002: vii–viii)

EXERCISE 1.3

1. Having read this poem and the poet's remarks about its significance to her, consider whether there are events, people and stories in your own life which might have a similar importance for you. If there are, think about the stories – and those who told them – that have inspired you.
2. Write a short description (one or two paragraphs) about any situation you regard as inspiring you to be who you are.

TWO REPRESENTING THE SELF

Because a sense of personal identity affects our interactions with others, it is not surprising that literature and film often deal with the implications of human development and transformation. For instance, when the little girl named Alice in Lewis Carroll's famous children's story, *Alice's Adventures in Wonderland*, falls down a rabbit hole, and then drinks from a bottle labelled 'Drink Me', strange things happen. She changes size rapidly and oddly. She meets very unusual creatures. All of this leaves her confused. But things get worse when she comes across an odd caterpillar, who is sitting on a mushroom and smoking a pipe called a hookah.

he Caterpillar and Alice looked at each other for some time in silence: at last the Caterpillar took the hookah out of its mouth, and addressed her in a languid, sleepy voice.

'Who are *you*?' said the Caterpillar.

This was not an encouraging opening for a conversation. Alice replied, rather shyly, 'I – I hardly know, sir, just at present – at least I know who I *was* when I got up this morning, but I think I must have been changed several times since then.'

'What do you mean by that?' said the Caterpillar sternly. 'Explain yourself!'

'I can't explain *myself*, I'm afraid, sir,' said Alice, 'because I'm not myself, you see.'

'I don't see,' said the Caterpillar.

'I'm afraid I can't put it more clearly,' Alice replied very politely, 'for I can't understand it myself to begin with; and being so many different sizes in a day is very confusing.'

'It isn't,' said the Caterpillar.

'Well, perhaps you haven't found it so yet,' said Alice; 'but when you have to turn into a chrysalis* – you will some day, you know – and then after that into a butterfly, I should think you'll feel it a little queer, won't you?'

'Not a bit,' said the Caterpillar.

'Well, perhaps your feelings may be different,' said Alice; 'all I know is, it would feel very queer to *me*.'

'You!' said the Caterpillar contemptuously. 'Who are *you*?'

Carroll, 1998: 40–41

* contemptuous: expressing a feeling that someone or something is unimportant or worthless

* metamorphosis: a change from one form to another, especially that undergone by insects as part of their life cycle

* chrysalis: the form of an insect, such as a moth, when encased in a hard shell during the process of metamorphosis

How much can our bodies change, without changing us in some deep, inner way?

When the Caterpillar first asks Alice 'Who are *you*?' he simply wants her to identify herself. The second time, though, the question 'Who are *you*?' has an added barb. The way he asks it suggests that the Caterpillar has no respect for Alice and places no value on her understanding of change. The contemptuous* tone tells us that the Caterpillar's question is a way of dismissing and devaluing Alice. For Alice, the recent rapid changes in her body, caused by drinking a strange, magical drink, have caused her to doubt her own identity. She has become unfamiliar with her own appearance. The Caterpillar, on the other hand, denies that change should be a source of confusion. He knows that he will undergo a process of metamorphosis* as an integral part of his life-cycle. Changing from a caterpillar into a chrysalis* and then into a butterfly is normal for him.

In Franz Kafka's short novel *The Metamorphosis* (1916) a young man wakes up one morning to find himself transformed into a giant beetle-like insect. The narrator stresses that this is not a dream and the story explores how this change wreaks havoc on the young man's identity. Here is the first paragraph of the story. Read it imagining that this has happened to you.

arch-shaped ribs, to whose dome the cover, about to slide off completely, could barely cling. His many legs, pitifully thin compared with the size of the rest of him, were waving helplessly before his eyes.

Kafka, 1981:1

When Gregor Samsa woke up one morning from unsettling dreams, he found himself changed in his bed into a monstrous vermin. He was lying on his back as hard as armor plate, and when he lifted his head a little, he saw his vaulted brown belly, sectioned by

Samsa knows who he is even though his body is unrecognizable. Other people, however, no longer relate to him in the same way as they did before. His experience is used as a symbol for human alienation in the modern age.

If you have a photograph of yourself taken ten or twenty years ago, look at it and then look into the mirror.

- ☺ How have you changed?
- ☺ What caused these changes?
- ☺ Have you changed psychologically as well as physically? If so, describe the changes that have occurred.
- ☺ Has any part of you remained constant? If so, which part? Why?
- ☺ Where do you think the greatest change in the identity of a person occurs over the years?

Personality

Although experts differ in their definition and understanding of personality, the term is generally used to describe deeply ingrained, relatively persistent patterns of thought, feeling and behaviour in a person. Like physical characteristics, personality also refers to what is unique about a particular person. In other words, characteristics (also known as traits) or combinations of characteristics (such as kindness, intelligence, aggression, competitiveness or reliability) are applied to individuals to distinguish them from other people. Used like this, the term personality covers many aspects of individuality.

The most obvious aspects are what is sometimes called 'temperament' – a person's typical emotional and behavioural reactions. Thus we might speak of someone as 'shy', 'outgoing' or 'quick-tempered' to describe the ways they behave or the way others perceive them. Some aspects of personality are less obvious because they are not necessarily visible to casual observers. These aspects of personality include abilities, beliefs, attitudes, values and motives. Intelligence, religious faith and personal attitudes concerning appropriate or inappropriate behaviour fall into this category. Unlike physical characteristics which are readily visible, personality is something that can be hidden. What people observe in others, then, are outward expressions of personality in the form of particular types of behaviour. We cannot always see the reasons why a person acts or reacts in a certain way. Yet, together with naming and physical description, personality is a means of categorizing and differentiating people.

The influence of genetics on personality is controversial and continues to be the focus of scientific research. Many would argue we are genetically predisposed (or 'programmed') to certain behavioural patterns, but that social, cultural and environmental influences also have a significant effect on personality. Schooling, for instance, influences a person's ability to perform certain tasks. Education also shapes people's attitudes to events and issues. Our concern, though, is not with the origins of personality. We are interested in how we think of ourselves as personalities, and with the ways we show or express our personalities to other people in action and writing.

Police squads investigating serial murder cases employ specialist psychologists to draw up psychological and social profiles of the killer or killers. By studying clues left at crime scenes and especially patterns of behaviour that emerge from each incident, these experts are able to draw up detailed profiles that assist in identifying suspects.

This quiz is not a serious, psychological evaluation. It is intended to be an enjoyable way for you to explore your personality.

PUTTING OURSELVES TO THE TEST ... FOR FUN!

What follows is a short personality test similar to those that often appear in magazines. We have included it as an opportunity for you to think about some of the ways in which personal identity is understood and represented. Various statements appear in the first column. For each statement, tick one box – Always, Usually, Sometimes or Never – that you think applies to you.

	Always	Usually	Sometimes	Never
1. I enjoy spending time with friends.				
2. I am very talkative and full of energy.				
3. I enjoy talking about myself.				
4. I think of myself as a relaxed person.				
5. I encourage other people to talk about themselves.				
6. I care about other people's feelings.				
7. I often criticize and judge other people.				

	Always	Usually	Sometimes	Never
8. I worry about things.				
9. I am calm in difficult situations.				
10. I enjoy working with other people as part of a group.				
11. I am quiet in a group and do not like to start a conversation.				
12. Other people think that I am a nervous person.				
13. Other people think I am fun to be with.				
14. I treat people rudely, especially if I don't like them.				
15. I am tolerant of other people's points of view.				
16. It is important to me that I should be well-liked.				
17. It is important to me that my appearance should make a good impression on others.				
18. I expect other people to agree with me and follow my advice.				
19. I am happy to help someone even if it causes me difficulty.				
20. I am honest with people even if I feel my opinions might be hurtful to them.				

What do you think your answers to this quiz reveal about your personality?

Here are descriptions of two very different personality types. Your answers to the first five statements above could place you closer to one category or the other. Where do you belong?

If you answered 'Never' to statements 1 to 5 you are an introvert:
You love spending time on your own. You find other people's company demanding and exhausting. You do not like socializing. You are inward-looking. Your idea of fun is being alone at home with a book for company. You really don't like parties and working in groups. Other people see you as being quiet, shy or reserved.

If you answered 'Always' to statements 1 to 5 you are an extrovert:
You are energized by spending time with other people. You love socializing, talking and being around others. You enjoy parties and social situations. You are talkative and need to communicate with the world around you. Your worst nightmare is being forced to spend much time alone. Your life is directed outwards: towards things and people around you.

EXERCISE 1.4

1. Would you say that either of these types accurately describes your personality?
2. Write down the characteristics that you think would be a more truthful representation of yourself. Think of the way that you behave in different situations; for instance, when you are by yourself, when you are with close friends and when you are in the company of strangers.
3. Do you feel and behave in exactly the same way in all these situations?
4. To what extent can you control or adapt your responses according to the situation in which you find yourself?

Generally, this kind of personality quiz works on a series of assumptions about people and how they view themselves. Most tests are not entirely accurate. At best, they can be used as starting points for thinking about aspects of your personality.

Personality tests tend to assume that people have a fixed and unchangeable personality. There are two problems with the concept of fixed personality types. The first is that a fixed personality type allows no room for development and change.

If one assumes that personalities are fixed from birth, then the personality of the child will become the personality of the adult. A fixed personality would not develop or alter with experience. The second problem is that the idea of a fixed personality does not take into account that people can often control what parts of their personality they choose to reveal in different circumstances.

If people do have some degree of control over their personality and how they show it, who and what we are is not just formed socially; our identity is also made by us, deliberately, by our own choice. (Of course, what we consider deliberate behaviour may itself be deeply socialized.) Finally, changes in the personality that we project suggests that who we are, to some extent, depends on how we present ourselves and how our presentations are viewed by other people.

THREE READING THE SELF

In this section, we will explore some of the purposes for which autobiography is used, and consider how the self is represented in such life writing.

Journeys of the self

The first writing you will encounter foregrounds a concept that occurs frequently in life writing: the idea of a journey. We have spoken, earlier in this chapter, of the fact that the self is in its own particular way a concept which has evolved, has travelled over time in a long process of thinking and re-thinking. It is not a static concept, nor one about which all people agree. In autobiographical writing, the idea of 'journey' is similarly important. It points to a sense of the self as changing, as moving through time and, very often, through different spaces or places. A sense of the individual as one who changes, moves and grows is important for life writing. Consider this as you read the extracts below, and be alert to how the concept of the journey is used by the author.

In the introduction to his memoir, the writer Adam Levin makes the following confession about an important period of his life:

I didn't know. With the generation before me already tragically lost, my own generation had buried its head in the sand. I read daily about Aids in the newspaper, I knew the extent of its spread and had some grasp on the politics of the crusade to manage it. And yet, despite being gay, thirty years old, and a resident of the country with the highest infection rate in the world, I was completely ignorant about the realities of this disease. I was bang in the centre of the Aids pandemic, and yet, if you'd asked me what Aids was really about on a daily basis, I wouldn't have known what to say. I had no sense of the experience of the progression of this disease. I was clueless as to the degree of pain and anxiety involved. Like so many of us, I was the victim of the secrecy and ignorance surrounding what has become the world's most pressing concern.

Often, while writing this memoir, I lost faith in its process. I wrestled with the egotism of writing sixty thousand words about myself, and I doubted its value. Many times, I abandoned the whole idea. But as unfortunate as the story of my suffering might be, the circumstances surrounding it have been extremely fortunate. The angels of care and affirmation have always been close at hand, and whatever doubts I still might have as to the significance of this manuscript, if there is any way I can express the depth of my gratitude for that support, it is by telling a story. And this is it.

When I first got sick, I looked for books that might prepare me for the journey ahead of me. I looked in the bookstores, I surfed Amazon, and yet I found nothing. This was no accident. In its own insidious way, the conspiracy to keep this disease walled in silence has triumphed. If this memoir helps to chip away at a single brick of that immense wall of silence, I will be greatly honoured. If my story can be of any solace or assistance to anyone battling the rigours of this disease, or to any of the people close to him or her, it will be my privilege to offer that. But this is not intended as a handbook for people with Aids: on a deeper, more intimate level, it is simply a story about lostness and love and life and how rarely it fails to surprise you.

At times I also struggled with the fears of personal exposure and worthlessness surrounding the publication of this book. But when I finally accepted that this unextraordinary story was possibly one worth sharing, finishing this book was one of the easiest things I'd ever done ... .

In the end, there is nothing simpler than telling a story when it is yours alone.

Levin, 2005: ix–xi

Levin goes on to discuss the difficulty of choosing a title for his autobiographical account:

 o I lay back and thought. I reflected on all the miraculous but exhausting African journeys of wonder I had chronicled in my first book *The Wonder Safaris*. I thought of that beautifully lyrical Swahili word for journey: 'safari'. And I realized that the hardest, most frightening safari of all had been the one that had not required a single step. It had been the journey in my head and through every aching nerve in my body.

The journey inside.

I searched for a word that might capture that whole ghastly, life-changing experience for myself. But I found nothing, and finally I surrendered to the fact that there wasn't a single word in the dictionary that resonated something so uniquely personal for me. And then my mischievous little brain finally figured out that if no word existed, I would simply have to make one up. And then, from somewhere deep in my subconscious, it came to me.

Somehow the curious ring of such a strange, invented word seemed perfectly appropriate for the scary unfamiliarity of the journey I had scribbled down. Over and over I sung the word to myself, until I learnt to pronounce it not as two words, 'Aids Safari', but rather with all the faith-drenched, rhythmic resonance of the phrase that rung out from the thick, marijuana-puffin' haze of my adolescence: 'Jah Rastafari!' I loved the way the sound concluded itself so triumphantly on the letter 'I', which was, after all, where it had all begun, and where it all ultimately ended up at. At I.

And so there you have it. As simply as a complicated lad like m'self could possibly put it: AIDSAFARI! A Memoir of My Journey with Aids.

Levin, 2005: xii–xiii

EXERCISE 1.5

There are several occasions within these two extracts from *Aidsafari* during which the writer expresses a sense of doubt.
1. What makes him feel so doubtful and how does he overcome doubt?
2. What ideas does the writer seem to have about writing? Why does he write?
3. Are there several purposes for this memoir, and what might they be?
4. What ideas or expressions do you find interesting in this writing?
5. How does the idea of journeying appear, and what does it mean here?
6. What impression does the writing give you about the writer?
7. What emotions does he refer to directly?
8. What other emotions are spoken of indirectly, or suggested by what is said here, and how it is said?

One aspect of the *Aidsafari* extracts worth thinking about is the use of figurative language to write the story of the self. Autobiography is not a dry, factual account of the events in the life of an individual. It is not a report, a profile, nor a police Identikit. Certainly, autobiographies do include factual information, and they describe events or experiences. But the form in which they do this is frequently creative and imaginative. Consider, for example, how Levin writes about the Aids pandemic:

In its own insidious way, the conspiracy to keep this disease walled in silence has triumphed. If this memoir helps to chip away at a single brick of that immense wall of silence, I will be greatly honoured. (Levin, 2005: xi)

Here, the experience of not finding adequate information about the disease with which he is living is expressed as meeting an 'immense wall of silence'. In our discussions earlier in this chapter, we noted that language is a symbolic system, a code which uses symbols to convey meaning. However, language is used both literally and figuratively. A literal meaning is the standard definition of a word, as it would appear in the dictionary. On the other hand, figurative language suggests other, less conventional meanings. It prompts one to imagine a number of mental images. Here, language is used to craft or shape ideas, extending the direct meaning towards further possibilities of significance. Quite simply, it is a way of saying more, by suggesting an array of further ways of seeing what is being directly described.

EXERCISE 1.6

1. Give some examples of how *Aidsafari* uses figurative language to comment on the author's experience of living with HIV and Aids.
2. What do you see, feel and imagine when you read each one?

Autobiographical writing is at times the creation of more than one voice. We tend to think of it as the voice of the solitary individual, the 'speaking I'. Yet it can be a collaborative form. In *Long Life ... Positive HIV Stories*, the writings of several women and men associated with the Cape Town Bambanani Women's Group are woven together to form a text that speaks of their separate lives. Art, dialogue, letters, photography and autobiographical writing together express the feelings and thoughts of members of the group. These are some of their words:

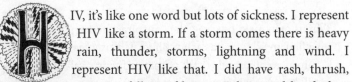

HIV, it's like one word but lots of sickness. I represent HIV like a storm. If a storm comes there is heavy rain, thunder, storms, lightning and wind. I represent HIV like that. I did have rash, thrush, falling of hair, coughing and headaches. … About the pot symbol on my painting. I like to cook. In that pot is the food, the veg, the green, me and healthy food. I want to dish for everyone … And fire represents me. The way I like people and I have that warmth in my body. My symbol of power I put in my head because the first thing I must do is think, before I do anything.

It's all over my body. It started to itch when I was eating the TB tablets and I told the nurses, these tablets are making my body itch. They said it was nothing. I finished the pills … It was terrible and I felt like going underground. When I looked at myself in the mirror I felt it's not me …

When I look at this picture I can see what I am, and what I'm not, and what I believe in, and what I don't. I can see that my finger is missing and that I have HIV, but also that I'm strong, very strong. … This picture of mine makes me happy and very strong, more than before. … I have power over this virus like when I'm working I stop thinking about it. That is why I put the symbol of mango in my brain. The mango got all those little things, fine things, like hairs that go in and stick out. My brain is just like a mango, I think a lot about other people's problems.

Morgan, Jonathan and the Bambanani Women's Group. 2005: 41, 56, 67–68

EXERCISE 1.7

1. As you read these descriptions, what do you notice about the attitudes expressed by the three writers?
2. How do they speak about living with HIV and Aids, and what images do they use?

Representation

The idea of representation is emphasized by the Bambanani writers. This is an important concept in thinking about any text, as it refers to the way in which writing shows, describes or symbolizes things. Representation, in the context of writing or art, means the way in which something is depicted or shown by the text or artwork. As you read autobiographical writing, ask yourself how the writers represent their lives. Likewise, when you read other kinds of writing (for example novels, poems, plays, advertisements, newspapers, or magazines), consider how the texts represent what they are talking about.

Representations of life experiences serve various purposes. Many people argue for the importance of this in relation to health and illness. Indeed, David Morris, an academic working in the field of medicine and literature, claims that human beings easily fall ill. He suggests that recovery is not simply a scientific or medical activity but that the ideas society has about disease are equally important in understanding and overcoming ill-health. He writes:

> illnesses, like texts, are amenable to various traditions of reading, both medical and non-medical, so that a Native American shaman will interpret them differently from a Western physician. Yet, illness is unique among social texts. It touches each of us, in our flesh, as we fall under the spell of internal events. Illness to is often thrust upon us, capable of interrupting every plan. It is a text we cannot put down or put off. (Morris, 1998: 6)

EXERCISE 1.8

1. What do you think about these ideas?
2. If you were asked to write about any illness that you have experienced, how do you think you might represent it?
3. Do you think that writing about the experience of sickness serves a purpose?

Lives in words

Let's continue our line of thought concerning autobiography by reflecting on a text which represents the life of one of the most revered figures of recent times. It also invokes the idea of journey and travel in its very title, *Long Walk to Freedom*, and is the world-famous autobiography of Nelson Mandela.

EXERCISE 1.9

Public figures are usually seen in a huge variety of ways, depending on what is known about them and how people regard them.

1. Write down five words that you think best describe how most people see Nelson Mandela.
2. Now write down five words which describe how you personally see him.
3. Do these two sets of words have anything in common? For instance, do they have positive or negative connotations? Do they deal with Mandela's career as a politician or with his private life?

Our sense of the person, Nelson Mandela, is determined by those aspects of his identity that we choose to focus on. Our sense of public figures is deeply affected by what we learn of them from the media, from what other people tell us, and from what we decide to believe. Similarly, it is affected by what such figures choose to reveal of themselves, and the images which they seek to project. Such choices have an enormous impact on our perceptions of identity.

Look at the Contents page of *Long Walk to Freedom*. The table of contents of a book provides valuable information about what we can expect as we read on.

CONTENTS

EXERCISE 1.10

1. Which chapters do you think deal with Mandela's personal life?
2. Which ones seem to deal with political activities and experiences?
3. What aspects do you think this autobiography will emphasize?
4. Why do you think the autobiography emphasizes the things it does?
5. Plan the Contents page of your own autobiography. What would each of your chapters be called?

The following excerpt from Nelson Mandela's life story is set in the 1940s, when he is twenty-three years old. He is living in Johannesburg and finds accommodation in the backyard room of a house belonging to a Mr Xhoma in Alexandra.

The Xhoma family had five daughters, each of them lovely, but the loveliest of all was named Didi. Didi was about my age and spent most of the week working as a domestic worker in a white suburb of Johannesburg. When I first moved to the house, I saw her only seldom and fleetingly. But later, when I made her acquaintance properly, I also fell in love with her. But Didi barely took any notice of me, and what she did notice was the fact that I owned only one patched-up suit and a single shirt, and that I did not present a figure much different from a tramp.

Every weekend Didi returned to Alexandra. She was brought home by a young man whom I assumed was her boyfriend, a flashy, well-to-do fellow who had a car, something that was most unusual. He wore expensive, double-breasted American suits and wide-brimmed hats, and paid a great deal of attention to his appearance. He must have been a gangster of some sort, but I cannot be sure. He would stand outside in the yard and put his hands in his waistcoat and look altogether superior. He greeted me politely, but I could see that he did not regard me as much competition.

I yearned to tell Didi I loved her, but I was afraid that my advances would be unwanted. I was hardly a Don Juan. Awkward and hesitant around girls, I did not know or understand the romantic games that others seemed to play effortlessly. On weekends, Didi's mother would sometimes ask her to bring out a plate of food to me. Didi would arrive on my doorstep with the plate and I could tell that she simply wanted to perform her errand as quickly as possible, but I would do my best to delay her. I would query her opinion on things, all sorts of questions. 'Now, what standard did you attain in school?' I would say. Standard five, she replied. 'Ah, well, you must go back to school,' I said. 'You are about the same age as I am,' I continued, 'and there is nothing wrong with returning to school at this age. Otherwise you will regret it when you are old. You must think seriously about your future. It is nice for you now because you are young and beautiful and have many admirers, but you need to have an independent profession.'

I realize that these are not the most romantic words that have ever been uttered by a young man to a young woman with whom he was in love, but I did not know what else to talk to her about. She listened seriously, but I could tell that she was not interested in me, that in fact she felt a bit superior to me.

I wanted to propose to her but I was unwilling to do so unless I was certain she would say yes. Although I loved her, I did not want to give her the satisfaction of rejecting me. I kept up my pursuit of her, but I was timid and hesitant. In love, unlike politics, caution is not usually a virtue. I was neither confident enough to think that I might succeed nor secure enough to bear the sense of failure if I did not.

I stayed at that house for about a year, and in the end, I uttered nothing about my feelings.

Mandela, 1994: 69–71

EXERCISE 1.11

1. Have you ever been in a situation similar to the one described in the passage? If you have, how did you react? Were you able to show your feelings?

2. Look up the following words in a dictionary. Write down their definitions and tick the words you would use to describe Mandela at this time. Add any other words that you think would be good descriptions of his actions.

   sophisticated, intelligent, naïve, insecure, articulate, proud, experienced, confident, awkward, romantic, foolish, suave, gregarious, principled

The following extract is from Nelson Mandela's account of his speech to the court during the famous Rivonia Treason Trial.

rose and faced the courtroom and read slowly.

I am the first accused.

I hold a Bachelor's degree in Arts, and practised as an attorney in Johannesburg for a number of years in partnership with Mr Oliver Tambo. I am a convicted prisoner, serving five years for leaving the country without a permit and for inciting people to go on strike at the end of May 1961.

I admit immediately that I was one of the persons who helped to form Umkhonto we Sizwe and that I played a prominent role in its affairs until I was arrested in August 1962.

At the outset, I want to say that the suggestion made by the state in its opening that the struggle in South Africa is under the influence of foreigners or Communists is wholly incorrect. I have done whatever I did, both as an individual and as a leader of my people, because of my experience in South Africa, and my own proudly felt African background, and not because of what any outsider might have said.

In my youth in the Transkei, I listened to the elders of my tribe telling stories of the old days. Amongst the tales they related to me were those of wars fought by our ancestors in defence of the fatherland. The names of Dingane and Bambatha, Hintsa and Makana, Squngthi and Dalasile, Moshoeshoe and Sekhukhuni were praised as the pride and glory of the entire African nation. I hoped then that life might offer me the opportunity to serve my people and make my own humble contribution to their freedom struggle. This is what has motivated me in all that I have done in relation to the charges made against me in this case.

Having said this, I must deal immediately and at some length with the question of violence. Some of the things so far told the court are true and some are untrue. I do not, however, deny that I planned sabotage. I did not plan it in a spirit of recklessness nor because I have any love of violence. I planned it as a result of a calm and sober assessment of the political situation that had arisen after any years of tyranny, exploitation, and oppression of my people by whites.

I wanted to impress upon the court that we had not acted irresponsibly or without thought to the ramifications of taking up violent action. I laid particular emphasis on our resolve to cause no harm to human life.

We of the ANC have always stood for a non-racial democracy, and we shrank from any action which might drive the races further apart than they already were. But the hard facts were that fifty years of non-violence had brought the African people nothing but more repressive legislation, and fewer and fewer rights. It may not be easy for this court to understand, but it is a fact that for a long time the people had been talking of violence – of the day when they would fight the white man and win back their country, and we, the leaders of the ANC, had nevertheless always prevailed upon them to avoid violence and to use peaceful methods. While some of us discussed this in May and June of 1961, it could not be denied that our policy to achieve a non-racial state by non-violence had achieved nothing, and that our followers were beginning to lose confidence in this policy and were developing disturbing ideas of terrorism ...

Umkhonto was formed in November 1961. When we took this decision, and subsequently formulated our plans, the ANC heritage of non-violence and racial harmony was very much with us. We felt that the country was drifting towards a civil war in which blacks and whites would fight each other. We viewed the situation with alarm. Civil war would mean the destruction of what the ANC stood for; with civil war racial peace would be more difficult than ever to achieve. We already have examples in South African history of the results of war. It has taken more than fifty years for the scars of the South African [Anglo-Boer] War to disappear. How much longer would it take to eradicate the scars of inter-racial civil war, which could not be fought without a great loss of life on both sides?

Sabotage, I said, offered the best hope for future race relations. The reaction of the white rulers to our first efforts were swift and brutal: sabotage was declared to be a crime punishable by death. We did not want civil war, I said, but we needed to be prepared for it.

Experience convinced us that rebellion would offer the government limitless opportunities for the indiscriminate slaughter of our people. But it was precisely because the soil of South Africa is already drenched with the blood of innocent Africans that we felt it our duty to make preparations as a long-term undertaking to use force in order to defend ourselves against force. If war were inevitable, we wanted the fight to be conducted on terms most favourable to our people. The fight which held out prospects best for us and the least risk of life to both sides was guerrilla warfare*. We decided therefore, in our preparations for the future, to make provision for the possibility of guerrilla warfare. [...]

* guerilla warfare: armed conflict, fought by fighters who are not members of a regular, state army, usually fought against a government or other power group which has a more formal army

I explained that at this stage in our discussions I left the country to attend the PAFMECSA conference and undergo military training. I said that I underwent training because if there was to be guerrilla war, I wanted to be able to stand and fight beside my own people. Even so, I believed that the possibilities of sabotage were far from exhausted and should be pursued with vigour.

I told the court of the dividing line between the ANC and MK, and how we made good-faith attempts to keep the two separate. This was our policy, but in practice, it was not so simple. Because of bannings and imprisonment, people often had to work in both organizations. Though this might have sometimes blurred the distinction, it did not abolish it. I disputed the allegations of the state that the aims and objects of the ANC and the Communist Party were one and the same. [...]

I told the court that I was not a Communist and had always regarded myself as an African patriot. I did not deny that I was attracted by the idea of a classless society, or that I had been influenced by Marxist thought. This was true of many leaders of the newly-independent states of Africa, who accepted the need for some form of socialism to enable their people to catch up with the advanced countries of the West.

> From my reading of Marxist literature and from conversations with Marxists, I have gained the impression that Communists regard the parliamentary system of the West as undemocratic and reactionary*. But, on the contrary, I am an admirer of such a system.
>
> The Magna Carta, the Petition of Rights and the Bill of Rights are documents which are held in veneration* by democrats throughout the world. I have great respect for British political institutions, and for the country's system of justice. I regard the British Parliament as the most democratic institution in the world, and the independence and impartiality of its judiciary never fail to arouse my admiration. The American Congress, the country's doctrine of separation of powers, as well as the independence of its judiciary, arouse in me similar sentiments.

* reactionary: conservative and opposed to radical or leftist ideas; usually the opposite of revolutionary

* veneration: great respect, for a person, thing or idea regarded as unusually valuable

I detailed the terrible disparities between black and white life in South Africa. In education, health, income, every aspect of life, blacks were barely at a subsistence level while whites had the highest standards in the world – and aimed to keep it that way. Whites, I said, often claimed that Africans in South Africa were better off than Africans in the rest of the continent. Our complaint, I said, was not that we were poor by comparison with the people in the rest of Africa, but that we were poor by comparison with the whites in our country, and that we were prevented by legislation from righting that imbalance.

The lack of human dignity experienced by Africans is the direct result of the policy of white supremacy. White supremacy implies black inferiority. Legislation designed to preserve white supremacy entrenches* this notion. Menial tasks in South Africa are invariably performed by Africans. When anything has to be carried or cleaned the white man looks around for an African to do it for him, whether the African is employed by him or not …

Poverty and the breakdown of family life have secondary effects. Children wander about the streets of the townships because they have no schools to go to, or no money to enable them to go to school, or no parents at home to see that they go to school, because both parents (if there are two) have to work to keep the family alive. This leads to a breakdown in moral standards, to an alarming rise in illegitimacy and to growing violence which erupts, not only politically, but everywhere …

Africans want a just share in the whole of South Africa; they want security and a stake in society. Above all, we want equal political rights, because without them our disabilities will be permanent. I know this sounds revolutionary to the whites in this country, because the majority of voters will be Africans. This makes the white man fear democracy …

This then is what the ANC is fighting for. Their struggle is a truly national one. It is a struggle of the African people, inspired by their own suffering and their own experience. It is a struggle for the right to live.

I had been reading my speech, and at this point I placed my papers on the defence table, and turned to face the judge. The courtroom became extremely quiet. I did not take my eyes off Justice de Wet as I spoke from memory the final words.

During my lifetime, I have dedicated myself to this struggle of the African people. I have fought against white domination, and I have fought against black domination.

I have cherished the ideal of a democratic and free society in which all persons live together in harmony and equal opportunities. It is an ideal which I hope to live for and to achieve. But if needs be, it is an ideal for which I am prepared to die.

The silence in the courtroom was now complete. At the end of the address, I simply sat down. I did not turn and face the gallery, though I felt all their eyes on me. The silence seemed to stretch for many minutes. But in fact it lasted probably not more than thirty seconds, and then from the gallery I heard what sounded like a great sigh, a deep, collective 'ummmm', followed by the cries of women.

Mandela, 1994: 317–322

EXERCISE 1.12

1. Look at the list of words, in the previous exercise, that you used to describe Nelson Mandela as a young man. Which of these words would you use to describe his courtroom personality and performance?
2. Are there other words that you would add?
3. Make a list of the issues that Nelson Mandela deals with in the Rivonia speech. What do these issues have in common?
4. What do the following words reveal about Nelson Mandela's personality? 'I do not, however, deny that I planned sabotage. I did not plan it in a spirit of recklessness nor because I have any love of violence. I planned it as a result of a calm and sober assessment of the political situation that had arisen after many years of tyranny, exploitation, and oppression of my people by whites.'
5. Does Mandela's Rivonia Treason Trial speech tell us anything about him as a person, or is it purely political?

The Rivonia Treason Trial speech appears to be Nelson Mandela's political manifesto, both personally and as a representative of the African National Congress. In explaining his actions, he is explaining the actions of his organization too. Throughout the speech and throughout *Long Walk to Freedom*, Mandela the person is almost inseparable from the cause that has shaped his life.

Of course, his speech also reveals much about the man's inner nature. His idealism, his commitment to democracy, his sense of human dignity, his insistence on equality and his opposition to all forms of injustice are obvious. Moreover, given the fact that he was facing the possibility of being sentenced to death, the Rivonia speech is a remarkable statement of personal courage.

Such honesty and directness, however, do not imply that this speech to the court was not carefully planned and structured. The words used are selected and placed in order to achieve the greatest possible effect. These are public statements uttered before a courtroom, and, since the press would publish the speech throughout the world, before a huge international audience. It stands to reason that he would want to make the best of his opportunity to outline his case. Thus, although we never doubt the sincerity of his statements, we are aware that these statements are formulated and delivered in a manner that will present a powerful and favourable image. This is particularly clear in the final paragraphs of the extract from the Rivonia Treason Trial speech. Notice how Mandela stops reading his speech and addresses the judge directly from memory.

EXERCISE 1.13

1. Why does Nelson Mandela address the judge directly towards the end of the speech? What effect does this direct, spoken (rather than read) statement have?
2. How does he characterize himself in the final words of his speech?
3. What does the reaction of the people in the courtroom suggest about the impact of the speech on its listeners?

The idea of writing an autobiography was first suggested to Mandela in 1975 while he was a prisoner on Robben Island:

One day, Kathy [Ahmed Kathrada], Walter [Sisulu] and I were talking in the courtyard when they suggested that I ought to write my memoirs. Kathy noted that the perfect time for such a book to be published would be on my sixtieth birthday. Walter said that such a story, if told truly and fairly, would serve to remind people of what we had fought and were still fighting for. He added that it could become a source of inspiration for young freedom fighters. The idea appealed to me, and during subsequent discussion, I agreed to go ahead. […]

We created an assembly line to process the manuscript. Each day I passed on what I wrote to Kathy, who reviewed the manuscript, and then read it to Walter. Kathy then wrote their comments in the margins. Walter and Kathy have never hesitated to criticize me, and I took their suggestions to heart, often incorporating their changes. This marked-up manuscript was then given to Laloo Chiba, who spent the next night transferring my writing to his own almost microscopic shorthand, reducing ten pages of foolscap to single small piece of paper. It would be Mac's [Maharaj's] job to smuggle the manuscript to the outside world.

[…] I wrote rapidly, completing a draft in four months. I did not hesitate over choosing a word or phrase. I covered the period from my birth through the Rivonia Trial, and ended with some notes about Robben Island.

I relived my experiences as I wrote about them. Those nights, as I wrote in silence, I could once again experience the sights and sounds of my youth in Qunu and Mqhekezwini; the excitement and fear of coming to Johannesburg; the tempests of the Youth League; the endless delays of the Treason Trial; the drama of Rivonia. It was like a waking dream and I attempted to transfer it to paper as simply and truthfully as I could.

Mandela, 1994: 415–416

Although this first draft of his memoirs was lost, the idea of recording his life story would lead to the publication of *Long Walk to Freedom* in 1994. This passage is interesting for reasons other than tracing the origins of the autobiography though. It also reveals other aspects of autobiographical writing we should think about.

Firstly, the writing is done for a purpose. In this case, Mandela's purpose in recording his life story was to remind people of the struggle for political liberation and to inspire a younger generation of freedom fighters. Given the purposes of the autobiography, it is not surprising that the text focuses more on public events and policies and less on private thoughts and experiences.

A second aspect of autobiographical writing revealed here is that writing is a selective process. In the case of an autobiography, and in memoirs especially, the writing relies on memory. The writer writes about what he or she remembers of the past. In the case of *Long Walk to Freedom*, the autobiography is a recollection of Mandela's past. It is also a selective portrayal of that past from his point of view. This raises interesting questions about whether autobiographies should be accepted as being absolutely true or not. People find it difficult to escape their personal preferences and biases. An autobiography may be factual, because it records events which really happened. But it is, and has to be, a subjective interpretation of those events. Other people might see and react to the same events in very different ways.

Autobiographies are not simply spontaneous stories about somebody's life. They are stories in which the author deliberately selects and arranges events in order to encourage the reader to see those events in particular ways.

It is impossible for an autobiography to encapsulate a whole life by telling every single detail about a person. Life is too complex and varied to permit a record of every detail. We do not remember all the events of our life with equal clarity. We do not always necessarily understand ourselves fully. Also, we never fully understand the meaning of our interactions with others. Finally, we may find it difficult to speak about certain things – especially those of a deeply personal or traumatic nature – in a direct way. The act of writing an autobiography is the act of reliving the past, in terms of both its joy and its pain.

In *Long Walk to Freedom* readers are aware that certain aspects of Nelson Mandela's life are emphasized at the expense of others. Although this autobiography is a thorough account of Mandela's life, the feelings of the inner, private person are usually concealed. Thus, while the autobiography documents hardship and struggle, it only hints at the author's inner feelings. The 'I' that narrates is often emotionally distant, even though this is his life story. Personal feeling and inner anguish are partly concealed by focusing on the details of outer events and actions.

The final autobiography we will look at here is one that shows the deep significance of a few, simple events in the life of the writer. The events selected for this story do not have much public significance, nor are they particularly unusual. They are, however, important in enabling the writer to show how she sees herself. She selects them to indicate what is deeply formative of her identity and suggest how she would like to be seen both by those who already know her and those who will meet her in the pages of this story.

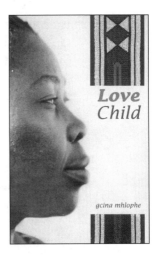

Transforming Moments

Gcina Mhlophe

I was seventeen years old and feeling very unsure of myself. With all my school work, I was doing exceptionally well and most of the teachers at the high school loved me – or they seemed to. My essays were the epitome of good work and they would be read by the whole class. I was probably proud of myself, even though I didn't really give it any serious thought. Somehow, my academic success did not do much for my confidence or give me any self-love. I thought I was very ugly and the fact that my hair was so hard to manage did not make things easier. I used to describe it as dry grass in winter. After a while, I even stopped combing it. I'd wash it and dry it, get dressed in my black skirt and white shirt, which were not as nice as those of the other girls, and off I'd go to school. To top it all, I had knock-knees and big feet! I was just so ugly and awkward – I hated myself. And, my God – I sat in the front desk! Miss-ugly-top-of-the class.

Our school was one of the biggest high schools in the Eastern Cape and we had a great school choir that simply collected trophies. I remember Bulelwa's voice every time I think of our choir. I used to close my eyes and enjoy listening to her sing. I don't know how many times I wished I had a tape recorder so that I could tape her voice and have the pleasure of listening to her for the rest of my life. I must say, I felt great on those rare afternoons when Bulelwa would come and study with me under the black wattle tree near the teachers' cottages. I loved that spot. And I also remember that Bulelwa would stand by me when some of the girls in our dormitory teased me about boys. They knew I was not very interested in boys and they would go on: 'But who would want to go out with her? She doesn't even try to look good!'

I remember this good-looking boy from Port Elizabeth who played rugby. It was half-way through the year and he still did not have a girlfriend. He was the star of our rugby team. I knew his name and I'd heard lots about how good he was, but I didn't really know him – I was not the one to go on the sports field. I was forever buried in my books. I read all the prescribed books for my year and then I read any other book or newspaper or magazine I could get my hands on. I read love stories by Barbara Cartland and Catherine Cookson; I read James Baldwin … I read so much you'd think that was the only thing that kept me alive. Often, by the time the teacher came to do certain books in class, I had long since finished them and was wishing we'd move on to something I didn't know. Boys in my class did not like me very much – except when they needed help with school work. But with Maths we all relied on one particular boy who scared me a lot. Sometimes the Maths genius did help us when he felt like it.

In the girls' dormitory, my bed was at the far corner, away from the entrance and far enough from the Matron too. So, long after the lights were switched off, my deep voice could be heard droning away, doing what we had termed 'coughing'; I used to 'cough' out chapters and chapters of our set books and history syllabus to my classmates, who'd generally left it too late to do their school work and prepare for whatever big test was round the corner. While I helped them out, it was also useful to me to do the 'coughing'. It helped to jog my memory, as generally, some time would have elapsed since I had read the set book, subsequently becoming engrossed in others that had nothing to do with the syllabus. Because of the 'coughing', some of the girls were forced to be my part-time friends. Then came the day when we were rehearsing a new school play and the boy from Port Elizabeth walked up to me and told me that he loved me and wished that I would try to love him too.

Well, I thought he was crazy! What did a good-looking boy like that want with me – and besides, I went to that school to study, not to sleep with boys! I told him so. He tried to convince me that he did not mean to rush things; I did not have to sleep with him – he just liked me and wanted to be my boyfriend. He said he really wanted to spend time with me and we could have good times together talking and reading, if that's what I wanted too. I asked him to please leave me alone.

Well, the Port Elizabeth boy didn't leave me alone, but many of the girls did. They thought he was too good for me. They claimed he was a city boy, and should therefore go for a city girl. There were many remarks too that I was ugly and did not have any fashionable clothes. Many girls now looked the other way when I walked towards them, and many unkind remarks were whispered behind my back. At first this annoyed me; I told whoever would listen that I didn't want anything to do with the handsome city boy – they could have him. But the hostility grew worse and the boy continued to follow me around. And then I began to find it funny. I looked at the girls who hated me and I wondered what would happen if I decided to accept the Rugby Star as my boyfriend. Sometimes, I laughed alone as I imagined what they could be whispering about me. Then I thought – well, he's not blind, he can see that I'm ugly, he can see that I don't have any fashionable clothes, he can see that I read too much. I thought, fine – I'll go out with him. He had chosen an unsuitable girl and set the whole school on fire. My English teacher thought it was really funny. He congratulated me for causing such a stir! It turned out that Sizwe, the Rugby Star, was a lovely person, and we'd become good friends by the time he left the school at the end of that year.

I carried on with my schoolwork and continued to please my sister in Johannesburg – she was the one paying for my education. I could imagine her face glowing when she received my good results and I wished that I could be there to see it. I was doing my Standard Nine then, and we'd just come back for the second semester after the winter holiday. Life was all right, everything was going the same as it always had. I'm not quite sure how it started, but as time went on, I had the feeling that my minister, Father Fikeni, had a soft spot for me. But then, maybe I don't have to explain too much. I think everyone has somebody in their lives who seems to like them for no particular reason – just like that. Sure, I was always well-behaved in church and I was one of the three girls who cut and arranged flowers for the church vases every Sunday morning. I had been kicked out of the school choir because my voice was too deep and I was impatiently told to sing tenor with the boys or leave. Everybody had laughed and I got the general feeling that my voice was not too good. So I left. That also added to my Miss-Ugly-Top-of-the-Class image. But the minister insisted that I be in the church choir, despite my protestations that my voice was ugly. He said my voice was strong and resonant – not ugly. That's the first time I heard the word resonant, and I liked it; so I joined the church choir.

Then there was this particular Friday afternoon; a group of lazy girls was walking back from school. The winter sun seemed as lazy as we were. We had just walked past the minister's house when a young boy ran up to tell me that Father Fikeni wanted to see me. I went with him and was about to walk into the kitchen, when the minister himself came out and gave me swift instructions to go and pack my weekend bag, because he and his wife were going to visit family in Tsolo and I was invited to come with them. I stood there at the top of the stairs open-mouthed, unable to move or speak . The minister looked at me and laughed out loud. He told me that we had less than an hour to go, so I should run. Without a word I turned and took all five steps in one big jump. Running at top speed, clutching my books tightly to my chest, I suddenly realized that I was not alone in the world

– everyone was staring at me. I tried to pull myself together and put a hand across my lips to hide my enormous grin.

Once in my dormitory, I did not know what to take or leave; I was not exactly used to going away on weekends. I quickly changed out of my school uniform and into my best dress. I ran to the bathroom to wet my hair a little so I could try to comb it. It was too painful to do a proper job but I sort of tugged and patted it down with my hand. When I thought it felt a bit better, I went and got my plastic bag with the few necessities for the weekend. I realized I had forgotten my nighty and hurried to get it from under my pillow. People were following me around curious but too proud to ask what was going on. I was not going to say a word till they asked!

Finally Nosisa grabbed me by the arm just as I was walking out the door. 'Aren't you going to tell us where you're going?'

That opened the door for everyone to ask me questions, all at the same time.

'I'm going with Father Fikeni to visit his family for the weekend; he said I must run,' was all I told them.

With that, I pulled my arm free and walked quickly out of the gate.

The drive to Tsolo was relaxing, with the sun setting ahead of us and me dreaming away in the back seat. The minister and his wife sat in front and they seemed to be at peace with themselves. Mrs Fikeni was a beautiful lady who did not talk too much. Many times in church, I would look at her and wish that some angel would come in to the church and ask me what I wanted. I knew exactly what I would ask for – I wanted to be as beautiful as the minister's wife.

That night, we went to bed at about ten, after the evening prayer. I fell asleep very quickly; maybe I was tired out from all the excitement. I was still excited when I woke up the next morning, to realize that no bells rang here to command me to wake up or go to the dining hall or school. I had a shower and went to help out in the kitchen. I liked the fact that I was not treated like some special guest who couldn't even do the dishes. I felt very much at home.

A short while after breakfast, we were all sitting on the veranda drinking some tea, with me seated next to the minister's wife. She was knitting a huge jersey with red and blue stripes. It looked so big I doubted it was hers, but she assured me it was – she said she liked it that way, long and big like a coat. I sat there, content, staring at her fast-moving hands and glancing every now and then into her face. It was as relaxed and beautiful as ever. She hardly even looked at her knitting, except when she ran out of wool or when she had to change colour. We were still sitting like that when Father Fikeni stood up, stretched his arms and said that it was time to go. Time to go where? I wondered, but only half-heartedly, still absorbed by his wife's busy hands. Presently, feeling his eyes on me, I looked up. Smiling, the minister suggested I might like to go with him. He said he had a surprise for me. I searched his face hopefully for a clue. But it gave nothing away. All he said, as I followed him into the house, was that he was going to a meeting and he thought I might be interested in seeing what goes on at such occasions. There was nothing for me to do but swallow my curiosity and get ready to go.

The meeting was held at a nearby village, at the chief's place. It was very well attended. Looking at all the people sitting on the grass, on rocks or wooden stools near the cattle kraal, I decided the whole village must have turned out for the occasion. We were late arrivals, but no one seemed to be too concerned. They made space for us to sit, while the speaker carried on and the people listened. I remember he was saying something about allowing cattle into the mealie fields, but only by agreement of all the people, and only once everyone had finished reaping their crops. His suggestion was something along those lines. Most people participated in the discussion that followed, which didn't seem to have much to do with me at all. I sat there quietly, trying to be interested, but not succeeding too well. And then, all of a sudden, this man – tall, with big shoulders and a very dark face – leaped up from the crowd, his eyes flashing this way and that way, as if he was on the alert for something. He wore a beautifully-made dark red hat with beads and long black feather on it. He had more beads around his neck and waist, and a leather skirt, with the front part reaching just above the knees and the back much longer and flowing behind. He carried a strong-looking sort of stick, with the tip made longer by a white oxtail attached to it. He held it in one hand and in the other, he had a big, red, almost blanket-like cloth, thrown casually over his arm. Everyone sat up expectantly. Father Fikeni looked at me with a big smile. The look in his eyes told me: 'This is your surprise now – enjoy!'

The brightly-dressed man started off by singing the praises of the chief's family, and then he sang about the chief's achievements, about the village people and about the great heroes of the past and present. His use of language was pure and flowing – and so were his movements. He leapt forward and hit the ground with his oxtail stick, hardly making a sound; I saw some people unconsciously imitating him. One minute, he would be praising, the next, he was reflective and critical. I had heard of *imbongi* – a praise poet – but I never dreamt that I'd see one in action. I was staring open-mouthed; even today, looking back, I still don't know exactly how to describe the feeling I had then. I only remember that when the man had finished and people moved forward to congratulate him, I was too tired even to clap my hands or join in the ululation and whistles … I simply sat there, and in my dreamy mind, saw myself in similar attire, doing what I had just seen the man do. I made the decision then and there that I was also a praise poet. That was a beautiful moment for me, to think of myself in that way. I shook a few people's hands and the minister introduced me to the chief, who thanked him for coming and laughingly asked what I was doing at such a meeting. And then the *imbongi* came to greet Father Fikeni. After their longish chat, I was introduced to him as a very good student – during which time I was frozen and dumb from disbelief and God knows what else. As I felt the poet's hot, sweaty hand holding mine, I felt baptized as a poet too. I think I wanted to say something clever, but all I could do that moment was smile and fidget with my button-holes. The poet went on to talk with other people, who called him Cira.

It was a Monday afternoon and I was lying on my stomach in my favourite spot under the black wattle trees when I wrote my first poem. I'd never had a child, but the great feeling that swept over me then was too overwhelming for words; I wondered whether that's how people feel when they have their first baby. I sat up and read it aloud. I liked the sound of my own voice, and I liked hearing the poem. I put the paper down and ran my fingers over my face to feel my features – the smile that wouldn't leave my face, my nose, my cheekbones, my eyes, my ears – including the pointy parts at the top that made my ears look like cups; I even felt my hair and I liked that too. For the first time, I liked the texture of my hard, curly hair and my face didn't feel so ugly – everything just felt fine. My voice sounded like it was a special voice, made specially to recite poems with dignity. Resonant – was that it? That's the day I fell in love with myself; everything about me was just perfect.

I collected my books and the towel I was lying on, stood up and stretched my limbs. I felt tall and fit. I felt like jumping and laughing until I could not laugh any more. I wanted tomorrow to come so that I could go and buy myself a new notebook to write my poems in. A woman praise poet – I'd never heard of one, but what did it matter? I could be the first one! I knew Father Fikeni would agree with me. I couldn't wait to see his face when I read him my poem. Across the fence, a big red cock flapped its wings and crowed loudly at me, as if in agreement.

Mhlophe, 2002: 1–8

In this account of her adolescence, Gcina Mhlophe's writing shows the moments in that period of her life which became touchstones* in her own development of a sense of self. She describes moments that contributed to her identity and sense of purpose.

* touchstones: things of great significance; standards against which other events or experiences are compared

EXERCISE 1.14

1. Does anything in particular strike you about this story?
2. What does the story show about how the writer sees herself?
3. How does she see herself in relation to others?
4. Why do certain people stand out as very important to her?
5. What feelings are expressed and what attitudes are revealed?
6. Think of the details she includes. What aspects of physical appearance are described?

7   What details are included about the physical context (for example, the sights and sounds of places)?
8. How are emotions and ideas described?
9. Which expressions or descriptions do you think are particularly effective? Why?

Writing our own lives

Mhlophe notes that the story you have just read

....

… was inspired by a question that an editor once asked me: 'What helped to create the writer that you are?' At the time, I couldn't take time off from my performance schedule to answer it, so I didn't do anything about it for a year. But the question stayed in my mind. And late one night, I simply had to make the journey down memory lane, stopping only to ponder over the events of the formative years of my life. (Mhlophe, 2002: vii)

....

EXERCISE 1.15

1. If you were to take a trip down memory lane, for the purposes of writing about your life, what details from your high school years might you select?
2. If you were to close your eyes and think yourself back to that time in your life, what or whom would you hear or see? What would you feel? What would you and others be doing?
3. Are there any voices, colours, smells, days, events or scenes that you recall vividly?
4. Do you remember particular tensions, joys, conflicts, or changes? What are they? Think about how you might describe them to someone who was not there.

5. Would you say that there were any 'transforming moments' for you? How would you put them into words and describe them?

Some psychologists believe that telling stories is the most profound way that humans speak about themselves. You do not have to be famous for your autobiography to be interesting. Many of the best autobiographies are about ordinary people. However, writing anything is difficult. There is nothing unusual in feeling apprehensive about writing. But writing something that pleases you is wonderful. It is well worth the effort involved.

To make writing easier, you can approach it step by step. Follow these ideas to get going:

START A WRITER'S JOURNAL

One of the keys to successful writing is constant practice. The more you write, the better your writing will be. You will become used to expressing yourself in writing if you do it frequently, and by keeping a writer's journal.

A writer's journal is a blank notebook in which you write down your experiences, thoughts, ideas and impressions every day. Write whatever comes to mind. Write about your life: your family, your job, your university courses, your groceries, events in the news or anything else that you are thinking about. (You could also use your writer's journal to jot down your responses to the questions that we ask throughout this book.) Don't worry about expressing yourself 'correctly' from the start. What is more important is that you write at least half a page every day.

As you write in your journal every day, you will gradually find it easier to express yourself in writing. You will gain practice in selecting and representing facts and experiences that are significant to you and interesting to a reader. (Always remember that you are writing for an audience, even an imaginary one.) Writing about your own life is a subjective exercise but is a practice that has been followed for hundreds of years.

KNOW YOUR OWN REASONS FOR WRITING

Writing is a form of communication. This means that you (a specific person) are writing about something (a particular topic) for someone (a specific audience). Knowing what your topic requires of you and your reasons for writing on that topic will help you to communicate your ideas more effectively. Suppose for a moment that you are to write about a particular experience you have had. Before you begin writing, it may be helpful if you ask yourself a few questions:

- How am I involved in the experience?
- What did I learn from it or gain from it?
- Why was it important to me?

These questions require you to think about yourself as the writer.

- What experience am I going to write about?
- What are the main details that I need to write down?
- What do I want my readers to know or understand?
- What impression do I want to create?

These questions deal with the topic and purpose of the writing.

- Who is going to read this piece of writing?
- Why are they going to read it?
- Do I have a casual or formal relationship with my readers?

These questions point to your audience; for example, your university lecturers.

Your answers to these questions will help you to select the material and the writing style that is most appropriate to the task that you have been asked to fulfil. We saw in the previous section that even autobiography, which we might think is the most truthful form of writing, can be written in such a way that it reflects particular positions or opinions.

EXERCISE 1.16

Try this exercise to test how a writer's topic, purpose and audience can influence the selection of material:

1. Choose four adjectives from the following list that you think describe you:
   clever, hard-working, independent, caring, creative, attractive, competent, skilful, practical, thoughtful, understanding, careful, tolerant, diplomatic, logical,

critical, fit, sporting, knowledgeable, forgiving, ambitious, persuasive, charming, friendly, sensitive, honest, persevering, energetic, decisive, domineering

2. Now imagine that you are describing yourself to someone you hope will become a partner in a love relationship. Which four adjectives would you choose?
3. Next, imagine that you are describing yourself to a person you hope will employ you. Which four adjectives would you choose?
4. Is there a difference between the sets of adjectives you chose?

You have certainly not changed much in the few seconds between answering these questions, but your answer to each one probably has. This shows that we represent ourselves *differently* to *different* people according to *different* aims. Or to put it another way, our representation of ourselves changes according to our audience and our *purpose*. We saw this in action earlier in the chapter, when we imagined a job interview.

EXERCISE 1.17

Now, if we asked you to write about an event in your life that had an especially profound impact on you, how would you go about it?

1. The first step is to choose the event you are going to write about. This event should be an experience that you remember in great detail (you as the writer should have a clear memory of it). It should also be an event that you think your reader will find interesting (it must be suitable for your audience). Thirdly, the event should have had a lasting effect on you, or on the way you feel (the topic should deal with things which you think are important). After you have decided on the experience you want to write about, your next step is to write down what happened to you, in the order in which you think it occurred. At this stage, you do not have to write in full sentences or perfect grammar. In the first draft of any piece of writing you should concentrate simply on getting your ideas down on paper.

2. Now stop and read through what you have written. Does your first draft include all the important details of the event you are describing? Will a reader be interested in reading what you have written? Telling the story of your life is more than just listing events. Readers are as interested in why things happened and how you felt about them as they are in the events themselves. Underlying causes, motives and people's personal feelings are often the most compelling aspects of any story. If you haven't written about these aspects in your first draft, try including them now.

3. To complete the writing of your autobiographical piece, ask yourself these questions:
   - How will my reader feel about me once they have read my story?
   - Do I want them to feel that way?

4. Depending on your answers to these questions, you might want to add descriptive words and images to your piece so that your reader can participate more fully in the experience being described. Vivid description will almost always make your writing more compelling and unique. Carefully planned, interesting writing is what will make your reader want to carry on reading. You might want to make many drafts of your piece before you feel it is finished.

5. Finally, when you are satisfied with your autobiographical piece, you may want to think about how you have chosen to represent yourself. Have you been absolutely truthful? Is your account an accurate version of what really happened? Do you think it's always important to be truthful and accurate? What does your own experience of writing autobiography suggest about the pitfalls and difficulties of representing the self?

2 Characterization: People and Points of View

IN THE PREVIOUS chapter we explored personal identity. You can think of that chapter as a discussion of the pronoun 'I' in various kinds of writing: your own and that of other people. In this chapter we are going to look at the pronoun 'you', which we use here as shorthand for the idea of 'other people'. We are going to look at *characters* in writing. Again, we will encourage you to try writing about characters yourself, as well as investigating the kinds of characters that have been written about in literature and other kinds of texts. We will end the chapter with a discussion of the ways in which you can write about characters in your essays.

ONE MEETING PEOPLE IN LITERATURE

These are some of the questions we are going to explore in this chapter:
- Why do you read fiction?
- What is fiction about?
- Who are the people we read about in literature?

A personal story

I have been reading literature (novels, poetry and drama) since I was a child. A few years ago, I tried to read A.S. Byatt's novel, *Possession*, which was recommended to me by several friends and several more colleagues. Unfortunately, I found myself unable to get past page 100. The reason was that I did not like one of the main characters in the novel, Roland Michell, who is a literary researcher and doctoral student in England. I found him dull, uninspired, uninspiring, and I did not care about his feelings, adventures or fortunes.

On the other hand, when I read *The Lord of the Rings* (by J. R. R. Tolkien), I find myself engrossed in the thoughts, feelings, life stories and adventures of the characters of Frodo, Sam and their friends. It is my liking for these 'people', whom I have never met and who do not exist outside of the pages of novels, that brings me back again and again to re-read *The Lord of the Rings*.

The last two paragraphs are very personal and subjective (they tell you about my impressions and likes and dislikes relating to fiction), and so they are not really acceptable academic discourse. All the same, they might give you some insight into why I read (and continue to read). In the end, I will enjoy a work of literature if it introduces me to characters whom I like and in whose adventures and fortunes I can take an interest; I do not enjoy them if I cannot form a sense of relationship with the characters in those works. This is not to say that I cannot *appreciate* or *understand* a literary text if I do not like the characters, because one's academic appreciation of literature does not depend only on one's impressions and tastes regarding people.

EXERCISE 2.1

1. What are your favourite literary texts? And your least favourite?
2. Why are your favourite works special to you? Is it because of their characters, plots or other aspects?
3. Can you identify with any of my reasons for enjoying literary works in the paragraphs above? Why/why not?

The *Oxford Advanced Learner's Dictionary* gives the following definition of the word 'character'.

character *noun*

QUALITIES/FEATURES | **1** [C, usually sing.] all the qualities and features that make a person, groups of people, and places different from others: *to have a strong/weak character; character traits/defects; The book gives a fascinating insight into Mrs Blair's character; Generosity is part of the American character; The character of the neighbourhood hasn't changed at all.* **2** [C usually sing, U] the way that sth is, or a particular quality or feature that a thing, an event or a place has: *the delicate character of the light in the evening; buildings that are very simple in character* **3** [U] (*approving*) strong personal qualities such as the ability to deal with difficult or dangerous situations: *Everyone admires her strength of character and determination; He showed great character returning to the sport after his accident; Adventure camps are considered to be character-building* (= meant to improve sb's strong qualities). **4** [U] (usually *approving*) the interesting or unusual quality that a place or a person has: *The modern hotels here have no real character; a face with a lot of character*

STRANGE/INTERESTING PERSON | **5** [C] (*informal*) (used with an adjective) a person, particularly an unpleasant or strange one: *There were some really strange characters hanging around the bar.* **6** [C] (*informal*) an interesting or unusual person: *She's a character!*

REPUTATION | **7** [C, U] (*formal*) the opinion that people have of you, particularly of whether you can be trusted or relied on: *a man of good character and integrity; She was a victim of character assassination* (= an unfair attack on the good opinion people had of her); *a slur/attack on his character*

IN BOOK/PLAY/MOVIE | **8** [C] a person or an animal in a book, play or film/movie: *a major/minor character in the book; cartoon characters*

SYMBOL/LETTER | **9** [C] a letter, sign, mark or symbol used in writing, printing or on computers: *Chinese characters; a line 30 characters long*

As this definition shows, there are several meanings of 'character'. The most common meaning is given first, namely the sum of all the qualities, traits, and features that distinguish a person (or group of people) from others. When we speak of someone's character, then, we mean the total collection of aspects about him or her that are unique. In practice, of course, we usually pick one or two outstanding traits by which to remember that person. These may be physical features or habits of interacting with other people. For example, if your father is very tall, you will be likely to remember that particular quality, or you might remember the nasty smile on the school bully's face.

Authors create characters in much the same way: by choosing important points and focusing on those before adding the details. Of course, the choice of details is important in itself.

Two of the other meanings given in the *Oxford Advanced Learner's Dictionary* are also important for this chapter. The definition mentions 'IN BOOK/PLAY/MOVIE **8** [C] a person or an animal in a book, play or film/movie' as the eighth possible meaning for this word (as we are going to see later, characters also appear in poems). The final meaning that is given is: 'SYMBOL/ LETTER **9** [C] a letter, sign, mark or symbol used in writing, printing or on computers'. I do not think it is a coincidence that *characters* in literature are made up of characters that are used in writing. It is as if the meaning of 'character' as a sign or letter helps to remind us that we only find literary characters in written texts, and that, for that reason, they are not quite the same kind of people as real ones. This is an important point, and we'll come back to it later.

Read the following extract from a famous novel, written during the Victorian era (1837–1901 in England) by one of the masters of creating characters in fiction.

David Copperfield
by Charles Dickens

 gnes laid aside her work, and replied, folding her hands upon one another, and looking pensively at me out of those beautiful soft eyes of hers: 'I believe he is going to enter into partnership with papa.'

'What? Uriah? That mean, fawning* fellow, worm himself into such promotion!' I cried indignantly. 'Have you made no remonstrance* about it, Agnes? Consider what a connexion it is likely to be. You must speak out. You must not allow your father to take such a mad step. You must prevent it, Agnes, while there's time.'

Still looking at me, Agnes shook her head while I was speaking, with a faint smile at my warmth: and then replied:

'You remember our last conversation about papa? It was not long after that – not more than two or three days when he gave me the first intimation* of what I tell you. It was sad to see him struggling between his desire to represent it to me as a matter of choice on his part, and his inability to conceal that it was forced upon him. I felt very sorry.'

'Forced upon him, Agnes! Who forces it upon him?'

'Uriah,' she replied, after a moment's hesitation, 'has made himself indispensable* to papa. He is subtle and watchful. He has mastered papa's weaknesses, fostered them, and taken advantage of them, until – to say all that I mean in a word, Trotwood, – until papa is afraid of him.'

Dickens, 1966: 428

Later in the same chapter, the narrator meets Uriah Heep. Here are his impressions:

I found Uriah Heep among the company, in a suit of black, and in deep humility. He told me, when I shook hands with him, that he was proud to be noticed by me, and that he really felt obliged* to me for my condescension*. I could have wished he had been less obliged to me, for he hovered about me in his gratitude all the rest of the evening; and whenever I said a word to Agnes, was sure, with his shadowless eyes and cadaverous* face, to be looking gauntly* down upon us from behind.

Dickens, 1966: 431

---

* fawning: trying to please others by paying them too much attention without being sincere
* remonstrance: protest

* intimation: sign

* indispensable: vital, very important

* obliged: in debt

* condescension: doing something that is below his social position: here, taking notice of the lowly Uriah

* cadaverous: from 'cadaver', a corpse

* gauntly: from 'gaunt', very thin; unhealthy-looking

Charles Dickens (1812–1870)

Charles Dickens is much loved for his great contribution to classical English literature. He is the quintessential* Victorian author: his epic stories, vivid characters and exhaustive depiction of contemporary life are unforgettable.

His own story is one of rags to riches. He was born in Portsmouth on February 7, 1812, to John and Elizabeth Dickens. The good fortune of being sent to school at the age of nine was short-lived because his father, inspiration for the character of Mr Micawber in *David Copperfield*, was imprisoned for bad debt. The entire family, apart from Charles, were sent to Marshalsea* along with their patriarch*. Charles was sent to work in Warren's blacking factory* and endured appalling conditions as well as loneliness and despair. After three years he was returned to school but the experience was never forgotten and became fictionalised in two of his better-known novels, *David Copperfield* and *Great Expectations*.

Like many others, he began his literary career as a journalist. His own father became a reporter and Charles began with *The Mirror of Parliament* and *The True Sun*. Then in 1833 he became parliamentary journalist for *The Morning Chronicle*. With new contacts in the press he was able to publish a series of sketches under the pseudonym* 'Boz'. In April 1836, he married Catherine Hogarth, daughter of George Hogarth who edited *Sketches by Boz*. Within the same month came the publication of the highly successful *Pickwick Papers*, and from that point on there was no looking back.

As well as a huge list of novels he published autobiography, edited weekly periodicals* including *Household Words* and *All Year Round*, wrote travel books and administered charitable organisations. He was also a theatre enthusiast*, wrote plays and performed before Queen Victoria in 1851. His energy was inexhaustible* and he spent much time abroad – for example lecturing against slavery in the United States and touring Italy with companions Augustus Egg and Wilkie Collins, a contemporary writer who inspired Dickens's final unfinished novel *The Mystery of Edwin Drood*.

He was estranged* from his wife in 1858 after the birth of their ten children, maintained relations with his mistress, the actress Ellen Ternan and died of a stroke in 1870. He is buried at Westminster Abbey.

(Online: BBC History, 6 March 2006)

* quintessential: the perfect example of something

* the Marshalsea: a notorious prison in Victorian England where people were sent when they could not pay their debts

* patriarch: male head of a family

* blacking factory: a factory that made polish for shoes and boots

* pseudonym: a false name, usually used when writing for public purposes

* periodicals: magazines or journals that appear regularly

* enthusiast: from 'enthusiasm', a person who has great enjoyment of something

* inexhaustible: did not run out

* estranged: a legal term meaning 'separated'

EXERCISE 2.2

1. What is your impression of Uriah Heep? Try to sum up the main features of his personality in one sentence, including adjectives that describe him well.

2. Do you think Uriah Heep will turn out to be a good character, working to help others, or the opposite?
3. How did you arrive at your opinion? Did Agnes's description of Uriah influence you more than the narrator's account of him?
4. Do you know anyone who is like Uriah in any way? If so, write a short description of that person.

If you have read *David Copperfield*, you will know that Uriah Heep turns out to be one of the book's worst villains: under the guise of careful politeness and a pretence of being humble, he studies his victims' personal weaknesses and uses his knowledge to enslave people so that he can gain power. There are a few clues to his nature in the extract above: Agnes's account of Uriah Heep's treatment of her father gives one example of his preying on other people's weaknesses. Once Uriah has tricked Agnes's father into accepting him as a business partner, he will gain access to the wealth and power in the business. He continues in the same way all through the narrative.

It is important for you to notice that Uriah Heep is presented *through* David Copperfield's impressions of him (the first mention of him occurs in Agnes's account, as David hears it). David Copperfield is calling himself 'Trotwood' at this point in the novel, so there are good reasons to doubt his own truthfulness. In other words, the text presents us with David's view of Agnes's view of Uriah, and then David's view of him. It is possible that both David and Agnes are biased against him, or that they do not know everything about him. For this reason, the text must be read carefully to gather more information, and decide what the 'truth' about him could be.

Now read another description of a famous character in literature. The description below, like the one from *David Copperfield*, is told by a first-person narrator (who writes as 'I', is involved in the plot and tells the story from his or her own 'point of view'. His name is Nick Carraway and he is describing one of the main characters in the novel, Tom Buchanan.

The Great Gatsby

by F. Scott Fitzgerald

* ends: a position in football
* anti-climax: a disappointing ending
* a string of polo ponies: polo is a game played on horseback that is similar to hockey. Ponies were specially bred for polo and were very expensive.
* supercilious: behaving towards other people as if you think you are better than they are
* arrogant: behaving towards other people in a way that shows you think you are more important than they are
* effeminate: womanly, feminine
* swank: to strut; to walk in a way that tries to impress people
* leverage: the ability to move or control other things or people
* fractiousness: from 'fractious', bad-tempered or easily upset
* paternal: fatherly, or 'talking down' to someone
* senior society: a club for students in their second year or above
* intimate: close; here, as in friendship
* wistfulness: longing for something in a sad way

Her [Daisy's] husband, [Tom Buchanan] among various physical accomplishments, had been one of the most powerful ends* that ever played football at New Haven – a national figure in a way, one of those men who reach such an acute limited excellence at twenty-one that everything afterward savours of anti-climax*. His family were enormously wealthy – even in college his freedom with money was a matter for reproach – but now he'd left Chicago and come East in a fashion that rather took your breath away: for instance, he'd brought down a string of polo ponies* from Lake Forest. It was hard to realize that a man in my own generation was wealthy enough to do that.

… He had changed since his New Haven years. Now he was a sturdy straw-haired man of thirty, with a rather hard mouth and a supercilious* manner. Two shining arrogant* eyes had established dominance over his face and gave him the appearance of always leaning aggressively forward. Not even the effeminate* swank* of his riding clothes could hide the enormous power of that body – he seemed to fill those glistening boots until he strained the top lacing, and you could see a great pack of muscle shifting when his shoulder moved under his thin coat. It was a body capable of enormous leverage* – a cruel body.

His speaking voice, a gruff husky tenor, added to the impression of fractiousness* he conveyed. There was a touch of paternal* contempt in it, even toward people he liked – and there were men at New Haven who had hated his guts.

'Now, don't think my opinion on these matters is final,' he seemed to say, 'just because I'm stronger and more of a man than you are.' We were in the same senior society*, and while we were never intimate* I always had the impression that he approved of me and wanted me to like him with some harsh, defiant wistfulness* of his own.

Fitzgerald, 1974: 12–13

EXERCISE 2.3

1. What is your impression of Tom Buchanan? Do you like him or not? Try to sum up his character, as represented in the extract above, in *four* of your own adjectives.
2. Have you ever met someone who resembled Tom in any way?
3. How does the narrator (who is telling the story) feel about Tom? How do you know?
4. What kind of masculinity does Tom convey to you? How do you feel about it?

Tom Buchanan is a complex character in *The Great Gatsby*. As the above extract shows, a great deal of his being is involved with the way he experiences his body. Nick sees him as having 'a cruel body' that could have 'enormous leverage' (in other words, it could move a great weight: this applies to people as well as to objects). Tom is portrayed as manipulative and controlling in the 'leverage' that he applies to other people, and it turns out that his effect in the novel is very damaging towards others. Although he is self-centred and arrogant, though, he is not all bad: he is capable of love (although not necessarily for his wife).

Our final character in this section is found in a novel that is written in the form of an imaginary letter to a friend. Its title is *So Long a Letter*, by the Senegalese writer Mariama Bâ. In the novel, a middle-aged widow, Ramatoulaye, explains her feelings to her lifelong friend, Aissatou, about her husband's second marriage.

So Long a Letter

by Mariama Bâ

I try to spot my faults in the failure of my marriage. I gave freely, gave more than I received. I am one of those who can realize themselves fully and bloom only when they form part of a couple. Even though I understand your choice, even though I respect the choice of

* liberated women: unlike
  Ramatoulaye, Aissatou
  decides to leave her husband
  when he takes a second wife,
  and in so doing she 'liberates'
  or frees herself from the
  restrictions of marriage
* a harmonious symphony
  of colours: the colours in
  Ramatoulaye's home work
  together like the notes in a
  symphony or beautiful piece
  of music, to create a pleasing
  whole
* mobilized: working together
  to achieve a particular aim;
  here, her husband's happiness
* anticipated: Ramatoulaye saw
  her husband's future desires
  and did something about
  them in advance
* laurels: signs of honour and
  praise; in ancient Rome, a
  crown of laurel leaves was
  given to the winner in a sports
  event
* trade union: an organized
  group of workers, who often
  bargain with their employers
  for better working conditions
* flouted: defied, openly
  scorned, rejected
* condescension: behaviour
  towards others that shows
  that she believes herself
  better than they are
* ideology: any particular set
  of beliefs held by a group of
  people

liberated women*, I have never conceived of happiness outside marriage.

I loved my house. You can testify to the fact that I made it a haven of peace where everything had its place, that I created a harmonious symphony of colours*. You know how soft-hearted I am, how much I loved Modou. You can testify to the fact that, mobilized* day and night in his service, I anticipated* his slightest desire.

I made peace with his family. Despite his desertion of our home, his father and mother and Tamsir, his brother, still continued to visit me often, as did his sisters. My children too grew up without much ado. Their success at school was my pride, just like laurels* thrown at the feet of my lord and master.

And Modou was no prisoner. He spent his time as he wished. I well understood his desire to let off steam. He fulfilled himself outside as he wished in his trade union* activities.

I am trying to pinpoint any weakness in the way I conducted myself. My social life may have been stormy and perhaps injured Modou's trade union career. Can a man, deceived and flouted* by his family, impose himself on others? Can a man whose wife does not do her job well honestly demand a fair reward for labour? Aggression and condescension* in a woman arouse contempt and hatred for her husband. If she is gracious, even without appealing to any ideology*, she can summon support for any action. In a word, a man's success depends on feminine support.

And I ask myself. I ask myself, why? Why did Modou detach himself? Why did he put Binetou between us?

You, very logically, may reply: 'Affections spring from nothing; sometimes a grimace, the carriage of a head can seduce a heart and keep it.'

I ask myself questions. The truth is that, despite everything, I remain faithful to the love of my youth. Aissatou, I cry for Modou, and I can do nothing about it.

Bâ, 1989: 55–56

Mariama Bâ

Senegalese teacher and writer, Mariama Bâ, was born into a well-to-do* family in Dakar, where she grew up. In the newly independent Senegal, Bâ's father became one of the first ministers of state. After Bâ's mother died she was raised in the traditional manner by her maternal grandparents. She received her early education in French, while at the same time attending Koranic* school. At school Bâ was a prominent* student. During the colonial period and later, girls faced a number of obstacles when they wanted to have a higher education. Bâ's grandparents did not plan to educate her beyond primary school, but her father's insistence on giving her an opportunity to continue her studies eventually prevailed*. She won the first prize in the entrance examination and entered the Ecole Normale de Rufisque, a teacher training college near Dakar. During this period she published her first book. It was non-fiction and dealt with colonial education in Senegal. At school she also wrote an essay which created a stir for its rejection of French policies in Africa.

In 1947 Bâ completed her schooling. She worked as an elementary-school teacher, married a politician, Obèye Diop, and had nine children. After twelve years, she was forced to resign due to poor health, and she then worked as a regional school inspector. When her marriage broke up, Bâ raised the children alone. A divorcee and 'a modern Muslim woman' as she characterized* herself, Bâ was active in women's associations, promoted education, championed women's rights, made speeches, and wrote articles in local newspapers.

Une si longue lettre (1980, *So Long a Letter*) is considered the classical statement of the female condition in Africa. The book won the first Noma Award for Publishing in Africa at the 1980 Frankfurt Book Fair, and made Bâ (in her 50s) world famous. Central themes in the novel are male-female relations in patriarchal* society, the survival of the caste system* and tradition of polygamy*, and its effects on the modern African family. 'Books are a weapon,' Bâ once said, 'a peaceful weapon perhaps, but they are a weapon.'

After a long illness, Bâ died of cancer in 1981, six months after *So Long a Letter* won the Noma Award for Literature. *Scarlet Song*, about the marriage between a European woman and an African man, was published posthumously*.

As a writer, Bâ emerged from the oral tradition of the Senegalese griot* women and wrote a 'speakerly text.' This tradition of orality in Senegal has been the major outlet for women's voices. The griot women – not controlled by society in ways other women are regarding speech – are given a license by society to say whatever they want without censorship. The tradition of the griot women is important to the Senegalese women, because it has always been one way of making themselves heard and listened to.'

(Adapted from: Pegasos website, www.kirjasto.sci.fi, 16 March 2006)

* well-to-do: wealthy, rich

* Koranic: based on the Qur'an or holy text of Islam
* prominent: important or well-known

* prevailed: won, succeeded or dominated

* characterized: described herself in words

* patriarchal society (or patriarchy): a system of power in society where males rule

* caste system: a system of ordering society according to the economic class into which people are born

* polygamy: a system whereby people are allowed to marry more than one person. In Africa, polygamy is seen in the custom of some men marrying more than one wife

* juxtaposition: placing things side by side

* posthumously: after her death

* griot: an African singer and oral storyteller

EXERCISE 2.4

1. Who are the main characters in this extract?
2. What are Ramatoulaye's main personal qualities?
3. Can you sum up Ramatoulaye's views on marriage?
4. Do you agree with her that 'In a word, a man's success depends on feminine support'? Why?

Ramatoulaye is a traditional Senegalese woman. She has twelve children, which probably means that she is middle-aged (between 40 and 55) and, in the passage above, she describes her attitude towards her marriage in the aftermath of her husband's having married a second wife (called Binetou). As Ramatoulaye explains her feelings, you may have found yourself either admiring her devotion to her husband (especially when she says she was 'mobilized day and night in his service') or wondering why she expended so much energy on pleasing him. Ramatoulaye is in the same position: torn by the pain of Modou's rejection, she reviews all the things she did in their marriage and wonders whether it was just a waste of energy, or whether she could have done more to ensure her husband's faithfulness to her. In this way, the reader is drawn into sharing Ramatoulaye's feelings and experiences.

How 'real' are characters in fiction?

You have now met three famous characters from novels: Uriah Heep, Tom Buchanan and Ramatoulaye. They are very different from one another: they come from different genders, different times in history, different countries and different cultures. All these aspects, besides their own personal qualities (such as Tom Buchanan's aggression or Ramatoulaye's devotion to her unfaithful husband) make them unique. Can you think of other characters who have impressed you or stayed in your memory?

It is clear from the start that characters in literature are not the same as people we meet. Literary characters (whether they appear in prose, drama or poetry) do not have a life outside the pages of the texts that represent them. Perhaps the most important aspect of this difference is that, while you have a body,

Uriah Heep does not. He is 'made up' entirely of words. These words appear on pages, to be read by readers, who then imagine the character according to their own thoughts about people. So there is no 'real' Uriah Heep (despite the rock group of the same name), Tom Buchanan or Ramatoulaye. When we 'meet' people in literature, we are meeting a word-picture of someone whom an author has imagined into being. It is the skill of the author to bring to life in words a person who does not exist, and to make readers take an interest in, and feel as if they have really met, that person. The character is *created* according to the author's imagination and intentions (the theme of the text, or what the author wants to achieve with that particular character) and then understood, or *interpreted*, by the reader, who will come to an individual understanding of that character. In the end, though, readers only have the words on a page to go by; we cannot call the character into our room to explain his or her decisions to us.

It is important to realize that, although readers get to know characters in fiction as if they were real people, they are not the same as real people we meet in our everyday lives. Baruch Hofman says:

....

To begin with, the imaginary beings who get into literature and who come swarming out of it into our consciousness are not people. They do not exist, except in our imaginations or as words on a page. They do not breathe; they have no body warmth; they cannot assault or embrace us. Nor do they figure as objects of our activity, except of our responsiveness. We cannot reason with them or interfere in their lives, any more than we can interfere with the lives of the dead. I may want to stop my brother from murdering his wife, and I can try to stop him, possibly even to some effect. I can do no such thing when Othello* is about to strangle Desdemona; all I can do, if I am watching the play, is bother the actor who is playing Othello and interfere with the pleasure of the audience in the theater.

Indeed, if the characters in literature are like people at all, in the ordinary sense, they are like dead people. The characters in literature, once they are 'written,' are finished like the dead. (Hofman, 1985: 59–60)

....

* Othello: by William Shakespeare, both a play and the name of the main character, who strangles his wife, Desdemona, because he believes, falsely, that she is being unfaithful to him.

All the same, there are some important similarities between characters in literature and real people. Both of them are modelled on our views of what a person should be like.

Copy the table below into your journal and fill in your own ideas.

My expectations and ideas of a person
He or she should have ...

Perhaps you included things like: history (every person has a life story); some qualities that relate to appearance; thoughts; emotions; likes and dislikes; habits, or things that person is most likely to do; a language; and so on. We expect the same thing when we meet people in literature. We expect that the text will give them a body (that is, by describing the way they look); will explain a little about their past; and will show them doing things, thinking, feeling and so on. In this way, characters take on a life of their own and readers come to feel as if we know them (that is, if the author has succeeded in making us take an interest in them).

One of the important things we realize on knowing a person for a short while is that most people are complex. They have good qualities as well as bad ones; they make mistakes in some areas, while succeeding in others; they have doubts and aspects of life that they have not resolved. This is also true of characters in literature, who, just like real people, do not always behave in the way we expect. The next extract gives us an example of a character who behaves in a very unusual way, given her situation.

Nervous Conditions

By Tsitsi Dangarembga

I was not sorry when my brother died. Nor am I apologising for my callousness*, as you may define it, my lack of feeling. For it is not that at all. I feel many things these days, much more than I was able to feel in the days when I was young and my brother died, and there are reasons for this more than the mere consequence* of age. Therefore I shall not apologise but begin by recalling the facts as I remember them that led up to my brother's death, the events that put me in a position to write this account. For though the event of my brother's passing and the events of my story cannot be separated, my story is not after all about death, but about my escape and Lucia's; about my mother's and Maiguru's entrapment; and about Nyasha's rebellion – Nyuha, far-minded and isolated, my uncle's daughter, whose rebellion may not in the end have been successful.

* callousness: not caring about other people's feelings or suffering

* consequence: result

Dangarembga, 2001: 1

Tsitsi Dangarembga

In 1959, Tsitsi Dangarembga was born in Rhodesia, now called Zimbabwe, in the town of Mutoko. Although born in Africa she spent her childhood, aged two to six, in Britain. She began her education in a British school but after returning to Rhodesia with her family, she concluded her early education, her A-levels, in a missionary school in the city of Mutare. Later, she went back to Britain to attend Cambridge University where she pursued a course of study in medicine. Dangarembga was not destined to stay in Britain; after becoming homesick and alienated she returned to her homeland of Rhodesia in 1980 just before it became Zimbabwe under black majority rule.

Although she returned to Rhodesia she still continued her educational pursuits. She began a course of study at the University of Harare in psychology. During her studies, Dangarembga held a job at a marketing agency as a copywriter for two years and was a member of the drama group affiliated with the university. This is where her early writing was given an avenue for expression. She wrote many of the plays that were put into production at the university. In 1983 she directed and wrote a play entitled *The Lost of the Soil*. She then became an active member of a theater group called Zambuko. This group was directed by Robert McLaren. While involved in this group she participated in the production of two plays, *Katshaa!* and *Mavambo*.

While involved in theater she also explored prose writing. In 1985, she published a short story in Sweden entitled 'The Letter' and in 1987, she published a play in Harare entitled *She No Longer Weeps*. Her real success came at age twenty-five with the publication of her novel *Nervous Conditions*. This novel was the first novel to be published in English by a black Zimbabwean woman. In 1989, this novel won her the African section of the Commonwealth Writers Prize. Prior to this award she had won a second prize in the Swedish aid-organization, SIDA, short story competition. After *Nervous Conditions* was published in Denmark, she made a trip there in 1991 to be part of the Images-of-Africa festival. Dangarembga continued her education in Berlin at the Deutsche Film und Fernseh Akademie where she studied film direction. While in school she made many film productions, including a documentary for German television. She then made the film entitled *Everyone's Child*, which has been shown worldwide at various festivals including the Dublin Film Festival.

(Emory University Department of English website, 21 April 2006)

The narrator (the person who speaks) in the extract is Tambudzai, whose nickname is Tambu, the younger sister of the brother who died, whose name is Nhamo. The first sentence of the extract, which is the reader's first encounter with Tambu, is designed to shock. We expect people to care about their family members and to feel grief when they die. It is all the more shocking, then, when we read that the uncaring sister is only eleven or twelve (having just completed Standard Three [Grade Five]) and that it is her only brother who has died. In many ways, the whole novel is an explanation of the first sentence and the reasons why Tambu does not mourn her brother's death.

EXERCISE 2.5

1. Without knowing any more about Tambu than the facts in the paragraph above, could you imagine reasons for her not to be sad about her brother's death?
2. How do you react to being told that a sister is not sad about her brother's death?
3. Does the first sentence make you think less highly of Tambu?

As the novel progresses, the readers learn that Tambu is passionate about going to school and being educated. She comes from a very poor family in rural Zimbabwe, who can only afford to send one child to school. As Nhamo is the only son (and sons are considered more valuable to educate than daughters), he is the lucky one who receives a place at school. When he dies, the opportunity to attend school passes to his sister Tambu. Tambu's frustration at not being allowed to attend school because it is thought to be more important to educate boys; her dislike of her brother's overbearing ways towards her and their younger sisters; and her desire for a chance to learn, and so escape rural poverty, all meet in the first sentence (though it is only on reading almost the whole novel that the reader can understand this). We do learn, though, from the dramatic first sentence that Tambu is not a person who always does what other people expect. In fact, she tends to do the opposite, and, later on in the novel, she rebels more and more against people's expectations of her. Tambu also tells the reader what the novel is going to be about: it is not about death, she says, but about escape.

Change and development

As Tambu escapes her position in small-town rural Zimbabwe through education, she changes as a person. Her view of her family, her situation and her place in history changes greatly. She develops a wider view of the conditions in which she has grown up and realizes that these conditions were created during the European colonial period, when colonizers treated indigenous African people as inferior; and they were also shaped by her society's habit of giving power to men while allowing women only secondary places and roles. Through realizing this, Tambu's anger towards her family for not giving her the opportunity to grow through education subsides a little and she comes closer to accepting them.

Many other characters in literature also change: indeed, readers might complain if they read a novel in which the main character stayed the same from the beginning to the end of the story. We would feel that this is not lifelike; not what we think life is about; not what we expect from a literary text, which, after all, is supposed to be 'like' real life, or to represent real life.

People change and develop throughout their lives, and so do literary characters. In fact, the way people change is a great

Verisimilitude and representation

Literary texts represent life experiences in words. (It does not matter whether these life experiences are imaginary or real.) The word 'represent' is important here because it has two meanings.

represent *verb*

ACT/SPEAK FOR SB | **1** [VN] [often passive] to be a member of a group of people and act or speak on their behalf at an event, a meeting, etc: *The competition attracted over 500 contestants representing 8 different countries; Local businesses are well represented on the committee* (= there are a lot of people from them on the committee); *The president was represented at the ceremony by the Vice-President*

re-present *verb* [VN] to give, show or send sth again, especially a cheque, bill, etc. that has not been paid.

The word is made up of two bits: 're' (meaning 'again') and 'present'. If we put them together, we can see that literature *presents* something to us as readers: but it does so in a repetitive way, that is, through language. The use of language distances the representation of experience in literature from the experience itself, so we cannot treat novels as true records of history or personal life experiences (indeed, often the language distorts or changes the way the experience appears). The perspective from which the writing is done has an impact on what the author includes and then on the representation that we encounter as readers.

On the other hand, readers expect texts that we read to be consistent with real life in some way. We want to read about people that we recognize or can identify with in some way. If the events in a play, novel or poem are too different from our knowledge of human experiences, we will feel alienated and find difficulty in responding to them. We call this aspect of writing *verisimilitude* (or 'true-to-life-ness'). Naturally, each reader expects something different from a 'life-like' piece of writing.

theme in literature, and 'novels of development' are so common as to have a special name from the German, *Bildungsroman*. These novels often follow the main character from youth through adolescence to adulthood, showing the important moments in their life and the way they change as they grow up into maturity. One well-known example is J. D. Salinger's *Catcher in the Rye*.

TWO CHARACTERS IN LITERATURE

Characters in literature are like people in real life, because they are modelled on real people, but readers cannot treat them as real. Instead, we have to limit our judgements to the information we are given about them in the texts in which they appear. Often, we get a lot of information about fictional characters, but sometimes we have to make guesses about them, too. We can gain of information from other people's descriptions of them. Here is an extract from the second scene of Shakespeare's play, *Macbeth*, which describes the title character:

ACT 1, SCENE 2
SCENE II.—[A camp.]

Alarum within. Enter KING DUNCAN, MALCOLM, DONALBAIN, LENOX, with Attendants, meeting a bleeding Captain.

DUN. What bloody man is that? He can report,
As seemeth by his plight, of the revolt
The newest state.

MAL. This is the Sergeant,
Who, like a good and hardy soldier, fought   5
'Gainst my captivity.—Hail, brave friend!
Say to the King the knowledge of the broil,
As thou didst leave it.

CAP. Doubtful it stood;
As two spent swimmers, that do cling together   10
And choke their art. The merciless Macdonwald
(Worthy to be a rebel, for to that
The multiplying villainies of nature
Do swarm upon him) from the western isles

Of Kernes and Gallowglasses is supplied;   15
And Fortune, on his damned quarrel smiling,
Show'd like a rebel's whore: but all's too weak;
For brave Macbeth (well he deserves that name),
Disdaining Fortune, with his brandish'd steel,
Which smok'd with bloody execution,   20
Like Valour's minion, carv'd out his passage,
Till he fac'd the slave;
Which ne'er shook hands, nor bade farewell to him,
Till he unseam'd him from the nave to th' chops,
And fix'd his head upon our battlements.   25

DUN. O valiant cousin! worthy gentleman!

The Captain's story tells the audience about a great warrior called Macbeth, who was not afraid to greet an enemy, but 'bravely' 'unseam'd him from the nave [the neck] to th' chops [to his buttocks]': in other words, Macbeth cut him open from his chin to the base of his stomach. Then he 'fix'd [the enemy's] head upon our battlements', probably as a sign of victory.

EXERCISE 2.6

1. What kind of person do you think Macbeth is, based on the information in the passage above? Which words give you your ideas about him?
2. What do you expect to happen to him in the course of the play? Do you think he will change at all?

One important source of information about characters in literature is what other characters say about them. We saw this in the passage from *David Copperfield*, when we heard about Uriah Heep first through Agnes's account of his interactions with her father. Of course, though, any character can only give his or her individual view of another character. For example, the Captain in the scene from *Macbeth* has a lower rank than Macbeth, and is therefore more easily impressed by Macbeth's feats in battle. When you read a novel or a play, you need to pay careful attention to the words used to describe other characters. But be aware that these probably will not provide a complete view or understanding of any one character.

Authors may use a variety of literary techniques to introduce us to their characters. As we saw in a previous exercise, real people have a number of qualities and attributes, including a life history, personal appearance, opinions, likes and dislikes. Usually the most important feature of the character is presented first.

Pride and Prejudice
by Jane Austen

Mr Bingley was good-looking and gentlemanlike; he had a pleasant countenance*, and easy, unaffected manners. His sisters were fine women, with an air of decided fashion. His brother-in-law, Mr Hurst, merely looked the gentleman; but his friend Mr Darcy soon drew the attention of the room by his fine, tall person*, handsome features, noble mien*, and the report which was in general circulation* within five minutes of his entrance, of his having ten thousand a year. The gentlemen pronounced him to be a fine figure of a man, the ladies declared he was much handsomer than Mr Bingley, and he was looked at with great admiration for about half the evening, till his manners gave a disgust which turned the tide of his popularity; for he was discovered to be proud, to be above his company, and above being pleased; and not all his large estate in Derbyshire could then save him from having a most forbidding*, disagreeable* countenance, and being unworthy to be compared with his friend.

* countenance: an old-fashioned word for 'face'
* fine, tall person: fine, tall body
* mien: a person's appearance or manner that shows how they are feeling
* in general circulation: everybody in the room knew about his fortune

* forbidding: seeming unfriendly and frightening
* disagreeable: unpleasant

Austen, 1990: 7–8

In this passage, the narrator tells us about the two most important men in the novel. First we learn about the way they look – Mr Bingley is said to be 'good-looking and gentlemanlike' and Mr Darcy is described as having a 'fine, tall person, handsome features, noble mien'. The two men are described 'from the outside', as it were: the narrator tells us how they would appear to an external observer. For this reason, we do not see what they are thinking or feeling: these details are hidden from the narrator. But their looks are not just descriptive details, though: they are important features of Mr Bingley and Mr Darcy. The two men have just moved to a new village, where many of the young women are looking for husbands. The women survey the newcomers to see if they might be suitable for them to marry. In this situation, good looks are a definite advantage.

But we also learn more than this. The narrator tells us about the behaviour and personality of the two men as well. Mr Bingley is described as having 'easy, unaffected manners', which please the people at the dance; but Mr Darcy's ways are not as popular. Indeed, as soon as the group finds out that he is 'proud … above his company, and above being pleased', they change their opinion of him altogether. Then they do not care if he is rich or not, and they even decide that he is not very handsome.

In this way, the paragraph also conveys some important aspects of the novel. It shows us that good looks and money are valuable assets for a woman to look for in a man; and it also shows us that a man must be friendly and pleasant in order to please other people. As the novel goes on, readers discover what a powerful fault Mr Darcy's pride is.

Another way of introducing a character is to describe what he or she feels or thinks, as you will see in the following passage.

The Loneliness of the Long-Distance Runner

by Alan Sillitoe

So as soon as I tell myself I'm the first man ever to be dropped into the world, and as soon as I take that first flying leap out into the frosty grass of an early morning when even birds haven't the heart to whistle, I get to thinking, and that's what I like. I go my rounds in a dream, turning at lane or footpath corners without knowing I'm turning, leaping brooks without knowing they're there, and shouting good morning to the early cow-milker without seeing him. It's a treat, being a long-distance runner, out in the world by yourself with not a soul to make you bad-tempered or tell you what to do or that there's a shop to break and enter a bit back from the next street. Sometimes I think that I've never been so free as during that couple of hours when I'm trotting up the path out of the gates and turning by that bare-faced, big-bellied oak tree at the lane end. Everything's dead, but good, because it's dead before coming alive, not dead after being alive. That's how I look at it. Mind you, I often feel frozen stiff at first. I can't feel my hands or feet or flesh at all, like I'm a ghost who wouldn't know the earth was under him if he didn't see it now and again through the mist. But even though some people would call this frost-pain suffering if they wrote about it to their mams in a letter, I don't, because I know that in half an hour I'm going to be warm, that by the time I get to the main road and am turning on to the wheatfield footpath by the bus stop I'm going to feel as hot as a potbellied stove and as happy as a dog with a tin tail.

Sillitoe, 1959: 160–161

The passage is told 'from the inside': it recounts the runner's thoughts as he sets out on his daily run. The reader is not told anything at all about what the runner looks like (or even his name), but we learn a great deal about the kinds of things that he thinks as he reflects on the pleasure he gains from running alone early in the morning. The long sentences that are used to convey the runner's thoughts are a way to show that he does not always finish a thought with a full stop, as one might finish a sentence on a page. Rather, thoughts flow into one another, as his attention shifts from one topic to another.

EXERCISE 2.7

Try doing some writing of your own now.
1. Write a paragraph about someone you know. Write it 'from the outside': describe the person's appearance and character, as well as their actions.

2. Now write another paragraph 'from the inside', describing a person's thoughts and feelings as if you were that person.
3. Which paragraph was easier to write? Why?

Readers get other information about characters in literature in a number of ways besides the two that we have just looked at. A text can tell the reader how the character looks; how they behave; what they say and do; how other people see them; or what they think and feel. As we read about characters interacting with others, we also get an idea of what they may be like.

What the narrator chooses to tell us about characters in fiction shapes the way readers respond to them. It is possible to read about a character in a novel whom the narrator does not like. In this case, it is likely that the reader will dislike the character, too. The characters in the next passage were created specifically by the author in order to give an example of disagreeable people.

Harry Potter and the Philosopher's Stone
by J.K. Rowling

Mr and Mrs Dursley, of number four, Privet Drive, were proud to say that they were perfectly normal, thank you very much. They were the last people you'd expect to be involved with anything strange or mysterious, because they just didn't hold with such nonsense.

Mr Dursley was the director of a firm called Grunnings, which made drills. He was a big, beefy man with hardly any neck, although he did have a very large moustache. Mrs Dursley was thin and blonde and had nearly twice the usual amount of neck, which came in very useful as she spent so much of her time craning over garden fences, spying on the neighbours. The Dursleys had a small son called Dudley and in their opinion there was no finer boy anywhere.

The Dursleys had everything they wanted, but they also had a secret, and their greatest fear was that somebody would discover it. They didn't think they could bear it if anyone found out about the Potters. Mrs Potter was Mrs Dursley's sister, but they hadn't met for several years; in fact, Mrs Dursley pretended she didn't have a sister, because her sister and her good-for-nothing husband were as unDursleyish as it is possible to be. The Dursleys knew that the Potters had a small son, too, but they had never even seen him. This boy was another good reason for keeping the Potters away; they didn't want Dudley mixing with a child like that.

Rowling, 1997: 7

As you can gather from the passage, Vernon and Petunia Dursley are neither caring nor particularly endearing. They have a blend of self-satisfaction and mediocrity that is found in suburban areas, where people's interest in the world around them does not extend beyond curiosity about their neighbours' business. As the novels unfold, though, it is clear that they are there to provide a contrast with the other adult characters in Harry's life, who are caring, interesting and much more likeable: in fact, all that they are not. The entire *Harry Potter* series is written (among other reasons) to demonstrate the difference between magical people (wizards, witches and so on), who have interesting lives; and non-magical people (called 'Muggles'), who are represented as being rather dull and lack any kind of inner depth.

Many 'bad' literary characters function in this way – as opposites of the 'good guys.' These kinds of characters are useful in fiction. Since a great deal of literature is about conflicts of various kinds, the 'bad guys' may be there to give the main characters someone to battle against. Their unpleasant qualities strengthen the good qualities possessed by the heroes of the texts, and sometimes their lack of ability can provide humour for the reader, too.

EXERCISE 2.8

1. Think of 'bad' or unpleasant characters in literary texts that you have read. What qualities make them unpleasant?
2. How do their actions show their undesirable personalities?
3. How do they help the author to get his or her message across? What is their role in the texts where they appear?

4. Write a description of a 'bad' character that you know from any text (it could be a novel, a play or a film). Try to sum them up in 10 lines.

THREE POINT OF VIEW

In the passages from *David Copperfield*, *The Great Gatsby*, *So Long a Letter* and *Nervous Conditions* which we read earlier, all the narrators speak as 'I'. Every fictional text has a narrator; to put it another way, every story is told by somebody. This simple fact has important implications for the point of view used in the story. Ursula K. Le Guin's handbook on creative writing says:

Point of view, POV for short and when scribbled in margins of manuscripts, is the technical term for describing *who is telling the story and what their relation to the story is*.

This person, if a character in the story, is called the *viewpoint character*. (The only other person it can be is the author.) (Le Guin, 1998: 83)

What Le Guin says implies that, whenever we tell a story, we adopt a particular perspective. In discussing literary texts we refer to the 'voice' that tells the story as the 'narrator': the narrator tells us, the readers, the story. Events and characters are presented from the narrator's point of view. It is easy to understand that the same story would be told differently if it were told from different points of view. Consider the two narratives below, which describe exactly the same event (a foreign princess entering a crowded room). A is told from the princess's point of view: B is told from the point of view of an observer in the crowd.

A: Princess Sefrid: First-Person Narration

I felt so strange and lonesome entering the room crowded with strangers that I wanted to turn around and run, but Rassa was right behind me, and I had to go ahead. People spoke to me, asked Rassa my name. In my confusion I couldn't tell one face from another or understand what people were saying to me, and answered them almost at random. Only for a moment I caught the glance of a person in the crowd, a woman looking directly at me, and there was a kindness in her eyes that made me long to go to her. She looked like somebody I could talk to.

B: Princess Sefrid: Observer-Narrator in Third Person

She wore Tufarian clothing, the heavy red robes Anna had not seen for fifteen years. Crowded forward by her owner, the Hemmian slavemaster called Rassa, the princess looked small, hunched, defensive, but she preserved around herself a space that was all her own. She was a captive, an exile, yet Anna saw in her young face the pride and kindness she had loved in the Tufarians, and longed to speak with her. (Le Guin, 1998: 83)

Many literary works are written using 'I'. This tells the reader that narrators (the people who tell the stories) are in the story; they are telling stories that happened to them. We call them *first-person* narrators because, in English, 'I' and 'we' are first-person pronouns, as the box on the right shows.

The first-person narrator is a technique that authors use when they want to tell a story where the narrator is part of the events. It has a number of interesting side-effects, though:

⊙ The narrator does not usually present the reader with objective information about him/herself. The reader has to infer, or gather, this information from clues in the text.

Pronouns in English

A pronoun is a word that takes the place of a noun (the name of a thing). In English there are seven pronouns: I, we, you, he, she, it and they. 'I' and 'we' are called first-person pronouns because we begin thinking and speaking from our own point of view; we write and speak about ourselves first.

'You' is the second- person pronoun because 'you' is the person we look at next, or second; 'you' are the next closest person to me.

'He, she or it' is used for someone or something that is more distant from me than 'you' are. For that reason, these are called third-person pronouns. 'They' is the third person plural because it refers to more than one thing.

☺ The narrator cannot be an objective observer and reporter of the events in the story, precisely because these events are presented as involving him or her. Rather, a first-person narrator will, inevitably, give a *subjective* view of the events (because no single person can have an entirely objective point of view on anything); he or she may even present a biased view of events. If the narrator's is the only voice in the text, then the reader can only know one point of view on the events that take place. This makes it difficult for the reader to know if the narrative is biased; one has to compare events in the text with what the narrator says about them and see if they measure up.

☺ A strongly biased first-person narrator is called an *unreliable* narrator. While all narratives are subjective (as you can see from the previous point), an unreliable narrator may conceal facts, or may make mistakes while relating events in the text. Most first-person narrators are reluctant to tell the reader about their own weaknesses and mistakes. A good example of an unreliable first-person narrator is Marlow in Joseph Conrad's *Heart of Darkness*, who does not tell the reader the full truth about his own decisions or motives in his search for Kurtz and what he does after Kurtz's death. In this case, the reader cannot rely entirely on the truth of the events narrated in the text. Instead, the reader must use other evidence in the text to construct his or her own version of things and events.

EXERCISE 2.9

Return to the three passages at the beginning of this chapter from *David Copperfield*, *The Great Gatsby* and *Nervous Conditions*. Write notes on whether you think the narrator of each passage is reliable or not (is he or she telling the truth about the story, as far as possible?) If you think any narrator is unreliable, give reasons based on the passage.

Of course, there are other forms and styles of narration as well. Literary critics have traditionally spoken about narrative in terms of 'first-person' or 'third-person' narration. Third-person narration refers to the way a story is told from the perspective, or point of view, of someone who is not one of the characters. The narrator in this case is outside the story and not a participant in its events. For example, I might wish to write a story assuming that I can see into the minds of all my characters; the way I wrote the story would be based on the idea that I know exactly what my characters think and feel. The narration is not limited to a particular character's point of view. This type of narrator is a 'third-person' or 'omniscient' narrator. 'Omniscience' refers to the idea that someone 'knows everything'. An omniscient narrator, therefore, presents the story from a point of view where he or she seems to know everything about the characters and their world. As readers, we can only know what we are told by the narrator with regard to characters' thoughts, feelings and motives. If an omniscient narrator presents us with a full and detailed picture of events and characters, we often tend to accept the narrator's point of view as our own. In other words, we tend to see the characters from the narrator's point of view and to share the narrator's opinion about the characters.

When we think about the 'voice' narrating a story, we need to think carefully about objectivity. A first-person narrator is most likely to offer a very subjective account. If the story is being told by a character, we have to take into account that he or she has particular interests, ideas, capacities and beliefs which will influence how the story is told. We might have to be very careful about taking the narrator's word as an objective or reliable interpretation of things.

But this problem is not limited only to first-person narration. On the face of it, a third-person or omniscient narrator should be more objective. However, it is important to note that this is not always the case. A third-person narrator may choose to focus on the thoughts, feelings and actions of one character only, and so foreground that character and his or her point of view. One effect of this narrative technique is to make the reader sympathize

Writing about point of view in poems

Narrative point of view is a central aspect of understanding and thinking about a literary work. In poetry, as in novels, we cannot assume that the ideas, attitudes and events shown in the poem are a direct expression of the poet's own life and experience. The 'voice' that speaks in the poem – the 'I' that narrates the poem – could be a character created by the poet to express a particular viewpoint or point of view. The ideas and feelings expressed in the poem may differ from those of the person who makes the poem. Although there might be significant similarities between the ideas and experiences of the writer and the situation described in the text, we cannot assume that they are identical. For this reason we refer to the voice in the poem as the 'speaker'. This allows us to think of the writer and the text as separate from each other.

with the character whose point of view is presented. Similarly, the narrator's opinions and world-view might affect the way in which she or he describes people. For example, if the narrator admires an aspect of a character's behaviour or personality, the description of that person will usually influence us to share the narrator's opinion. In the same way, a negative description from the narrator would affect our feelings about events or characters.

In the following poem, the speaker signs the 'letter' as 'YOUR MOTHER'. This should alert you to the fact that the speaker is not the same as the poet, who has a man's name (Charles). The poet has created an imaginary speaker to express the feelings of longing and need for children's support, which are common among parents whose children are away from home. Now read the poem and answer the questions that follow.

A Letter to a Son
Charles Mungoshi

Now the pumpkin is ripe.
We are only a few days from
the year's first mealie cob.
The cows are giving us lots of milk.
Taken in the round it isn't a bad year at all   5
if it weren't for your father.
Your father's back is back again
and all the work has fallen on my shoulders.
Your little brothers and sisters are doing
fine at the day-school. Only Rindai   10
is becoming a problem. You will remember
we wrote you – did you get our letter?
you didn't answer – you see, since your
father's back started we haven't been able
to raise enough to send your sister Rindai   15
to secondary school. She spends most of her time
crying by the well. It's mainly because of her
that I am writing this letter.
I had thought you would be with us last Christmas

then I thought maybe you were too busy   20
and you would make it at Easter –
it was then your father nearly left us, son.
Then I thought I would come to you some time
before the cold season settled in – you know how
I simply hate that time of year   25
but then your father went down again
and this time worse than any time before.
We were beginning to think he would never see
another sowing season. I asked your sister Rindai
to write you but your father would have none of it   30
– you know how stubborn he can get when
he has to lie in bed all day or gets
one of those queer notions of his that
everybody is deserting him!
Now, Tambu, don't think I am asking for money   35
although we had to borrow a little from
those who have it to get your father to hospital
and you know how he hates having to borrow!
That is all I wanted to tell you.
I do hope that you will be with us this July.   40
It's so long since we heard from you –
I hope this letter finds you at the old address.
It is the only address we know.
                    YOUR MOTHER

Moffett and Mphahlele (eds), 2002: 213–214

EXERCISE 2.10

1. Who are the main characters in the poem?
2. What is your impression of them? Which words or
   phrases make you think this?
3. What is not said in the poem?
4. What is the real reason for the letter?
5. What kind of son is being addressed here?
6. Which lines, words or phrases appeal most to you? Why?

You will probably get the idea that, although the mother does not say so, she is gently scolding her son for not doing his duty towards the family. The whole poem is an exercise in *not* saying what is really meant: for example, the mother says 'it isn't a bad year at all' (line 5), but the details that she relates later in the poem show that it is a very bad year indeed, with the father unable to work and the family thrown into poverty as a result. You need to work out why the letter is being written and what the mother wants from her son (although she does not ask him directly to do anything). It is also interesting to explore the way she subtly tries to persuade her son to do as she wants. She does this by telling him what she does not want – for example, she claims she is not asking for money, while the background to the poem is all about the family's lack of money (to send the sister to secondary school, and even to afford hospital treatment for the father).

Now imagine that you are the son who is addressed in the poem, and that you have received the letter. Write a letter back to your mother. Begin with the words, 'Dear Mother' and go on from there. You can write your letter in the form of a poem, if you wish; try, whether you write in prose or in verse, to use the same matter-of-fact tone that is used in the original poem (even when you are conveying emotions to the reader).

Other first-person narrators

Issues relating to the intricacies of point of view and characterization are of course not limited to these two novels. Among the huge number of texts which explore issues similar to these are *Jane Eyre* by Charlotte Brontë, *Great Expectations* by Charles Dickens and *Catcher in the Rye* by J. D. Salinger. Reading any of them would provide many opportunities for exploring these concepts further.

One of the earliest novels written in English was published in the 1760s by Laurence Sterne. At the time the book was highly controversial and was criticised by many leading figures of the day for moral and literary reasons. The title of the novel is *The Life and Opinions of Tristram Shandy, Gentleman*. It presents a picture of the fictional character named Tristram Shandy. Or at least, that is what it almost does – in fact, the book says very little about the life of the character and does not reveal much about his opinions either. Instead, it focuses extensively on the other characters who spend time with Tristram Shandy, and reveals quite a lot about the narrator's personality. One of the many interesting things about this book is what this says about writing about the self and identity. To me, it seems that the very difficulty of describing a 'self' is shown by the way in which the book is 'about' a self who is so seldom revealed. But more than this, the narrator also examines the question of when a 'self' begins. The book begins by stating that it is necessary to describe the moment at which Tristram Shandy was conceived if the book is going to talk about the life of Tristram Shandy. In other words, the problem of a 'self' is taken back to the time before that self was born.

Many other books also explore this problem, though in a different way. One example is Salman Rushdie's novel *Midnight's Children*, which was first published in 1982. In this novel, the opening scenes focus on the character Saleem. He starts to describe his own identity in terms of the moment of his birth, which he claims as very important to his identity, although he then goes on to revise even this. Within the next few paragraphs, he characterizes his identity in different terms by saying that who he is depends on events and people that precede his birth. His 'self' is, in a way, 'made' by these factors, as they contribute to the way that he understands himself and to the stories he tells people about himself and his identity.

FOUR CAN THEMBA'S 'THE SUIT'

In this section we are going to apply the ideas and concepts of characterization, context and perspective that we explored in the previous two sections to a short story by Can Themba called 'The Suit'. We have chosen this story because it is centrally concerned with character – what people feel, what they expect and why they behave as they do. After reading it, we are going to do some detective work.

Strategies for reading the text

* The main idea is the most important idea in each paragraph.
* The argument of a text is the way in which ideas are arranged logically in a text to make a certain point.
* The themes are the abstract ideas which are expressed by the argument.

We suggest that you preview a text to get a general impression of its content by means of skimming and scanning. Good readers often skim through a text and note the most important ideas before reading it more intensively. When you have discovered the main ideas of a text and are satisfied that you understand its basic content, you can begin to look at it in more detail to find its main ideas*, arguments* and themes*.

Often, if we list the main ideas in a text, we can produce a summary of the argument; that is, we can make a list of how the ideas are arranged in the text. The themes of the text might give us an indication of the writer's purpose and intention. One theory about literature states that readers, however, should not necessarily believe everything that they read. Instead, they read critically and think about the writer's purpose, intention and tone in writing the text. Does the writer want to *inform* the reader? Does the writer perhaps aim at *persuading* the reader to do something or to think about something in a certain way? Do we know the writer's and / or the narrator's opinion from what is said and from the way in which it is said? Very often, the writer's purpose in writing the text and his or her opinions about the topic are veiled. The writer does not tell the reader explicitly why they are writing and how they are feeling, which is why we should read critically and carefully. Readers can get clues about the writer's or narrator's intentions and opinions by focusing on emotive words that are used in the text. Some words have strong emotional connotations. Emotive words are often used in advertisements and politics, for instance, because they are effective in persuading people to buy a product or believe an idea.

Often writers seem to be writing objectively and giving factual information. However, if we look at the words they choose to describe people and situations, we see that the writing is also, in many ways, subjective (that is, it is written from the writer's point of view).

Can Themba (1924–1968)

Can Themba was born in Marabastad, Pretoria, in 1924. He studied at the University of Fort Hare and later worked in Johannesburg as an English teacher and a journalist on *Drum* and *The Golden City Post*. After being declared a banned person by the National Party government, he left for Swaziland in 1963 and died there in Manzini in 1968.

Adey *et al.*, 1986: 195

The setting of 'The Suit'

The setting of a novel or play is the place and time in which the action happens. 'The Suit' is set in Sophiatown, which was a freehold area in Johannesburg where black people were legally able to own property, even into the early years of apartheid. Unlike the other racially divided suburbs of the time, people from different racial groups lived there. The suburb had a vibrant culture where jazz and other local music and poetry were written and performed. The people who lived there loved Sophiatown passionately, and it featured in many poems, short stories and autobiographies. However, in the mid-1950s Sophiatown was bulldozed under the regime of H. F. Verwoerd and re-classified as a white area called Triomf (Afrikaans for 'triumph'). With the political changes of the 1990s, Triomf became known again by its original name, Sophiatown.

The Suit
by Can Themba

Five-thirty in the morning, and the candlewick bedspread frowned as the man under it stirred. He did not like to wake his wife lying by his side – as yet – so he crawled up and out by careful peristalsis*. But before he tiptoed out of his room with shoes and socks under his arm, he leaned over and peered at the sleeping serenity* of his wife: to him a daily matutinal* miracle.

He grinned and yawned simultaneously, offering his wordless Te Deum* to whatever gods for the goodness of life; for the pure beauty of his wife; for the strength surging through his willing body; for the even, unperturbed rhythms of his passage through days and months and years – it must be – to heaven.

Then he slipped soundlessly into the kitchen. He flipped aside the curtain of the kitchen window, and saw outside a thin drizzle, the type that can soak one to the skin, and that could go on for days and days. He wondered, head aslant, why the rain in Sophiatown always came in the morning when workers had to creep out of their burrows; and then at how blistering heatwaves

* peristalsis: the muscular contraction of the digestive system. In this context, it describes a slow movement, similar to that of a worm.

* serenity: calm or tranquility

* matutinal: morning

* Te Deum: a prayer or hymn in praise of God.

Philemon thinks his life is 'good' and his wife is 'pure' and 'beautiful'. For this reason he is grateful for his life.

came during the day when messengers had to run errands all over; and then at how the rain came back when workers knocked off and had to scurry home.

He smiled at the odd caprice of the heavens, and tossed his head at the naughty incongruity, as if, 'Ai, but the gods!'

From behind the kitchen door, he removed an old rain cape, peeling off in places, and swung it over his head. He dashed for the lavatory, nearly slipping in a pool of muddy water, but he reached the door.[1] Aw, blast, someone had made it before him. Well, that is the toll of staying in a yard where twenty … thirty other people have to share the same lean-to. He was dancing and burning in that climactic moment when trouser-fly will not come wide soon enough. He stepped round the lavatory and watched the streamlets of rainwater quickly wash away the jet of tension that spouted from him. The infinite after-relief. Then he dashed back to his kitchen. He grabbed the old baby-bathtub hanging on a nail under the slight shelter of the garden roof-edge. He opened a large wooden box and quickly filled the bathtub with coal. Then he inched his way back to the kitchen door and inside.

He was huh-huh-huhing one of those fugitive tunes that cannot be hidden, but often just occur and linger naggingly in the head. The fire he was making soon licked up cheerfully, in mood with his contentment.

He had a trick for these morning chores. When the fire in the old stove warmed up, the water kettle humming on it, he gathered and laid ready the things he would need for the day: brief case and the files that go with it; the book that he was reading currently; the letters of his lawyer boss which he usually posted before he reached the office; his wife's and his own dry-cleaning slips for the Sixty-Minutes; his lunch tin solicitously* prepared the night before by his attentive wife; and, today, the battered rain cape. By the time the kettle on the stove sang (before it actually boiled), he poured water from it into a wash basin, refilled and replaced it on the stove. Then he washed himself carefully: across the eyes, under, in and out the armpits, down the torso and in between the legs. The ritual was thorough, though no white man a-complaining of the smell of wogs knows anything about it. Then he dressed himself fastidiously. By this time he was ready to prepare breakfast.[2]

Despite his circumstances, Philemon remains positive and content.

[1] What kind of life does this sentence describe?

This description of Philemon's surroundings in Sophiatown does not seem to match Philemon's ideas about the quality of his own life.

* solicitously: showing great concern

[2] The way Philemon washes himself is described as a 'ritual', a word which could have a religious meaning. It links to other words such as 'pure', 'Te Deum' and 'serenity'. What do these words suggest about Philemon's view of his wife and his marriage? What do the words 'thorough' and 'fastidiously' suggest about Philemon's character?

Breakfast! How he enjoyed taking in a tray of warm breakfast to his wife, cuddled in bed. To appear there in his supremest immaculacy, tray in hand when his wife comes out of ether to behold him. These things we blacks want to do for our own … not fawningly for the whites for whom we bloody well got to do it. He felt, he denied, that he was one of those who believed in putting his wife in her place even if she was a good wife. Not he.

Matilda, too, appreciated her husband's kindness, and only put her foot down when he offered to wash up also. 'Off with you,' she scolded him on his way.[3]

At the bus-stop he was a little sorry to see that jovial old Maphikela was in a queue for a bus ahead of him, He would miss Maphikela's raucous laughter and uninhibited, bawdy conversations in fortissimo*. Maphikela hailed him nevertheless. He thought he noticed hesitation in the old man, and a slight clouding of his countenance, but the old man shouted back at him, saying that he would wait for him at the terminus in town.

Philemon considered this morning trip to town with garrulous* old Maphikela as his daily bulletin. All the township news was generously reported by loud-mouthed heralds, and spiritedly* discussed by the bus at large. Of course, 'news' included views on bosses (scurrilous), the Government (rude), Ghana and Russia (idolatrous), America and the West (sympathetically ridiculing), and boxing (bloodthirsty). But it was always stimulating and surprisingly comprehensive for so short a trip. And there was no law of libel.

Maphikela was standing under one of those token bus-stop shelters that never keep out rain nor wind nor sun-heat. Philemon easily located him by his noisy ribbing of some office boys in their khaki-green uniforms. They walked together into town, but from Maphikela's suddenly subdued manner, Philemon gathered that there was something serious coming up. Maybe a loan.[4]

Eventually, Maphikela came out with it.

'Son,' he said sadly, 'if I could've avoided this, believe you me I would, but my wife is nagging the spice out of my life for not talking to you about it.'

It just did not become blustering old Maphikela to sound so grave and Philemon took compassion* upon him.

This shows us how Philemon would like his wife and others to see him.

[3] What do these sentences reveal about the roles of men and women in the society that Philemon and Matilda live in? What do they suggest about Matilda's attitude to her husband and his duties?

* fortissimo: a musical term indicating loud volume

* garrulous: very talkative
* spiritedly: enthusiastically

The narrator seems to suggest that, despite any opinions to the contrary, township dwellers are knowledgeable, informed and interested in ideas and current events.

[4] Maphikela's face suddenly looks worried or sad. How does this statement prepare the reader for what he is going to tell Philemon?

* compassion: feeling of deep sympathy and sorrow for another person stricken by misfortune

5 Why do you think Maphikela is reluctant to tell Philemon the news?

The 'infinitely delicate mechanism' seems to refer to the careful construction Philemon has built in his own head about the world around him and his role in it. In Philemon's mind he and his life are perfect. However, at the first hint of trouble, his life seems to be in danger of collapsing.

* miasmata: unhealthy or unpleasant smells

* viscera: the organs of the body in the abdomen

The descriptive words used here are an indication to the reader that something dangerous, 'menacing' or life-threatening is about to happen.

* subjugation: defeat; to gain mastery or control

6 Look at how Philemon's entire character seems to have been reversed. Previously, the expression of unease on Maphikela's face filled Philemon with concern or compassion. Now, however, he is described as 'merciless.' If Philemon's will is 'merciless,' what do we expect of the way he might treat his wife?

'Go ahead, dad,' he said generously. 'You know you can talk to me about anything.

The old man gave a pathetic smile. 'We-e-e-ll, it's not really any of our business … er … but my wife felt … you see. Damn it all! I wish these women would not snoop around so much.'5 Then he rushed it. 'Anyway, it seems there's a young man who's going to visit your wife every morning … ah … for these last bloomin' three months. And that wife of mine swears by her heathen gods you don't know a thing about it.'

It was not quite like the explosion of a devastating bomb. It was more like the critical breakdown in an infinitely delicate piece of mechanism. From outside the machine just seemed to have gone dead. But deep in its innermost recesses, menacing electrical flashes were leaping from coil to coil, and hot, viscous molten metal was creeping upon the fuel tanks … Philemon heard gears grinding and screaming in his head …

'Dad,' he said hoarsely, 'I … I have to go back home.'

He turned round and did not hear old Maphikela's anxious, 'Steady, son. Steady, son.'

The bus ride home was a torture of numb dread and suffocating despair. Though the bus was now emptier Philemon suffered crushing claustrophobia. There were immense washerwomen whose immense bundles of soiled laundry seemed to baulk and menace him. From those bundles crept miasmata* of sweaty intimacies that sent nauseous waves up and down from his viscera*. Then the wild swaying of the bus as it negotiated Mayfair Circle hurtled him sickeningly from side to side. Some of the younger women shrieked delightedly to the driver, 'Fuduga! … Stir the pot!' as he swung his steering-wheel this way and that. Normally, the crazy tilting of the bus gave him a prickling exhilaration. But now …

He felt like getting out of there, screamingly, elbowing everything out of his way. He wished this insane trip were over, and then again, he recoiled at the thought of getting home. He made a tremendous resolve to gather in all the torn, tingling threads of his nerves contorting in the raw. By a merciless act of will, he kept them in subjugation* as he stepped out of the bus back in the Victoria Road terminus, Sophiatown.6

The calm he achieved was tense … but he could think now …
he could take a decision …

With almost boyishly innocent urgency, he rushed through
his kitchen into his bedroom. In the lightning flash that the eye
can whip, he saw it all … the man beside his wife … the chestnut
arm around her neck … the ruffled candlewick bed spread … the
suit across the chair. But he affected not to see.

He opened the wardrobe door, and as he dug into it, he
cheerfully spoke to his wife, 'Fancy, Tilly, I forgot to take my
pass. I had already reached town and was going to walk up to the
office. If it hadn't been for wonderful old Mr Maphikela … '

A swooshing noise of violent retreat and the clap of his bedroom
window stopped him. He came from behind the wardrobe door
and looked out from the open window. A man clad only in vest
and underpants was running down the street. Slowly he turned
around and contemplated … the suit.

Philemon lifted it gingerly under his arm and looked at the
stark horror in Matilda's eyes. She was now sitting up in bed. Her
mouth twitched, but her throat raised no words.[7]

'Ha,' he said, 'I see we have a visitor,' indicating the blue suit.
'We really must show some of our hospitality. But first, I must
phone my boss that I can't come to work today … mmmm-er,
my wife's not well. Be back in a moment, then we can make
arrangements.'

He took the suit along.[8]

When he returned he found Matilda weeping on the bed. He
dropped the suit beside her, pulled up the chair, turned it round
so that its back came in front of him, sat down, brought his chin
onto his folded arms before him, and waited for her.

After a while the convulsions of her shoulders ceased. She saw
a smug man with an odd smile and meaningless inscrutability*
in his eyes. He spoke to her with very little noticeable emotion; if
anything, with a flutter of humour.

'We have a visitor, Tilly.' His mouth curved ever so slightly.
'I'd like him to be treated with the greatest of consideration.
He will eat every meal with us and share all we have. Since we
have no spare room, he'd better sleep in here. But the point is,
Tilly, that you will meticulously look after him. If he vanishes or

This reaction seems
prophetic of his treatment
of Matilda. Notice that
Philemon has not thought
of Matilda even once. He
is only concerned with his
own anger. In one glance
Philemon sees exactly what
is going on: Matilda is in bed
with another man, whose
suit is draped over the chair.
But he pretends not to have
seen it.

[7] If Philemon has always been
merciful and good to his wife
(as he believes he has), then
why is she so terrified of him
now?

[8] Why do you think Philemon
focuses on the suit and not on
Matilda?

* inscrutable: impossible to
understand

For the first time we glimpse
the world from Matilda's
perspective. The Philemon
that Matilda sees is not the
Philemon we have 'seen'
riding on the bus. Matilda
does not see that Philemon
is upset, but rather that he
is unfeeling about what has
happened and even feels
pleased with himself and
amused by the situation.

She ducks because she expects him to beat her.

9 Consider Philemon's behaviour from Matilda's perspective. Note the threatening tone of his voice and content of his words. Is this the same Philemon we saw in the first part of the story? What made his character change?

'Stern masculinity' implies that the house was 'cruel, strict and uncompromising' even before Matilda's unfaithfulness was detected.

The use of words and phrases such as 'gripped', 'overwhelming, undisciplined force', 'catapult', and 'glowed fiercely' emphasize the power of this force.

10 For the first time Philemon looks at his wife and considers her motives. What is this 'overwhelming, undisciplined force', this 'essence'? Is this essence love? Is it sexual desire? What does the death of this essence imply about their relationship from now on?

* dexterous: skilled or efficient

anything else happens to him ...' A shaft of evil shot from his eye ... 'Matilda, I'll kill you.'

He rose from the chair and looked with incongruous supplication at her. He told her to put the fellow in the wardrobe for the time being. As she passed him to get the suit, he turned to go. She ducked frantically, and he stopped.

'You don't seem to understand me, Matilda. There's to be no violence in this house if you and I can help it. So just look after that suit.' He went out.[9]

He went out to the Sophiatown Post Office, which is placed on the exact line between Sophiatown and the white man's surly Westdene. He posted his boss's letters, and walked to the beer hall at the tail end of Western Native Township. He had never been inside it before, but somehow the thunderous din laved his bruised spirit. He stayed there all day.

He returned home for supper ... and surprise. His dingy little home had been transformed, and the air of stern masculinity it had hitherto contained had been wiped away to be replaced by anxious feminine touches here and there. There were even gay, colourful curtains swirling in the kitchen window. The old-fashioned coal-stove gleamed in its blackness. A clean, chequered oilcloth on the table. Supper ready.

Then she appeared in the doorway of the bedroom. Heavens! Here was the woman he had married; the young, fresh, cocoa-coloured maid who had sent rushes of emotion shuddering through him. And the dress she wore brought out all the girlishness of her, hidden so long beneath German print. But no hint of coquettishness, although she stood in the doorway and slid her arm up the jamb, and shyly slanted her head to the other shoulder. She smiled weakly.

What makes a woman like this experiment with adultery? He wondered.

Philemon closed his eyes and gripped the seat of his chair on both sides as some overwhelming, undisciplined force sought to catapult him towards her. For a moment some essence glowed fiercely within him, then sank back into itself and died ... [10]

He sighed and smiled sadly back at her, 'I'm hungry, Tilly.'

The spell snapped, and she was galvanized into action. She prepared his supper with dexterous* hands that trembled a little only when they hesitated in mid-air. She took her seat opposite him, regarded him curiously, clasped her hands waiting for his prayer, but in her heart she murmured some other, much more urgent prayer of her own.

'Matilda!' he barked, 'Our visitor!' The sheer savagery with which he cracked at her jerked her up, but only when she saw the brute cruelty in his face did she run out of the room, toppling the chair behind her.

She returned with the suit on a hanger, and stood there quivering like a feather. She looked at him with helpless dismay. The demonical rage in his face was evaporating, but his heavy breathing still rocked his thorax above the table, to and fro.

'Put a chair, there.' He indicated with a languid gesture of his arm. She moved like a ghost as she drew a chair to the table.

'Now seat our friend at the table ... no, no, not like that. Put him in front of the chair, and place him on the seat so that he becomes indeed the third person.'

Philemon went on relentlessly: 'Dish up for him. Generously. I imagine he hasn't had a morsel all day, the poor devil.'[11]

She served the suit. The act was so ridiculous that she carried it out with a bitter sense of humiliation. He came back to sit down and plunge into his meal. No grace was said for the first time in this house. With his mouth full, he indicated by a toss of his head that she should sit down in her place. She did so. Glancing at her plate, the thought occurred to her that someone, after a long famine, was served a sumptuous supper, but as the food reached her mouth it turned to sawdust. Where had she heard it?[12]

Matilda could not eat. She suddenly broke into tears.

Philemon took no notice of her weeping. After supper, he casually gathered the dishes and started washing up. He flung a dry cloth at her without saying a word. She rose and went to stand by his side drying up. But for their wordlessness, they seemed a very devoted couple.

After washing up, he took the suit and turned to her. 'That's how I want it every meal, every day.' Then he walked into the bedroom.

So it was. After that first breakdown, Matilda began to feel that her punishment was not too severe, considering the heinousness of the crime. She tried to put a joke into it, but by slow, unconscious

Matilda tries to calm down her husband's anger by being even more submissive to him than she has been before. She tries to make things beautiful, but her efforts are those of a woman who is very scared ('anxious').

Words like 'barked', 'savagery' and 'cruelty' are all associated with cruel and inhuman behaviour. Words like 'quivering' and 'dismay' describe Matilda's fear and helplessness.

[11] Philemon has no mercy and is enjoying his wife's humiliation. Do you think Philemon behaves in an appropriate way?

[12] Think of the pure, almost religious way in which Philemon saw himself at the beginning of the story. Does this behaviour, motivated by 'demonical rage,' concur with how he saw himself?

Note how Philemon rules Matilda.

Matilda is completely submissive and begins to think that her punishment suits the wickedness ('heinousness') of her mistake. Even though she does not admit it, the daily tension of the ritual with the suit affects her nerves.

Matilda's humiliation becomes public here, reminiscent of the Biblical story of the crucifixion, where Christ carries his cross in public. Matilda is still paying for her 'sin', for which her husband never forgives her.

13 Why is Philemon reading this particular book?

Philemon refers to the suit in terms that appear to be friendly, such as 'the old chap' and 'our friend.' However, he is sarcastic and takes every opportunity to remind Matilda of her unfaithfulness.

We get a glimpse here of Matilda's feelings. She is reaching the end of her tether. Her first desire is to resolve the issue with Philemon, but she fears his rage. The society in which she lives sees men as superior to women. Although Matilda would like to be free of this oppressive marriage, she does not have the courage to confront Philemon or to leave him.

degrees, the strain nibbled at her. Philemon did not harass her much more, so long as the ritual with the confounded suit was conscientiously followed.

Only once, he got one of his malevolent brainwaves. He got it into his head that 'our visitor' needed an outing. Accordingly, the suit was taken to the dry-cleaners during the week, and, come Sunday, they had to take it out for a walk. Both Philemon and Matilda dressed for the occasion. Matilda had to carry the suit on its hanger over her back and the three of them strolled leisurely along Ray Street. They passed the church crowd in front of the famous Anglican Mission of Christ the King. Though the worshippers saw nothing unusual in them, Matilda felt, searing through her, red-hot needles of embarrassment, and every needlepoint was a public eye piercing into her degradation.

But Philemon walked casually on. He led her down Ray Street and turned into Main Road. He stopped often to look into shop windows or to greet a friend passing by. They went up Toby Street, turned into Edward Road, and back home. To Philemon the outing was free of incident, but to Matilda it was one long, excruciating incident.

At home, he grabbed a book on abnormal psychology, flung himself into a chair and calmly said to her, 'Give the old chap a rest, will you, Tilly?'13

In the bedroom, Matilda said to herself that things could not go on like this. She thought of how she could bring the matter to a head with Philemon; have it out with him for once and for all. But the memory of his face, that first day she had forgotten to entertain the suit, stayed her. She thought of running away, but where to? Home? What could she tell her old-fashioned mother had happened between Philemon and her? All right, run away clean then. She thought of many young married girls who were divorcees now, who had won their freedom.

What had happened to Staff Nurse Kakile? The woman drank heavily now, and when she got drunk, the boys of Sophiatown passed her around and called her the Cesspot.

Matilda shuddered.

An idea struck her. There were still decent, married women around Sophiatown.14 She remembered how after the private schools had been forced to close with the advent of Bantu

Education, Father Harringway of the Anglican Mission had organized Cultural Clubs. One, she seemed to remember, was for married women. If only she could lose herself in some cultural activity, find absolution for her conscience in some doing good; that would blur her blasted home life, would restore her self-respect. After all, Philemon had not broadcast her disgrace abroad … nobody knew; not one of Sophiatown's slander-mongers suspected how vulnerable she was. She must go and see Mrs Montjane about joining a Cultural Club. She must ask Philemon now if she might … she must ask him nicely.

She got up and walked into the other room where Philemon was reading quietly. She dreaded disturbing him, did not know how to begin talking to him. They had talked so little for so long. She went and stood in front of him, looking silently upon his deep concentration. Presently, he looked up with a frown on his face.

Then she dared, 'Phil, I'd like to join one of those Cultural Clubs for married women. Would you mind?'

He wrinkled his nose and rubbed it between thumb and index finger as he considered the request. But he had caught the note of anxiety of in her voice and thought he knew what it meant.

'Mmmm,' he said, nodding. 'I think that's a good idea. You can't be moping around here all day. Yes, you may, Tilly.' Then he returned to his book.[15]

The Cultural Club idea was wonderful. She found women like herself, with time (if not with tragedy) on their hands, engaged in wholesome, refreshing activities. The atmosphere was cheerful and cathartic*. They learned things and they did things. They organized fêtes, bazaars, youth activities, sport, music, self-help and community projects. She got involved in committees, meetings, debates, conferences. It was for her a whole new venture into humancraft, and her personality blossomed. Philemon gave her all the rein she wanted.

Now, abiding by that silly ritual at home seemed a little thing … a very little thing …

Then one day she decided to organize a little party for her friends and their husbands. Philemon was very decent about it. He said it was all right. He even gave her extra money for it. Of

[14] Does Matilda see herself as one of the 'decent, married women', or has she come to see herself as Philemon sees her?

Matilda does not have the courage to confront Philemon, so she hopes to 'lose herself' – to forget about her terrible situation by doing something good and having contact with other people.

[15] Why do you think he allows her to participate in the activities of the women's club?

* cathartic: therapeutic

This sentence has an ominous tone. Philemon will allow Matilda freedom ('gave her rein'), but only for a short while before he will 'rein her in' again.

Matilda tries to persuade herself that her fate is not as bad as it seems.

* castigation: punishment

The way in which Philemon treats Matilda has an impact on him too.

More religious imagery that seems to suggest that things are improving for Matilda. The Biblical reference is to Jesus' feeding more than 5000 people by miraculously multiplying five loaves of bread and two fishes.

* edict: official statement issued by an authority. The word reveals the power Philemon wields.

Matilda has grown and regained some of her self-respect.

Again, Philemon is amused and delights in his wife's humiliation.

Philemon exploits the situation to the full and wields all the power he has over her to humiliate her in front of the guests.

An albatross is a large sea bird. Can Themba is referring to a famous epic poem, 'The Rime of the Ancient Mariner', where a sailor kills an albatross and this cruelty brings him bad luck. He is forced to wear the dead bird around his neck to show his guilt. Matilda's 'albatross' is the suit, the symbol of her guilt.

course, she knew nothing of the strain he himself suffered from his mode of castigation*.

There was a week of hectic preparation. Philemon stepped out of its cluttering way as best he could. So many things seemed to be taking place simultaneously. New dresses were made. Cakes were baked; three different orders of meat prepared; beef for the uninvited chancers; mutton for the normal guests; turkey and chicken for the inner pith of the club's core. To Philemon, it looked as if Matilda planned to feed the multitude on the Mount with no aid of miracles.

On the Sunday of the party, Philemon saw Matilda's guests. He was surprised by the handsome grace with which she received them. There was a long table with enticing foods and flowers and serviettes. Matilda placed all her guests round the table, and the party was ready to begin in the mock-formal township fashion. Outside a steady rumble of conversation went on where the human odds and ends of every Sophiatown party had their 'share'.

Matilda caught a curious look on Philemon's face. He tried to disguise his edict* when he said, 'Er – the guest of honour.'

But Matilda took a chance, She begged, 'Just this once, Phil.'

He became livid. 'Matilda!' he shouted. 'Get our visitor!' Then with incisive sarcasm, 'Or are you ashamed of him?'

She went ash-grey; but there was nothing for it but to fetch her albatross. She came back and squeezed a chair into some corner, and placed the suit on it. Then slowly she placed a plate of food before it. For a while the guests were dumbfounded. Then curiosity flooded in. They talked at the same time. 'What's the idea, Philemon?' … 'Why must she serve a suit?' … 'What's happening?' Some just giggled in a silly way. Philemon carelessly swung his head towards Matilda. 'You better ask my wife. She knows the fellow best.'

All interest beamed upon poor Matilda. For a moment she could not speak, all enveloped in misery. Then she said, unconvincingly, 'It's just a game that my husband and I play at mealtime.' They roared with laughter. Philemon let her get away with it.

The party went on, and every time Philemon's glare sent Matilda scurrying to serve the suit each course; the guests were no-end amused by the persistent mock-seriousness with which husband and wife played out their little game. Only, to Matilda, it was no joke; it was a hot poker* down her throat. After the party, Philemon went off with one of the guests who promised to show him a joint 'that sells genuine stuff, boy, genuine stuff.'

Reeling drunk, late that sabbath, he crashed through his kitchen door, towards his bedroom. Then he saw her.

They have a way of saying in the argot* of Sophiatown, 'Cook out of the head!' signifying that someone was impacted with such violent shock that whatever whiffs of alcohol still wandered through his head were instantaneously evaporated and the man stood sober before stark reality.

There she lay, curled as if just before she died she begged for a little love, implored some implacable lover to cuddle her a little … just this once … just this once more. [16]

In screwish anguish, Philemon cried, 'Tilly!'

In literature, writers exploit language in every possible way to make readers interpret their stories and characters in certain ways. If we read critically to identify their emphasis, tone and use of emotive words, and if we question their purpose, we will get a clearer idea of the events and characters that writers describe.

'The Suit' is about a failing relationship between a husband and wife. Thinking about how you would behave in a similar situation can help you to understand the story and your response to it more clearly.

- ⊕ Have you ever been involved in a relationship in which your partner cheated on you? If so, how did you discover that the person was dishonest to you and had another lover? How did you feel?

- ⊕ Even if you have not had such an experience, how do you imagine you would feel if you discovered that your partner had been unfaithful to you?

- ⊕ If your partner was having an affair with another person, would you prefer your friends to tell you about it, or would you rather not know? Why?

- ⊕ Would you consider taking revenge on your partner and the lover? Why? Do you think revenge would make you feel better about the whole matter in the long run?

Philemon exploits the situation to the full and wields all the power he has over her to humiliate her in front of the guests. The guests do not realize that the situation is serious; there is no game involved, but a malicious ritual.

* poker: metal bar for poking fires

He has tried to escape by drinking alcohol.

* argot: language specific to one group of people

[16] Even in her death she is begging for love. Did she receive such love from Philemon? Why did she have an affair?

'Screwish anguish' is an image of extreme torture and pain.

Investigating the text

'The Suit' is a challenging story that raises difficult questions about human behaviour and relationships. It was called 'a psychological thriller' by the famous South African poet, Chris van Wyk, who was a contemporary of Can Themba, because of the way the story builds up unspoken emotions to the final breaking point and tragedy. Some of the questions readers might ask are: Who are these characters and why do they behave in the ways they do? Is Philemon's treatment of Matilda fair or not? Is he justified in punishing her for being unfaithful to him? Why does Matilda kill herself? Can we hold Philemon responsible for her death?

Fortunately, we can develop skills to help us read and understand texts. Like police detectives who might investigate the facts surrounding Matilda's death, we need to become literary detectives who have to sift through the layers of evidence provided in the text.

Looking for clues: the plot

At the beginning of our literary detective work, we need to find out what happens in the story under investigation. The literary term for the series of events (or happenings) in a story is the plot. Plot is important, because our knowledge of what happens will influence the way we see characters and the motives for their behaviour.

You can use a timeline, like the one below, to summarize the plot of a story. A good understanding of the order of events allows us to see how they are linked and to decide on the causes and effects of specific actions and attitudes.

①	②	③
Philemon leaves for work	Maphikela tells Philemon about Matilda's affair	Philemon finds Matilda with her lover

Notice how the timeline shows only the important events, in the exact order in which they occur. You can copy the timeline and complete it after you have read the story.

Looking for clues: the context and setting

The events in a story always occur in a particular context. Context refers to the set of circumstances in which something takes place. Context includes the place where and the time when events occur. Setting means the location where the events take place. If we can understand the background against which things happen, we have better insight into the events and the characters, and ultimately the meaning of the story. As literary detectives we would ask:

⊙ How does the context direct and shape the motives and the actions of characters?

⊙ To what extent have the realities of a particular time and place influenced the actions shown in the text?

The events in 'The Suit' take place in Sophiatown before black people were removed by the National Party government. The narrator's description of Philemon's surroundings gives us clues about living conditions in Sophiatown at this time.

Poverty, over-crowding and inadequate facilities typify the environment in which Philemon and Matilda live. We can imagine that these difficult conditions have had an impact on the characters and their behaviour. Is there any suggestion that they act as they do because of their living conditions? Or is the behaviour of the characters in contrast to what we, the readers, might expect given the circumstances? There is seldom a direct, uncomplicated relationship between characters and their environments. Some characters may even come into conflict with aspects of or people in their environments. Nevertheless, we need to assess the extent to which circumstances help to explain the characters and their actions.

Looking for clues: meeting the characters

Philemon and Matilda are the central characters in 'The Suit'. Neither character is fixed or static in behaviour or personality; rather, they both change as the story progresses (as real people do in different situations). As we read through the story our impression of these characters changes as we see them in different situations.

We might see Philemon in at least five ways as we read through the story, as:

- a devoted husband,
- a hard-working man and a good friend,
- a cold, authoritarian and vengeful husband,
- a cruel man who takes pleasure in humiliating others, and
- a remorseful person in pain.

Each of these different ways of seeing Philemon occurs as we see him from different points of view, especially when we see his actions in the face of crisis. Together, these different points of view provide the reader with an integrated picture of his character. As we know, all people have different facets to their personalities. The same person might be both strict and compassionate, patient in one situation and irritable in another, or loving in some contexts and cruel in others. These different facets of character combine to form a unique identity. As we read 'The Suit' we continually adjust our idea of Philemon's identity (and the identities of the other characters).

In the case of Philemon, we realize that the picture that we have formed of him early on in the story might not be an entirely accurate or complete view of his character. Certain aspects of his personality are concealed or are only hinted at indirectly.

Look at the first three paragraphs of the story. What kind of man do they describe? What kind of man does Philemon appear to be?

Philemon sees himself as a devoted husband and his wife as a 'serene' and 'pure' woman. However, the moment he discovers that Matilda is having an affair with another man, his personality seems to change. In stories, as in life, it is often in times of crisis that a person is most likely to reveal hidden aspects of their character. At the first hint of trouble, Philemon exposes a side to his character that is not evident from the opening descriptions of a contented married man in a happy domestic environment. The internal tensions within Philemon's personality are revealed by Philemon's reaction to Maphikela's information that Matilda is being visited by a strange man.

Philemon's immediate, devastating suspicion is in conflict with his thoughts and ideas at the beginning of the story. Would a loving, trusting husband who believes in the purity of his wife be swayed by an unproven suggestion of her unfaithfulness? It seems as though Philemon's notion that their lives are perfect clashes with the way he actually behaves when his beliefs are put to the test. In crisis, Philemon's character crumbles and falls apart. We have two different character portrayals of Philemon now: Philemon as he appears at the beginning of the story, and Philemon as he responds to Maphikela's news.

Consider:

- Do you think Philemon has a realistic idea of what his wife is like? Do you think Matilda can live up to Philemon's expectations of her as a perfect wife?

- How does the image of Philemon conveyed in the first page of the story contrast with his behaviour towards Matilda later in the story?

- Consider his response to Matilda after he has discovered her unfaithfulness. Does this mean that Philemon is actually an incredibly cruel and vindictive character?

- Now consider Philemon's response when he discovers his wife's body. Is this the response of a cruel and vindictive man?

Now that we have considered Philemon as a character and the different ways he is presented throughout the story, we need to look at Matilda and how she sees the world. We also need to think about how she is seen by other people.

EXERCISE 2.11

Copy and complete the table on the next page to compare points of view on Matilda before and after her unfaithfulness is discovered.

	Matilda's view of herself	Philemon's view of Matilda
Before her unfaithfulness is discovered		
After her unfaithfulness has been discovered		
Before she joins the Cultural Club		
After she joins the Cultural Club		

Matilda's character changes over the course of the events depicted in the story. Immediately after Philemon has caught her in bed with another man, Matilda tries to please her husband by making their house and herself beautiful.

What we have read gives reason to suspect that Matilda has a low sense of self-esteem (she does not think highly of herself). The text of the story also tells us that she is afraid of what might happen to her should she have to survive on her own, without a husband. When Matilda joins the Cultural Club her attitude towards herself begins to change. She slowly discovers a new sense of self-worth. It is partly as a result of these changes that Matilda's death by suicide is so shocking.

Character and meaning

An understanding of the relationship between character and events (plot) can help us understand the hidden motives and reasons for the behaviour of the people we meet in life and in stories. Can Themba's short story raises many pertinent questions about character and behaviour. What we think about the issues it raises will depend both on how well we have understood the story and on the attitudes that we bring to bear on its events. Some of these attitudes, particularly those concerned with women and culture, are explored later in this book. For the meantime, we need to be aware that any response to a literary text is complex.

EXERCISE 2.12

1. Why is Matilda unfaithful to her husband?
2. How do you expect Philemon to behave when he discovers that his wife has been unfaithful?
3. How does Philemon actually respond to the discovery of his wife in bed with her lover? Does he respond in the way one would expect?
3. Is Philemon's response to his wife's infidelity appropriate?
4. Can you think of other ways in which he could have responded that might have been better for both of them?
5. Is Philemon justified in choosing to continue punishing his wife in the way he does, long after she has been unfaithful?
6. Is there any specific point at which Philemon should have forgiven her?

The narrative viewpoint

In our earlier discussion of first-person and third-person narrators, we noticed that the narrator's point of view may influence readers to sympathize with certain characters more than others. In 'The Suit' the narrative voice leads the reader into seeing the characters in particular ways. For example, when we finish reading 'The Suit', we might be appalled by Philemon's behaviour, and we might be horrified by the consequences of his actions. However, most readers are also, probably, left with some sympathy for him. Why does this happen? What is it that makes our reactions to Philemon so complicated and even contradictory?

One important influence on us is the narrator's technique of concentrating on Philemon's emotions and point of view at important stages in the story. Think about the end of the story in particular – his emotions are described in forceful and unusual terms ('In screwish anguish, Philemon cried, "Tilly!"'). Even though we might feel that Philemon is to blame for Matilda's suicide, the narrator tells us that he suffers terrible emotional pain because of her death. Since we as readers might also feel upset by the story, and especially by Matilda's suicide, there is a sense in which we are led by this to identify with Philemon. In sharing similar reactions with him we also share a similar point of view on the suicide. At least to some extent, we see things the way he sees them.

Another aspect that affects the way we see him is the ending of the story. Why does the narrator choose to end the story at Philemon's anguish? What feelings go into that anguish? Why is there no resolution to his guilt? By leaving the story at the point where he discovers his wife's death, the narrator also leaves the reader at an unresolved stage. We cannot fully put together our feelings of blame towards him for his emotional cruelty to his wife and our sympathy for the knowledge that he has finally gone too far in his revenge. These feelings mirror the way Philemon probably feels about himself.

FIVE DESCRIBING PEOPLE

In Chapter One we said that successful writing was more than simply listing events, and that, as writers, we need to take care to interest our readers. In this section, we will explore some methods of writing about people descriptively. Descriptive writing creates interest because it allows readers to visualize more vividly the scene, event or person being described. When we write descriptively, we usually use special kinds of words, called *adjectives* and *adverbs*.

ADJECTIVES

Adjectives are words that give us information about nouns, making them more specific and more detailed.

In English, adjectives can be used in different places in a sentence:

⊗ before nouns, as in 'a *colourful* flag'

ADVERBS

Adverbs are words that modify or describe verbs. Adverbs answer the questions 'how?', 'when?' and 'where?' about verbs. They often end in '-ly', as you can see in the examples below.

We can use adverbs for different purposes:

- after linking verbs such as 'be', 'seem' and 'look'; for example, 'You look *elegant*' and 'She is *clever*'
- after pronouns ending in 'somebody', 'someone', 'something' and 'somewhere'; for example, 'somewhere *quiet*', or 'something *entertaining*'.

Adverbs can describe verbs (actions) in greater detail; for example, 'She smiles *cheerfully*.'

We can use adverbs for emphasis, for example, 'He has *definitely* committed the crime.'

Adverbs can also modify adjectives; for example, 'I am *extremely* confused.'

Adverbs can modify whole sentences, for example, '*Unfortunately*, you have arrived too late for the examination.'

Adjectives and adverbs can be graded to indicate their intensity. They can also be compared. The most common intensifier is 'very', as in 'He is very angry'. There are three degrees of comparison: for instance, 'cold', 'colder', 'coldest'; 'good', 'better', 'best'.

EXERCISE 2.13

1. Now try using adjectives and adverbs to describe someone. You need not describe an invented character; it may be someone you know.
2. Choose no more than six adjectives that you think best describe the person. Some of your adjectives should describe the person's appearance and some should describe his or her personality. Think of how they dress and what they look like. What is their voice like? Do they have any peculiar characteristics that set them aside from other people?
3. Now choose adverbs to describe this person's actions.
4. Use these adjectives and adverbs to help you write a paragraph about the person you have chosen to describe. Try to give your reader a clear picture of what they are like and how they behave.

Now read the advice of a famous author on the use of adjectives and adverbs in fiction.

* overindulge: eat too much of something

* qualifier: a word, usually an adjective or adverb, that describes another word in a particular way

Adjectives and adverbs are rich and good and fattening. The main thing is not to overindulge*.

If the quality that the adverb indicates can be put in the verb itself (they ran quickly = they raced) or the quality the adjective indicates can be put in the noun itself (a growling voice = a growl), the prose will be cleaner, more intense, more vivid.

In Chapter Five of *The Elements of Style*, Strunk and White talk about the abuse of qualifiers*. The qualifiers I myself have to look out for are 'kind of,' 'sort of,' and 'just' – and always, always 'very.' You might just look at your own writing to see if you have some very favorite qualifiers that you kind of use just a little too often.

Some adjectives and adverbs have become meaningless through literary overuse. 'Great' seldom carries the weight it ought to carry. 'Suddenly' seldom means anything at all; it's a mere transition device, a noise – 'He was walking down the street. Suddenly he saw her.' 'Somehow' is a weasel word; it means the author didn't want to bother thinking out the story – 'Somehow she just knew … .' 'Somehow they made it to the asteroid … .' When I teach science fiction I ban the word. Nothing can happen 'somehow.'

I would recommend to all [writers and] storytellers a watchful attitude and a thoughtful, careful choice of adjectives and adverbs, because the bakery shop of English is rich beyond belief … (Le Guin, 1998: 61–62)

Now try reading a paragraph by a master of description (Charles Dickens). Pick out all the adjectives and adverbs and try to identify what they add to the picture of Magwitch, the villain of the story.

… A fearful man, all in coarse gray, with a great iron on his leg. A man with no hat, and with broken shoes, and with an old rag tied round his head. A man who had been soaked in water, and smothered in mud, and lamed by stones, and cut by flints, and stung by nettles, and torn by briars; who limped, and shivered, and glared and growled; and whose teech chattered in his head as he seized me by the chin. (Dickens, 1993: 2)

....

The passage uses very few adjectives, and no adverbs at all; yet it conveys a powerful feeling of menace in the figure of the man who appears out of nowhere to young Pip (the narrator). Now that you have read it, go back to the paragraphs you have just written and try to use stronger nouns and verbs instead of some of the adjectives and adverbs you used to describe someone.

Describing other people: actions

Authors do not create characters only by using adjectives. Fantasy author, Terry Pratchett, for instance, says that one should not 'describe' fictional characters: one should, instead, allow their personalities to emerge from what they do and say. This idea is based on the assumption that a character will speak and behave in a certain way, in accordance with his or her nature. Of course, the author still has to create and visualize that character, but the idea is that the author also uses actions to characterize the person. Certainly we gain most of our insight into the people we know from what they say and do, not only from what they look like.

Fleshing my characters
by Deborah Moggach

nce a character has gelled it's an unmistakable sensation, like an engine starting up within one's body. From then onwards, one is driven by this other person, seeing things through their eyes, shuffling around the shops as a 57-year-old divorced man and practically feeling one has grown a beard.

Moggach in Boylan (ed.), 1993

It is challenging to convey someone's character in a life-like manner. Words often do not say exactly what we would like them to say. It is hard to find exactly the right expressions to indicate changes in the tone of a voice or shifts in facial expression. Your descriptive writing is more likely to be successful if you have observed your subject closely and selected those details which are most important or revealing. More importantly, you will have to spend time thinking about your choice of descriptive words and editing your original transcript.

Writing drafts

Writing is a process. Even the most experienced writers write more than one draft of something. They go through a process of drafting, revising and rewriting until they are happy with the finished product. This is true both when you are writing an assignment essay and when you write a creative piece such as a poem or short story. When you write, you should follow these steps:

1. Carefully examine the topic on which you are to write; focus on what the topic requires you to write about.
2. Generate ideas about the topic. This is the planning stage of writing. Just write down ideas as they come to mind. Don't worry about putting your ideas down in a grammatical or well-phrased way at this stage. You could simply list ideas, make a mind-map or write down key words.
3. Now you are ready to write the first draft. Select the best ideas from the planning stage, put them together in sentences and organize these sentences into paragraphs.
4. The next stage is revision. Read through your first draft. Is your message clear? Is your writing interesting? Did you include all the relevant details?
5. Write the second draft, incorporating the improvements on your first draft. Now check the grammatical correctness of your piece of writing. Did you write full sentences? Have you used the correct tenses? Have you used punctuation marks correctly? Is your spelling correct?
6. Finally, revise your writing until you are satisfied with it. Be sure to write an effective concluding paragraph to bring the piece of writing to a close. Ask someone you know (and trust) to read through what you have written and to comment on it.

EXERCISE 2.14

To end this chapter, we are going to put these steps into practice. Use the steps above to write a description of a member of your family. Your description could take any form you like: a paragraph or two, a poem, a story, a letter to someone or an article for a magazine. Finally, show your work to other people who know that person and ask them what they think of it.

3 Made for Each Other: Ideas about Gender

THE PREVIOUS CHAPTER looked at how we think, speak about and represent ourselves and other people. In this chapter we will explore a particular aspect of identity, or 'being oneself', namely gender (we can also call this 'femininity' or 'masculinity': being feminine or masculine). We are going to read texts that have been written about gender and think about how gender influences the reading and writing of texts. As you work through this chapter, aim to spend some time developing your own understanding of gender, language and representation.

This chapter contains a variety of texts. There are extracts from literature and philosophy for you to read, information boxes providing you with interesting facts, and a number of writing exercises for you to do. All these texts are intended to help you understand what 'gender' means. As you work through them, you will need to think about the stereotypes and assumptions that surround gender. We hope that you will come to realize how people's views about gender shape our thinking about ourselves as well as the people we meet and interact with each day.

Historically, the study of gender began with women protesting against the roles that society prescribed for them. Thus, this chapter touches briefly on women's movements and the development of feminism. But in recent years more and more people have come to realize that it is not only women who possess gender: men are also 'gendered'. This chapter, then, looks at some of the ways in which gender applies to men and masculinity. But we cannot hope to cover all the ideas that have ever been thought or written about gender. Rather, you should use this chapter as a springboard for beginning to think about an important aspect of human life.

1. What is the *first* thing you notice about a new person you meet? Do you notice his or her age, race or gender (or other aspects)?
2. Who has power to make decisions in your family or community? Is it older people, or people with the most experience? Men? Women?
3. How has being a girl or a boy, a man or a woman, shaped your life?
4. What does it mean to be a girl or a boy, a man or a woman?

These are some of the questions we are going to explore in this chapter.

ONE GENDER

From the cradle to the grave

The first thing a doctor says when a baby is born is, 'It's a girl' or 'It's a boy'. This statement begins a story about how gender is created and lived through the whole life of a person. Right from early childhood, we tend to dress boys in blue (this practice dates from the time when blue was considered the colour of heaven, and since boys were thought to come from heaven, they were dressed in the same colour) and girls in pink to distinguish them from boys. In our time, pink has come to be associated with softness, fluffiness and, well, being decorative (rather than useful). From the day of birth on, we associate girls and boys with different qualities and different ways of being.

This situation continues. The box below gives a list of toys that parents and friends might buy for a small child. Separate the list into the ones you would buy for a boy, the ones you would buy for a girl, and those you would buy for a child of either sex.

> a ball; a doll; building blocks; paints; toy plates and cutlery; a toy car; a teddy bear; a toy wand; a Lego set; toy soldiers; animal toys; a skipping rope; a bicycle; a funny mask; face paints; toy tools; marbles; a toy radio; alphabet blocks; a toy helicopter; a drum

You probably divided the list along these lines, or something similar:

Boys: ball; building blocks; toy car; Lego set; toy soldier; bicycle; toy tools; marbles; toy helicopter

Girls: doll; paints; toy plates and cutlery; teddy bear; toy wand; skipping rope; face paints

Either sex: animal toys; funny mask; marbles; toy radio; alphabet blocks; drum

Why do we buy certain toys for girls and others for boys? Obviously we expect girls and boys to like different things, but why is this? Or do the toys we provide for children actually steer them into certain likes and dislikes?

There is no doubt that we do expect boys and girls to like and do different things. Indeed, we expect them to *be* different things – to exhibit different personality characteristics – as well. Among these expectations are: we anticipate that boys will enjoy physical activities, be 'rough' and do well at sport; we expect girls to be more interested in verbal activities, domestic games and artistic pursuits (in fact, to be less physical than boys). When children start school, we expect boys to behave worse than girls, to get involved in more physical fights in the playground and, later in school, we think they will be more intelligent than girls (at least in mathematics and physical science, which are seen as more important than languages and other human sciences). We expect girls to behave better and to be more intelligent in verbal matters, but not to get too involved in sport or physical conflict.

People often discuss what makes children the way they are. There are two sides to this argument. Some people believe that people behave in accordance with expectations for their gender because they are born with it. This opinion is the foundation of statements like, 'What else can you expect from a girl/boy/man/woman?' It holds that being masculine or feminine is part of one's nature. Other people believe that social forces, such as our families, our schools and people around us, make us the way we are. We develop 'masculine' or 'feminine' behaviour in response to what we learn as we are growing up. This view holds that our gender is a result of nurture, or the way we are brought up. As you read this chapter, you will encounter these points of view often.

Discuss these issues with people around you:

☺ When we say things like 'Boys are rougher than girls' or 'Girls talk more than boys', are we *observing* what children do, or are we *imposing* our ideas about gender on children?

☺ Do the different things people expect from boys and girls actually *create* these tendencies?

☺ Do children live up to what adults expect from them? And do they then learn to act out a certain role depending on their sex? (This is called a self-fulfilling prophecy.)

Eventually, people grow up, still embroiled in a system of roles based on whether they are male or female. By the time we reach adulthood, though, we are so used to the conventions surrounding 'being male' or 'being female' that they seem quite normal to us. We do not notice that the expectations of other people (our parents, siblings, teachers and peers) have shaped the way we see ourselves and other people from the beginning of our education in social life. In other words, it may not be natural for boys or

Stereotypes

The Oxford Advanced Learner's Dictionary defines 'stereotype' as:

noun a fixed idea or image that many people have of a particular person or thing, but which is often not true in reality: *cultural/gender/racial stereotypes*

A gender stereotype is the result of thinking along these lines: 'That person is a man (or a woman), so he (or she) must be ... '. For example, one might think that, because Joe is a man, he must enjoy watching sport on TV. Or, if Naledi is a woman, someone who doesn't know her might think that she must be good at cooking just because she is a woman. It doesn't take much thought to see the flaws in this kind of thinking.

Stereotypes result from assumptions – ideas that we receive from our culture and community (either through our family life, or through education). We generally do not question them. Everyone holds assumptions – we could not get through life without assuming, for example, that our cars will work in the morning – but they can be dangerous when we do not think about them carefully and critically or when we apply them to people without considering differences between individuals.

men to be 'sporty' and girls or women to be 'domestic'; males may not be born 'more rational' than females; and men may not be born leaders, while women may not be born mothers. These are only a few of the expectations and norms that come into play in our understanding of what it means to be a boy or a girl, a man or a woman. Things that we expect give rise to *stereotypes* and *assumptions* about other people.

The shape of people's bodies – whether they have a male or a female body – influences the roles they may play in the groups they live in (the family, school, the workplace, and so on). In earlier times, people believed that the division of human activity (often known as 'the division of labour') into 'men's stuff,' such as sport, and 'women's stuff,' such as cooking, was a natural result of having a particular kind of body. This is no longer as widely

Clothes maketh the man (or woman)

Let's take an obvious example: clothes. In traditional Western societies, girls and women wear dresses, while boys and men wear trousers; and we all know that only women wear high heels and make-up. This pattern is enacted for us daily, and so we do not stop to question why it is so. It seems 'natural' to us: it is 'just the way things are'. The truth is, though, that so-called 'natural' habits of behaviour are learned over many years, and may not be natural or inborn at all. There is no universal reason why women should dress in a certain way (following a particular dress code) and men should dress in another way. In fact, conventional Western dress codes for men and women are not the only possible ones at all. Scottish men wear skirts called kilts for ceremonial occasions, and many men in Asian, Indian and African cultures wear clothes that look like dresses. As you probably know, too, clothes are more than mere coverings for our bodies or protection against the weather: they also make statements about how we want to be seen.

Clothes are an important marker of gender difference; they also have an impact on what the people wearing them can do. A girl in a dress cannot climb a tree or hang upside-down easily; a pencil skirt and high heels do not allow one to run fast; clothes for boys and men allow them to move more easily (while concealing 'sexualized' parts of the body, of course). Women tend to wear more decorations on their bodies, such as jewellery, scarves and make-up, than men do. Is this merely because, in our societies, women tend to be the ones who are 'chased' by men looking for sexual partners and so they need to make themselves more attractive to men? Or are these decorations, as advertising and other media would have us believe, an important part of a woman's care for herself? Why don't most Western men usually wear such decorations?

When you read works of literature (poetry or fiction), try to imagine what the characters could be wearing and how this reflects their gender.

accepted as before. Nowadays we tend to think that gender roles, instead of being natural or given, are constructed by the societies we live in.

Three keywords: sex, gender and desire

The *Oxford Advanced Learner's Dictionary* provides the same definition for the words 'sex' and 'gender'. The meaning of both words is given as 'the condition of being male or female'. In practice, though, we tend to use the words in connection with different meanings. We use 'sex' to refer to the shape of a person's body: whether they have a male or a female body. 'Gender' is used to mean the social role that a person plays, based on whether they are male or female, and we use the words 'masculine' and 'feminine' when we want to speak about gender.

Gender need not mean the same as sex: a man could be more 'masculine' or more 'feminine', and so could a woman. Not all women conform to what we think of as 'feminine' at all, and not all men like to behave in terms of socially accepted ideas of being 'masculine'. The descriptions 'masculine' and 'feminine' themselves need to be thought about in detail, as they have a very important influence on how people see themselves and others. The expression 'Boys don't cry' is only one example of popular views of masculinity: Can you think of others? And what about our views of femininity? Another way to think about this is in terms of 'real men' and 'real women'. What does a 'real man' or a 'real woman' think or do? How does he or she look?

'Lady' versus 'woman': Denotation and connotation

The primary or most obvious dictionary meaning of 'lady' and 'woman' is an adult human female. That is, they both have the same denotation (they 'point to' the same thing). But they have very different connotations, which are additional meanings, associations or values attached to them. We cannot use them interchangeably. See the next exercise.

EXERCISE 3.2

The following sentences all contain the word 'lady' or the word 'woman'. (Many of them come from popular sayings, or have been said by famous people.) Try changing each sentence by substituting the other word and see if the new sentence means the same as the first version.

1. It is a lady's privilege to change her mind.
2. 'What do women want?' (Sigmund Freud, father of psychoanalysis)
3. Ladies are never rude.
4. A woman should be barefoot, pregnant and in the kitchen.
5. The Queen is a real lady.
6. 'The children of a real woman do not grow thin or die.' (Batswana proverb)
7. Behind every great man is a woman.

This exercise is designed to show you that there is a vast difference between the meanings surrounding 'lady' and 'woman'. While a woman can be any adult human female, a lady is a particular kind of woman. The meanings attached to the word 'lady' include refinement, lack of aggression (even passivity), beauty and the appreciation of beauty, and a degree of class or style.

'Ladies' do not, for example, usually get dirty doing heavy manual work, and they are often to be found in lounges, drinking tea. They never do anything that is rude or unbecoming, such as losing their tempers or blowing their noses. Their power and influence is domestic rather than public. In short, they do not get involved in the important activities of human life. Women, on the other hand, have a much more interesting and active life.

Do you agree? What meanings do you associate with the words 'lady' and 'woman'?

The feminist movement

Many women throughout history have protested against the roles that were assigned to them by their parents and societies. They did not like being confined to their homes and expected to do only domestic duties or spend all their time raising children. Instead, they went out into the world and pursued their own interests. The box on the left gives some examples.

But, if women have not always liked the roles that are given to them, men may also feel burdened by people's expectations about masculinity. Sometimes it is difficult to grow up as a boy, despite what people may think about boys having a better deal or having the best of everything. This is usually because their families expect them to carry on the family name and to contribute financially to their family's well-being.

Here is a humorous piece from a short story about the difficulties of being a man in the United States. Read it and see whether you can identify with anything it says about being a man or a woman.

Address to the National Federation of Associations Convention, Minneapolis, June 12, 1993
by Garrison Keillor

Here's what they won't tell you in class:

Girls had it better from the beginning, don't kid yourself. They were allowed to play in the house, where the books were and the adults, and boys were sent outside like livestock. Boys were noisy and rough, and girls were nice, so they got to stay and we had to go. Boys ran around in the yard with toy guns going *kksshh-kksshh*, fighting wars for made-up reasons and arguing about who was dead, while girls stayed inside and played with dolls, creating complex family groups and learning to solve problems through negotiation* and role-playing. Which gender is better equipped, on the whole, to live an adult life, would you guess? (APPLAUSE, SHOUTS) Is there any doubt about this? Is it even *close*?

Adolescence hits boys harder than it does girls. Girls bleed a little and their breasts pop out, big deal, but adolescence lands on a guy with both feet, a bad hormone experience. You are crazed with madness. Your body is engulfed by chemicals of rage and despair, you pound, you shriek, you batter your head against the trees. You come away wounded, feeling that life is unknowable, can never be understood, only endured and sometimes cheated.

Women know about life and social life and how to get along with others, and they are sensitive to beauty, and at the same time they can yell louder. They know all about guys, having been exposed to guy life and guy b.s.* since forever, and guys know nothing about girls except that they want one desperately. Which gender is better equipped to manipulate* the other?

The father of a daughter, for example, is nothing but a high-class hostage. A father turns a stony face to his sons, berates* them, shakes his antlers, paws the ground, snorts, runs them off into the underbrush, but when his daughter puts her arm over his shoulder and says, 'Daddy, I need to ask you something,' he is a pat of butter in a hot frying pan. The butter thinks to itself, 'This time I really am going to remain rectangular,' and then it feels very relaxed, and then it smells smoke.

Men adore women. Our mothers taught us to. Women do not adore men; women are amused by men, we are a source of chuckles. That's because women are the makers of life, and we aren't. We will never be able to carry life within our bodies, never breast-feed. We get more than our share of loot and we are, for some reason, incredibly brave and funny and inventive, and yet our role in procreation basically is to get crazy and howl and spray our seed in all directions.

Keillor, 1993: 12–13

* negotiation: discussion between people who are trying to reach an agreement

* guy b.s.: male nonsense, literally 'bullshit'

* manipulate: control or influence somebody, sometimes in a dishonest way

* berates: scolds

EXERCISE 3.3

1. Did this piece amuse you? Why?
2. Did anything in the extract sound familiar? Explain.

Let's look at the main ideas in the extract.

First, this is not an extract from a real speech, but, rather, a fictional one (it did not really take place). The speaker is addressing a group of men and discussing his views on being a man. He explains that 'guys' (men) feel inferior to women, for a number of reasons; the most important is that women are the 'makers of life' because they can bear children and men are not and cannot. Do you agree with him?

The image of women created in this extract is of sophisticated, refined beings who have finely-developed social skills, due to having been allowed to play inside and act out family situations. Furthermore, the speaker says, women are amused by men rather than 'adoring' them. Does this ring true for you?

Finally, the speaker argues that girls 'have it better' because they are allowed to play sophisticated, enjoyable games inside while boys are seen as undesirable (noisy and rough) and so are exiled from the company of girls. While girls grow up familiar with 'guy stuff', guys are not allowed to get to know anything about girls, and so they find girls strange (although highly desirable). Do you agree with this view?

There are other views on being masculine, too. One powerful image is provided by the idea of 'macho' and 'machismo'.

> **machismo** *noun* [U] (from *Spanish*, usually *disapproving*) aggressive male behaviour that emphasizes the importance of being strong rather than being intelligent and sensitive
>
> **macho** *adj.* (usually *disapproving*) male in an aggressive way: *He's too macho to ever admit he was wrong; macho pride/posturing*

We can find typical examples of 'macho' behaviour in many works of literature. Here is one example.

The Kite Runner

by Khaled Hosseini

e crossed the residential street* and were trekking through a barren patch of rough land that led to the hill when, suddenly, a rock struck Hassan in the back. We whirled around and my heart dropped. Assef and two of his friends, Wali and Kamal, were approaching us.

Assef was the son of one of my father's friends, Mahmood, an airline pilot. His family lived a few streets south of our home, in a posh, high-walled compound with palm trees. If you were a kid living in the Wazir Akbar Khan section of Kabul, you knew about Assef and his famous stainless-steel brass knuckles*, hopefully not through personal experience. Born to a German mother and an Afghan father, the blond, blue-eyed Assef towered over the other kids. His well-earned reputation for savagery preceded him on the streets. Flanked by his obeying friends, he walked the neighborhood like a Khan* strolling through his land with his eager-to-please entourage*. His word was law, and if you needed a little legal education, then those brass knuckles were just the right teaching tool. I saw him use those knuckles once on a kid from the Karteh-Char district. I will never forget how Assef's blue eyes glinted with a light not entirely sane and how he grinned, how he *grinned*, as he pummeled that poor kid unconscious. Some of the boys in Wazir Akbar Khan had nicknamed him Assef *Goshkor*, or Assef 'the Ear Eater.' Of course, none of them dared utter it to his face unless they wished to suffer the same fate as the poor kid who had unwittingly inspired the nickname when he had fought Assef over a kite and ended up fishing his right ear from a muddy gutter. Years later, I learned an English word for the creature that Assef was, a word for which a good Farsi* equivalent does not exist: 'sociopath'*.

His blue eyes flicked to Hassan. 'Afghanistan is the land of Pashtuns. It always has been, always will be. We are the true Afghans, the pure Afghans, not this Flat-Nose here. His people pollute our homeland, our *watan*. They dirty our blood.' He

* **residential street:** a street where people live, as opposed to a street in a business area or an open space

* **brass knuckles:** false knuckles made of brass that fit over Assef's real knuckles and give him a more powerful punch

* **Khan:** a title given to rulers in some Muslim countries

* **entourage:** group of followers

* **Farsi:** a Middle Eastern language

* **sociopath:** a person who has a mental illness; may behave aggressively

made a sweeping, grandiose gesture with his hands. 'Afghanistan for Pashtuns, I say. That's my vision.'

Assef shifted his gaze to me again. He looked like someone coming out of a good dream. 'Too late for Hitler,' he said. 'But not for us.'

He reached for something from the back pocket of his jeans. 'I'll ask the president to do what the king didn't have the *quwat** to do. To rid Afghanistan of all the dirty, *kasseef** Hazaras.'

'Just let us go, Assef,' I said, hating the way my voice trembled. 'We're not bothering you.'

'Oh, you're bothering me,' Assef said. And I saw with a sinking heart what he had fished out of his pocket. Of course. His stainless steel brass knuckles sparkled in the sun. 'You're bothering me very much. In fact, you bother me more than this Hazara here. How can you talk to him, play with him, let him touch you?' he said, his voice dripping with disgust. Wali and Kamal nodded in agreement. Assef narrowed his eyes. Shook his head. When he spoke again, he sounded as baffled as he looked. 'How can you call him your 'friend'?'

But he's not my friend! I almost blurted. *He's my servant!* Had I really thought that? Of course I hadn't. I hadn't. I treated Hassan well, just like a friend, better even, more like a brother. But if so, then why, when Baba's friends came to visit with their kids, didn't I ever include Hassan in our games? Why did I play with Hassan only when no one else was around?

Assef slipped on the brass knuckles. Gave me an icy look. 'You're part of the problem, Amir. If idiots like you and your father didn't take these people in, we'd be rid of them by now. They'd all just go rot in Hazarajat where they belong. You're a disgrace to Afghanistan.'

I looked in his crazy eyes and saw that he meant it. He *really* meant to hurt me. Assef raised his fist and came for me.

There was a flurry of rapid movement behind me. Out of the corner of my eye, I saw Hassan bend down and stand up quickly. Assef's eyes flicked to something behind me and widened with surprise. I saw that same look of astonishment on Kamal and Wali's faces as they too saw what had happened behind me.

I turned and came face to face with Hassan's slingshot. Hassan had pulled the wide elastic band all the way back. In the cup was

* quwat: courage

* kasseef: lower-class or inferior

a rock the size of a walnut. Hassan held the slingshot pointed directly at Assef's face. His hand trembled with the strain of the pulled elastic band and beads of sweat had erupted on his brow.

'Please leave us alone, Agha*,' Hassan said in a flat tone. He'd referred to Assef as 'Agha,' and I wondered briefly what it must be like to live with such an ingrained sense of one's place in a hierarchy*.

Assef gritted his teeth. 'Put it down, you motherless* Hazara.'

'Please leave us be, Agha,' Hassan said.

Assef smiled. 'Maybe you didn't notice, but there are three of us and two of you.'

Hassan shrugged. To an outsider, he didn't look scared. But Hassan's face was my earliest memory and I knew all of its subtle nuances, knew each and every twitch and flicker that ever rippled across it. And I saw that he was scared. He was scared plenty.

'You are right, Agha. But perhaps you didn't notice that I am the one holding the slingshot. If you make a move, they'll have to change your nickname from Assef 'the EarEater' to 'One-Eyed Assef,' because I have this rock pointed at your left eye.' He said this so flatly that even I had to strain to hear the fear that I knew hid under that calm voice.

Hosseini, 2003: 33–37

---

* Agha: a term of respect, roughly equivalent to 'Sir'

* hierarchy: a system of social value, with people organized from the least important to the most important

* motherless: in many cultures, the worst form of insult is to insult another person's mother

Assef and his friends pride themselves on their masculinity, which, for them, means dominating other people. They associate male power with racial or class superiority. At the time when the above incident takes place, society in Afghanistan (as in many other countries) was divided along class and ethnic lines. Pashtuns, who had money and could afford a wealthy lifestyle, include Assef and Amir. Hazaras were similar to gypsies and belonged to the servant class, who were much poorer than Pashtuns. Part of Assef's confidence in attacking Amir and Hassan comes from his 'superior' class; but the greatest part of it comes from his ideas about maleness. His brass knuckles and the two friends who flank him (but do not initiate any action in the fight) only reinforce his security in being aggressive towards weaker people. When he harasses and intimidates Amir and Hassan, he believes that he is being a tough guy. In another context, though, Assef's behaviour would be called bullying. Hassan shows a different approach to masculinity when he stands up to Assef and forces him to retreat.

EXERCISE 3.4

1. What do you think about Assef's approach to being male?
2. What is your response to Hassan's version of being male?
3. Which one do you prefer? Why?
4. Can you imagine girls behaving as any of the three characters in the passage above do? Why/why not?

The speaker in the passage above is Amir, whose ideas about masculinity change throughout the novel. Assef believes that 'being a real man' or 'being macho' gives him the right to hurt people, while Hassan is much gentler, while still displaying considerable bravery in his defence of his friend.

Boys and girls are brought up differently and, as a result, grow up differently **because** they are boys or girls. The expectations that we have of boy-children and girl-children develop into expectations that we have of men and women; and these, in turn, become the roles that people play in their families and communities. Here are some common expectations that people hold in relation to the two genders:

Men ...	Women ...
like physical activity, such as sport, building or repairing their homes.	like domestic activities, such as cooking, decorating their homes and washing clothes.
are rational (or even, intellectual).	are emotional.
don't show their feelings (as in the saying, 'Boys don't cry').	can't be relied on to stay calm.
have stronger muscles than women.	are physically weak and therefore need to be protected by men.
are natural leaders in the workplace and the home.	are naturally good at caring for children.
(Add your own ideas here.)	(Add your own ideas here.)

Of course, the descriptions in the table above are are generalizations – statements about everyone in a particular group of people, which might not be true for every single person in that group.

Sexuality (or desire)

We do not usually speak of someone as having a female or male 'sexuality'. 'Sexuality' usually means sexual orientation, or the choices that people make about having sex. The people we have sex with often become our life partners because we love them. So the practice of sexuality is tied up with the system of marriage. We are taught (by our parents, by books, films, magazines and television) to look for a person of the opposite sex to love and desire. In many societies, marriage and family produces a home with a man, a woman and some children – who are intended, in turn, to produce their own offspring. Some people choose partners of the same sex, and there are many variations on the family unit.

Like our ideas about gender roles, beliefs about sexuality also reflect prejudices and assumptions. For instance, some people think that women are less interested in having sex than men, or that it is 'unfeminine' for a woman to enjoy sex or to express sexual desire. Then there is the commonly held belief that men need to have many sexual partners while women only need or want one partner. Throughout Western history, these beliefs have given men more sexual freedom than women; they have also ensured that women remained sexually faithful to the men they married. As a result, men could be sure that their wives' children were also theirs, and they could be certain that they were leaving their property

Some more facts about marriage

Another controversial practice in marriage is polygamy, the custom of a man marrying more than one wife. It is practiced in Africa, India, China, the Arab states, by Mormons in the United States, and by orthodox Muslims everywhere. In its favour, it may be seen to provide co-wives financial security and also with a form of sisterhood in their situations. But it also raises problems in relationships between the wives and the ways in which the husband divides his time, attention and sexual energies among his wives. It is very controversial, because some women do not like sharing their husbands with other wives; they may feel that it is unfaithful; or they may feel 'put down' by a system which gives certain wives more power than others. Many women, including South African-born Bessie Head and Senegalese Mariama Bâ, criticize polygamy quite energetically because of its negative effects on women. What do you think?

to the right children. Land and inheritance rights have always been very important in places where there is fierce competition for space.

In many cultures, including in African countries, women are seen as valuable property belonging to their fathers. This is demonstrated by the custom of the prospective husband asking the bride's father for permission to marry his daughter (and even paying 'lobola' for the privilege). While this may seem an honourable tradition, one may assume that the woman's choice in the matter is not important – it is her father's wish and approval that count. After marriage, a wife 'belongs to' her husband, almost like any other piece of property. An unmarried woman is often treated with pity and the unspoken question is asked, 'What was wrong with her? Why couldn't she find a husband?'

Once a woman is married, most cultures expect that she will bear a child or children. In many African societies, having children during the engagement period is encouraged. A childless woman is shamed, as though it were her fault that she could not have children and there is nothing wrong with her husband (in other words, men are perfect by nature). Her husband is not seen in quite the same guilty light. In many cultures, it is also very important to men that the women they marry should have no sexual experience. Many women who have had sex before marriage are seen as 'dirty' and much less attractive to a prospective husband, while nobody asks the man whether *he* is a virgin or not. After marriage, women are expected to be 'chaste' or sexually faithful to their husbands.

Born to hunt

Many common ideas or assumptions about men, women and the relationships between them are reflected in the following short extract.

....

Man is a hunter by nature. He likes to chase his game. His pleasure lies in the pursuit. With capture and possession there often comes lack of interest; so that the wise woman restrains herself at such passionate moments, in order that he may be kept eager in his pursuit. (Cole in Sian, 1994: 13)

....

The assumptions in the passage are not expressed directly, since the writer uses metaphorical language to make her point. The writer speaks about relationships between men and women, but uses the metaphor of hunting to convey her ideas to readers. Now that you have read the extract, copy and complete the table that follows. This table lists some of the assumptions that appear in the extract. Next to each assumption, write down how you feel about it, whether you agree with it or not and why.

EXERCISE 3.5

Assumption	My feelings and reactions
A man is a hunter.	
A man likes to 'hunt' and chase a woman.	
Although a man likes to chase a woman, he doesn't like actually succeeding.	
After a man has successfully achieved a relationship with a woman, he loses interest in her.	
A woman should play hard to get, because this will keep the man interested in her.	

Hysteria and ideas about women

Many Western ideas about politics, culture and society are based on ancient Greek models. The word 'hysteria' comes from the ancient Greek word for womb (*hystera*), and this connection links

Metaphor

A metaphor is an implied comparison. The word 'metaphorical' refers to our habit of using words in ways that are different from their obvious or 'literal' meanings. 'Metaphor' is language used to suggest that something is 'as if' it is something else, although the words 'as if' do not appear on the page.

For example: You are my sunshine. (This does not mean that the person is really the speaker's sunshine. It means that he or she shares the sun's features: he or she brings light, warmth, happiness and life. The sun and the person are being compared.)

When a metaphor describes something – a thing, a person or an idea – as if it were something else, it suggests that there are similarities between it and the thing it is described as. It implies that they have some of the same characteristics and makes connections between things that are not necessarily or directly connected. Metaphors make descriptions in writing more interesting and powerful, but this is not their only use. A metaphor is a condensed form of language, communicating a great deal of meaning in a few words.

hysteria and being female from the earliest times of civilization. Ancient Greek doctors, following the ideas of the famous doctor Hippocrates, thought that a woman's womb or uterus did not stay in a fixed spot in her body. They thought that it moved around, and that this movement caused the woman's body to react in various ways. In particular, when the womb reached the area around the heart, it blocked the blood flow and caused the woman to feel faint, excitable, short of breath and irrational. They said then that the woman was being *hysterikos*, or 'hysterical'. Relying on this idea about women's wombs, the logic behind the invention of the term 'hysterical' would be: since it seems 'natural' for a woman to have a womb (uterus), it also seems 'natural' for her to behave hysterically. It seemed 'unnatural' for a man to be hysterical. Behaviour of that sort, when performed by a man, would be called 'unmanly' and 'womanish'.

Influenced by Greek ideas on this subject, the ancient Romans referred to the woman's womb as an animal that needed to be driven back into its lair. This suggests that they saw the womb and its alleged effects as dangerous and wild. It also suggests a view of women as threatening, inferior and animal-like, needing to be tamed. Roman medical practices included methods for treating illnesses related to the womb; they would apply substances and objects to the woman's body in order to push the womb back to where it was allegedly meant to be. These practices were brutal and caused great suffering for women. They also show that the ideas that people have about one another have deeply important consequences (results). In this example, such consequences could include pain and even death.

Beliefs about hysteria continued to focus on women for many years. People still thought of hysterical behaviour as typical of women (some people still believe this). In the nineteenth century, the French doctor Jean Charcot conducted research into hysteria. The patients he studied were mostly women. The word 'hysteria' was used to describe illnesses such as blindness and the loss of speech when it was unclear what had caused the condition. In this way, mysterious illnesses became associated with women, and with the idea of hysteria. Nowadays, we call these symptoms *psychosomatic*, indicating that the way we think has a direct influence on the physical body.

SUMMARY

The chain of ideas associating women with hysteria goes like this:

1. Women's sexual organs (their wombs) are wild and unpredictable.

2. These organs make women behave in uncontrollable ways.

3. Women are at the mercy of their sexual organs, which produce their emotions.

4. Men do not have the same sexual organs, so they are not prone to emotional extremes and excesses. They are much more rational than women.

5. Men do not have to take women's emotions seriously; they should treat women's emotions as one would treat the feelings of a child, and try to bring women back under control.

These ideas may seem illogical and far-fetched – for example, plenty of men lose control and give in to emotional outbursts – but traces of them can still be seen today. Remember this the next time you (or anybody around you) are tempted to label a woman as 'hysterical'!

TWO FEMINISM IN EUROPE AND THE UNITED STATES

During the Victorian era (1837–1901, when Queen Victoria ruled Britain and all its colonies), women were seen as weak and only fit for domestic life, and were supposed to aspire to the ideal of being 'the angel in the house', self-sacrificing, 'cultured' and obedient. In other words, they were not allowed to seek employment or to earn their own money. They were, therefore, financially dependent on men for support. A woman had to find a husband, or she was likely to face severe financial difficulties which would keep her dependent on her parents and family for support.

This arrangement had negative implications for both men and women. Men had to find jobs that would pay them enough to support their wives and children; women had to stay at home and look after their homes and children. Now there is nothing wrong in men finding lucrative careers, and nothing wrong in women devoting themselves to the care of their homes and children; but being *forced* into these roles made many people (mostly women) very uncomfortable. Some men did not like being corporate executives, and many women loved their families, but still wished for a more stimulating life with their own financial independence. The system of assigning people to roles in the workplace and at home, with men being assigned to the 'important' task of having careers and earning money while women were generally not expected to work outside their homes after marriage, placed enormous strain on both men and women. What we call 'first-wave' feminism began to focus on absolute rights such as suffrage (the right to vote), and most Western countries eventually gave women this right in the early part of the 20th century – but only after persistent demonstrations, jail, hunger strikes and a world war that proved women were able to do the work of men in every aspect of communal life.

Here is an extract from one of the most famous novels of the Victorian era, *Middlemarch* by George Eliot (the assumed name of the writer Mary Ann Evans). The extract gives the thoughts of one of the main characters, Dorothea Brooke, about her future as a woman in her small-town society. Dorothea is unique in her interest in academic and political affairs, but her sense of being trapped is typical of many women in the Victorian age.

What could she do, what ought she to do? She, hardly more than a budding woman, but yet with an active conscience and a great mental need, not to be satisfied by a girlish instruction comparable to the nibblings and judgments of a discursive* mouse … . The intensity of her religious disposition, the coercion* it exercised over her life, was but one aspect of a nature altogether ardent*, theoretic*, and intellectually consequent*; and with such a nature, struggling in the bands of a narrow teaching, hemmed in by a social life which seemed nothing but a labyrinth of petty courses*, a walled-in maze of small paths that led no whither*, the outcome was sure to strike others as at once exaggeration and inconsistency. (Eliot, 2001: 28–29)

---

* discursive: in relation to discourse or language: here, Dorothea feels like a mouse compared to people around her who have more power in language than she does.

* coercion: being forced to do something

* ardent: passionate, very enthusiastic, showing strong feelings

* theoretic: abstract, more interested in theory than in practical matters

* consequent: an old-fashioned word for consistent

* courses: paths

* no whither: nowhere

EXERCISE 3.6

1. Why is Dorothea so unhappy with her life and prospects?
2. Do you think Dorothea has a good reason to be discontented with the role that her community expects her to fill?
3. Would Dorothea be able to look forward to a different kind of life (a happier one) if she were a man?

Dorothea is discontented because she feels that her life is limited to a 'small' sphere of influence, in which she cannot achieve very much and cannot fulfil her dreams of doing something substantial and good for the less fortunate people around her. The men around Dorothea – her uncle, Mr Brooke, her suitor, Sir James Chettam, and the ancient Mr Casaubon, whom she eventually marries – cannot understand Dorothea's ideals and aspirations. She continues to pursue them, though, undertaking many charitable projects in the village where she lives, until she meets and falls in love with Will Ladislaw, whom she marries, and (apparently) settles down into domestic life with no memory of her earlier dreams at all.

In a similar way to Dorothea, women in America in the 1950s, shortly after the Second World War (1939–1945), were also relegated to their homes. As with the First World War, which helped give the vote to women in Britain and the USA, the Second World War involved many men in the armed forces, with the result that women stayed behind and ran the countries' essential services such as transport, communications and working in factories. At the end of the War, the soldiers returned home and women were 'freed' from the burden of having to work just to ensure that the country was provided with essentials. Most people expected that the nation's women would be delighted to be free of the hardships of work and able to occupy themselves with their homes.

But this was not the case, as the sociologist, Betty Friedan, found out. Friedan and her friends all completed a questionnaire about their feelings of satisfaction with themselves and their lives. She found out that they all suffered from 'the problem that has no name': feelings of discontent, dissatisfaction, lack of fulfillment and even depression. Friedan's name for the problem was the title of her book: *The Feminine Mystique* (published in 1963). In her book, she argues that it is false to expect women to find all their fulfillment in their husbands, homes and children. They also need stimulation for themselves, and she argues that, although people expected that women would be delighted to be returned to their 'rightful' places (at home), the truth was the opposite. Many women complained of depression, lack of motivation and dissatisfaction when they were not given anything more challenging to do than raise children and attend to domestic work. Friedan concludes that the assumption that women like domestic activity more than working life must be wrong. She goes on to argue that this assumption has been the reason for women to be denied education after school and to say that this practice must be stopped immediately, so that the doors to learning and empowerment could be opened to women.

Betty Friedan's book, *The Feminine Mystique*, is important in the development of 'the women's movement' (also known as feminism) because it is part of 'second-wave feminism'. This period was concerned with the issue of economic and other forms of equality, including the ability to have careers in addition to motherhood, or the right to choose not to have children.

In this movement, women campaigned extensively for equal rights with men. These included equal access to education; equal pay for equal work; and equal citizenship rights. Although the feminists of the second wave met with a great deal of opposition and accusations of being 'unfeminine' and 'aggressive', most of the rights they campaigned for have been achieved. In South Africa today, for example, it is against constitutional law (the highest law in the land) to discriminate against anyone on the basis of their gender. This means that employers have to give women equal chances for appointment and promotion in the workplace with men, and that women are equal to men in public life. But does this mean that men and women have equal power and rights in *all* areas of life?

Third-wave feminists would say no, because women are still expected to do most of the housework and child-care, while having high-powered jobs at the same time. The poem below explains some of the feelings of a feminist in the late twentieth century:

Because we're women
by Joyce Stevens

Because our work is never done
and under or unpaid or boring or repetitious
and we're the first to get the sack
and what we look like is more important than what we do
and if we get raped it's our fault
and if we get bashed we must have provoked it
and if we raise our voices we're nagging bitches
and if we enjoy sex we're nymphos*
and if we don't we're frigid*

* nymphos: short for nymphomaniacs (women who are addicted to sex)

* frigid: sexually unfeeling

and if we love women it's because we can't get a real man
and if we ask our doctor too many questions we're neurotic
and/or pushy
and if we expect community care for children we're selfish
and if we stand up for our rights we're aggressive and
unfeminine
and if we don't we're typical weak females
and if we want to get married we're out to trap a man
and if we don't we're unnatural
and because we still can't get an adequate safe contraceptive*
but men can walk on the moon
and if we can't cope or don't want a pregnancy
we're made to feel guilty about abortion
and for lots and lots of other reasons
we are part of the women's liberation movement

* contraceptive: medicine or device used by women to prevent themselves getting pregnant

Gender inequality

This leads us to consider a claim made by Michael Kimmel, who has written numerous books about gender. Kimmel writes:

> Gender is not simply a system of classification, by which biological males and biological females are sorted, separated and socialized into equivalent sex roles. Gender also expresses the universal inequality between women and men. When we speak about gender we also speak about hierarchy, power, and inequality, not simply difference.
>
> So the two tasks of any study of gender, it seems to me, are to explain both difference and inequality, or, to be alliterative, *difference* and *dominance*. Every general explanation of gender must address two central questions, and their ancillary derivative questions.
>
> First: *Why is it that virtually every single society differentiates people on the basis of gender?* Why are women and men perceived as different in every known society? What are the differences that are perceived? Why is gender at least one – if not the central – basis for the division of labor?

Second: *Why is it that virtually every known society is also based on male dominance?* Why does virtually every society divide social, political, and economic resources unequally between the genders? And why is it that men always get more? Why is a gendered division of labor also an unequal division of labor? Why are women's tasks and men's tasks valued differently? (Kimmel, 2000: 1–2)

Kimmel is claiming here that the system of 'gendering' people (or giving them gender roles) has two results: it produces *difference* between women and men, and it creates male *dominance*, in which men have more power and more resources than women. We are going to stop here and consider whether we agree with these ideas.

IDEA ONE: MEN AND WOMEN ARE DIFFERENT

Some people believe that men and women simply are different and there is nothing to be done about it. (Kimmel humorously calls this 'the interplanetary theory' of gender difference, implying that it speaks about women and men as if they came from different planets.) Individuals, then, need to accept the innate differences between women and men and all the consequences of this difference. One consequence is that they cannot communicate meaningfully with one another, or can do so only in limited ways.

EXERCISE 3.7

Do you agree that men and women are innately different? Give reasons from your own experience to support your point of view.

IDEA TWO: MEN DOMINATE WOMEN

This idea means that men have more power and a greater share of the good things in life than women do. They get more education (women are considered 'not worth educating' since they are only going to get married and, after marriage, look after children, anyway); more money, greater political power, more freedom, more opportunities to make important decisions and more say in how their communities function than women do. They achieve this by not allowing women to have access to these desirable things, abilities and resources. In other words, men keep women in an inferior, second-rate position.

EXERCISE 3.8

Do you agree that men have 'a better deal' than women in society generally? Give reasons from your own experience to support your point of view.

In support of the idea that men dominate women, you could consider five people you know who have leadership or management positions in their workplaces, and who receive the highest salaries. It's very likely that most or all of these people will be men. Or you could consider the gender balance in a group of leaders (for example, the Cabinet of South Africa or any other community leadership group). Once again, it is likely that most of the leaders, the people who are empowered to make the decisions in their communities, will turn out to be men, although this has changed in South Africa since 1994. The country has one of the highest numbers of female politicians in the world, although the numbers of men and women who are leaders are still far from equal.

TWO LANGUAGE AND GENDER

If we accept that men have more power and resources than women, we have to ask how this has been achieved. It is undoubtedly the result of several strategies (such as denying education to women). One very powerful tool for giving power to one group while withholding it from another is language. Language is important for a number of reasons:

- Language is not simply the product of our thinking about the world; it actually *shapes* the way we think about ourselves and our worlds.

- Language is made by culture, holds cultural values and transmits those cultural values to other people.

- Stories are made out of language. One of the oldest ways in which older members of a community teach values to children is through stories. Africa is particularly rich in oral tradition. Stories (including all kinds of narratives, such as fairy-tales, myths and legends) are not free of values, but actively teach values to their audiences.

Let's look at one tiny example of the power of language to create and sustain gender inequality: the pronoun. A pronoun is a little piece of language – one word that takes the place of a noun, or the name of something. For example, you might write, 'That *table* (noun, or name of the thing) has claw feet. *It* (pronoun) must be an antique.' But when we use pronouns for people, the matter becomes more complicated. While many other languages do not, English has two pronouns for people: *he* and *she*. Which one do you use when you do not know the sex of the person who is being referred to? Take the following riddle as an example:

A young man is brought into a hospital after he has been seriously injured in a car accident that killed his father, who was also in the car with him. He is taken to the hospital's operating theatre, where the surgeon on duty says, 'I cannot operate on that man. He is my son.'

Why can the surgeon not operate on the young man?

It takes most people some time to figure out the reason, which is that the surgeon is the young man's mother. This is because we do not expect surgeons (who are highly-paid, specialist doctors) to be women, much less mothers. The lack of a pronoun (he or she) to refer to the surgeon in the story only underlines the fact that hardly any surgeons in our societies are women. The same goes for doctors, professors, politicians, CEOs of large businesses and nuclear scientists – even though there are plenty of women in these professions.

It used to be common practice to use the pronoun 'he' to refer to people in general. When *all* people are meant, the term is usually 'man' or 'mankind'. Both of these practices imply that women do not count. Aristotle was a famous philosopher in Greece in the fourth century BCE, but, like most men of his time, he was sexist. In ancient Greece, men were at the top of the power hierarchy. All other people, including women, children and slaves, were seen unquestioningly as inferior to men and were kept in far lower positions. When Aristotle wrote, 'Man is a rational animal', he believed he was giving a definition of human nature in general. But what he was really doing, through his use of 'man' to refer to all human beings, was to imply that women are irrational, emotional, and not to be depended upon because of their defective intellectual abilities. Although you may think it is ridiculous to think about women like this, Aristotle sincerely believed that women were less valuable than men, as the following quotation shows:

....

… this holds true not only of man, but of other animals also, for tame animals are naturally better than wild ones, and it is advantageous that both should be under subjection to man; for this is productive of their common safety: so is it naturally with the male and the female; the one is superior, the other inferior; the one governs, the other is governed …
(Aristotle, Online Free Library, 21 April 2006)

....

Guidelines for Non-Sexist Use of Language

by Virginia L. Warren, Chapman College
APA Committee on the Status of Women in the Profession

For several reasons we, as philosophers, should be particularly sensitive to the issue of non-sexist language – that is, language whose 'use creates, constitutes, promotes, or exploits an unfair or irrelevant distinction between the sexes' (Vetterling-Braggin, 1981: 3). First, our profession has long focused on language. Accordingly, we are attuned to the emotive force of words and to the ways in which language influences thought and behavior. Second, we pride ourselves on our willingness to question assumptions. Yet the uncritical use of sexist language may blind us to our having adopted a particular value-laden perspective. Such blindness may systematically distort our theories and interfere with the careers and lives of many of our colleagues and students, both female and male. Third, as scholars and teachers we pursue truth wherever it leads: to the reform of our ordinary concepts and beliefs and, if necessary, of our everyday language.

Our readers and listeners may have been receiving a message that we never intended to send. Rather than encouraging a superficial recasting of words, these guidelines are designed to foster a deeper appreciation of how easily bias slips into our thoughts and theories.

THE GENERIC* USE OF 'MAN' AND 'HE'

* generic: applying to all cases (here, to men and women)

The generic use of 'man' and 'he' (and 'his', 'him', 'himself') is commonly considered gender-neutral. The case against the generic use of these terms does not rest on rare instances in which they refer ambiguously to 'male' or 'human being'. Rather, *every* occurrence of their generic use is problematic.

First, Janice Moulton persuasively argues, in 'The Myth of the Neutral "Man"' (in Vetterling-Braggin, 1981: 100–115; revised from Vetterling-Braggin, *et al*, 1977: 124–37), that 'he' and 'man' used generically are really not gender-neutral terms at all. ('Person' and 'human' are genuinely gender-neutral.) As evidence, Moulton offers many examples of statements in which 'man' and 'he' *unambiguously* refer to all humanity, rather than to males alone, yet are false, funny, or insulting. For example, 'Some men are female' is irredeemably odd, while 'Some human beings are female' is fine. Similarly, 'Each applicant is to list the name of his husband or wife' is odd; and even using 'his spouse' disquiets more than using 'his or her spouse.'

Second, empirical evidence supports Moulton's claim that *regardless of the author's intention* the generic 'man' is *not* interpreted gender neutrally. Casey Miller and Kate Swift (1976) cite a study in which college students chose pictures to illustrate chapters of a sociology textbook. Those with chapters entitled 'Society,' 'Industrial Life,' and 'Political Behaviour' tended to select pictures of both females and males. However, when the same chapters were named 'Social Man,' 'Industrial Man,' and 'Political Man,' students of both sexes tended to select pictures of males only. With some chapters the differences [between the two groups] reached magnitudes of 30 to 40 percent. The authors concluded, 'This is rather convincing evidence that when you use the word man generically, people do tend to think male, and tend not to think female' (Miller and Swift, 1976: 21). This study also finds that the generic 'man' leaves out more than women: 'As the image of capitalist, playboy, and hard hat are called forth by the word 'man', so is the other side of the coin called forth by 'behaviour' or 'life' – women, children, minorities, dissent and protest' (Miller and Swift, 1976: 23).

Third, using the generic 'he' and 'man' is problematic because it often leads us to omit the distinctive elements of female experience and behavior. For example, a sentence beginning, 'If a student is conscientious, *he* is probably a good ... ', will likely be ended with 'son' – even though 'good son,' 'good daughter,' and 'good child' connote different things. If the sentence had begun, 'A conscientious student is probably a good ... ' a likely finale would be 'son or daughter' or 'child.'

In sum, there are convincing reasons, both empirical and conceptual, for avoiding the generic 'he' and 'man' and for specifically including females. Hence, it is inadequate to state in an opening footnote that, for the remainder of the letter, article or book, 'he' shall stand for 'he or she' and 'man' for all humanity. What authors intend is not the issue. Good intentions not carried through are not good enough.

ADDRESSING THE PROFESSIONAL

Forms of address indicate attitudes about status and/or worth. Children often go by first names while calling adults by surname and title. Whenever males are referred to by title, use the appropriate title for female professionals (Ms, Dr, Professor), rather than their first names.

SEXUAL STEREOTYPING: DISTORTIONS AND SILENCE

One way that sexual stereotypes enter philosophic discourse is through examples. Since philosophic examples are usually illustrative, it is often thought that their presuppositions need not be checked for sexist content. However, examples may manifest sexist bias: (a) through embodying explicit or implicit sexual stereotypes (e.g., by contrasting female beauty with male success, or by using this hackneyed example of a complex question: 'When did you stop beating your wife?'); (b) through adopting a male perspective (as when using the generic 'man' or 'he' leads one to say 'his wife'); and (c) through silence – the absence of examples explicitly referring to women.

A second mode of entry for sexual stereotypes has been through the labelling of some roles as predominantly male or female. To assume that all lawyers or epistemologists* are male deletes the female segment of the profession and reinforces the assumption that only males are 'proper' professionals. Moreover, to assume that homemaking and child-rearing tasks are the primary concern of all and only women excludes males from these roles, even as it ignores women's other concerns.

> * epistemologists: philosophers, people who deal with questions of knowledge

Finally, omitting women's distinctive interests and experience also perpetuates* sexual stereotypes. The generic use of 'he' and 'man' are part of the more general problem of women's 'invisibility' in philosophic discourse. Some empirical* data on sexist language indicate that if women are not *specifically included* (e.g., through using females in examples, or the term 'he or she'), even genuinely gender-neutral prose (e.g., using plural pronouns) tends to be heard as referring to males only.

> * perpetuates: continues

> * empirical: based on facts

SUMMARY OF GUIDELINES FOR THE NON-SEXIST USE OF LANGUAGE

When constructing examples and theories, remember to *include* those human activities, interests, and points of view which traditionally have been associated with females.

Eliminate the generic use of 'he' by:

☺ using plural nouns

☺ deleting 'he', 'his', and 'him' altogether

☺ substituting articles ('the', 'a', 'an') for 'his'; and 'who' for 'he'

☺ substituting 'one', 'we', or 'you'

☺ minimizing use of indefinite pronouns (e.g., 'everybody', 'someone')

☺ using the passive voice [use sparingly]

☺ substituting nouns for pronouns [use sparingly].

Eliminate the generic use of 'man':

☺ for 'man', substitute 'person'/'people', 'individual(s)', 'human(s)', 'human being(s)'

☺ for 'mankind', substitute 'humankind', 'humanity', 'the human race'

☺ for 'manhood', substitute 'adulthood', 'maturity'

☺ delete unnecessary references to generic 'man'.

Eliminate sexism when addressing persons formally by:

☺ using 'Ms' instead of 'Miss' or 'Mrs', even when a woman's marital status is known

☺ using a married woman's first name instead of her husband's (e.g., 'Ms Annabelle Lee' not 'Mrs Herman Lee')

☺ using the corresponding title for females ('Ms', 'Dr', 'Prof') whenever a title is appropriate for males

☺ using 'Dear Colleague' or 'Editor' or 'Professor', etc. in letters to unknown persons (instead of 'Dear Sir', 'Gentlemen').

Eliminate sexual stereotyping of roles by:

☺ using the same term (which avoids the generic 'man') for both females and males (e.g., 'department chair' or 'chairperson'), or by using the corresponding verb (e.g., 'to chair')

✪ not calling attention to irrelevancies (e.g., 'lady lawyer', 'male nurse').

EXAMPLE OF SEXIST LANGUAGE WITH NON-SEXIST ALTERNATIVES

Example	Preferred Alternative	Comment
1. The philosopher uses his reason to guide him.	Philosophers use their reason to guide them.	Use *plural* nouns.
	OR: The philosopher uses reason as a guide.	*Delete* 'he', 'his', or 'him' altogether, rewording if necessary.
2. The student did it and he was glad.	The student did it and was glad.	*Delete* 'he', using compound verbs.
3. The department chair must submit his budget by March 1st.	The department chair must submit a budget by March 1st.	Use *articles* ('the', 'a', 'an') instead of personal pronouns.
	OR: The budget must be submitted by the department chair by March 1st.	Use *passive voice* for verbs. (Use sparingly.)
4. If the writer plans ahead, he will save a lot of effort.	The writer who plans ahead will save a lot of effort.	Use '*who*' for 'he'.
5. Take seriously what your Dean says about falling enrollments. He knows about current demographic trends.	Take seriously what your Dean says about falling enrollments. This person knows about current demographic trends.	Substitute a *noun* for the pronoun. (Use sparingly.)
6. As someone grows older, he grows more reflective.	As one grows older, one grows more reflective.	Use '*one*', '*you*', '*we*', instead of indefinite pronouns.
	OR: In growing older, people grow more reflective.	Or reword, *deleting pronouns* altogether.
	CONTROVERSIAL (FOR INFORMAL CONTEXTS ONLY): As someone grows older, they grow more reflective.	The National Council of Teachers of English (1975: 3) says, 'In all but strictly formal usage, plural pronouns have become acceptable substitutes for the masculine singular' following an indefinite pronoun. Kett and Underwood (1978: 38) predict that such informal usage will eventually become acceptable in all contexts.

Example	Preferred Alternative	Comment
7. Students are different: one may be assertive in his interpersonal relations, while another may be timid in his approach to the world.	Students are different: one may relate to others assertively, while another may approach the world timidly.	*Delete* 'his', rewording.
	OR: Students are different: one may be assertive in his or her interpersonal relations, while another may be timid in approaching the world.	Use '*he or she*, '*his* or *her*' sparingly, in conjunction with other methods. ('Himself or herself' is awkward. 'S/he' breaks down when one comes to 'her/his'.) 'She or he' and 'her or him' are fine. *Be consistent*: do not begin by using 'he or she' and lapse into the generic 'he'. Avoid 'he (she)', 'men (and women)', etc., since including females parenthetically* suggests that females are an afterthought.
	OR: Students are different: one may be assertive in her interpersonal relations, while another may be timid in his approach to the world.	*Alternate masculine and feminine pronouns* when giving examples. (CAUTION: avoid reinforcing sexual stereotypes. Switching 'her' and 'his' in the preferred alternative results in a sentence as sexist as the original.).
8. 'When a nurse comes on duty she . . .' is as sexist as 'When a physician comes on duty he . . .'		Use the above methods to avoid the generic 'she' for traditionally female occupations.
9. Consider what the ordinary (common) man thinks about justice.	Consider what ordinary people (individuals) think about justice.	Using the plural noun avoids the generic '*he*' later on.
10. Reason is what distinguishes man from other animals.	Reason is what distinguishes humans (human beings) from other animals.	When '*man*' is used to contrast species, substitute '*humans*' or '*human beings*'. Use '*who*' for '*he*'.
11. For Aristotle, man is, above all, Political Man.	Aristotle regarded human beings as inherently political.	No non-sexist counterparts to '*Political Man*', '*Economic Man*', etc. preserve the exact flavour of these terms – perhaps because they focus on stereotypically male behavior. Note that much of '*Economic Woman's*' labour is still unpaid, and hence is excluded from the G.N.P.* Sexist language may camouflage a theory's sexist assumptions.

* parenthetically: between brackets

* G.N.P.: Gross National Product; calculation of a nation's wealth based on individual earnings.

Example	Preferred Alternative	Comment
12. The brotherhood of man	the human family	
Feelings of brotherhood or fraternity	feelings of kinship, solidarity, affection collegiality, unity, congeniality, community	
The Founding Fathers	the Founders (founding leaders)	
The Father of relativity theory	the founder (initiator) of relativity theory	
13. Dear Sir, Gentlemen (to an unknown person)	Dear Colleague, Dear Editor, Dear Professor, Dear Staff Member, etc.	Do not presume that people are male until proven otherwise. Do not use 'Dear Sir' or 'Gentlemen' just because you are sure that there are no women on that committee.
Dear Sir, Dear Mr Green (when first name and sex are unknown)	Dear Professor (Doctor, Editor) Green, Dear J. Green	If 'To Whom it May Concern' seems too brusque and all else fails, adopt a modified memo style ('Attention: Order Department') or omit the salutation entirely.
Dear Mrs Green (when a female's marital status is unknown)	Dear Ms Green, Dear J. Green, Dear Jean Green	Do not presume that women are married until proven otherwise.
14. Man and wife	husband and wife	
Men ... ladies; or men ... girls	men ... women	Of course, if the ages are right, 'men ... girls' may be appropriate, as may 'women ... boys'.
Three male students and two co-eds*	five students (two females and three males)	
15. Males and females	females and males	Varying the order (if the content does not require the conventional order) both counters the implication that males take priority over females, and enlivens discourse by avoiding cliché.*
Husbands and wives	wives and husbands	
Men and women	women and men	
Sons and daughters	daughters and sons	
Descendants of Adam and Eve	descendants of Eve and Adam	
His and her	her and his	

* co-eds: female students   * cliché: an expression that has lost its force through over-use

Example	Preferred Alternative	Comment
16. Congressman, Congresswoman	U.S. Representative, member of Congress	Choose non-sexist labels for occupations.
Poetess, stewardess, fireman, lady lawyer, male nurse, woman doctor	poet, flight attendant, firefighter, lawyer, nurse, doctor	The terms *'lawyer'*, *'nurse'* and *'doctor'* include both males and females.
17. Cautious men and timid women	cautious women and men; cautious people; timid men and women; timid people	Choose adjectives carefully. Sometimes we intend to attribute the same trait to females and males; yet, through choosing two stereotyped adjectives, we imply either that the two groups have different traits or that readers should evaluate the same trait differently for females and males. (Note: some adjectives have a different emotive or descriptive meaning when predicated of one sex or the other.)
Ambitious men and aggressive women	ambitious men and women; ambitious people; aggressive women and men; aggressive people	

APA Online, Guidelines for Non-Sexist Use of Language, 21 April 2006

In order to focus your mind on your reactions, answer the following questions.

EXERCISE 3.9

1. How do you react to the ideas presented in this article?
2. Do you agree or disagree with the basic claim that people ought to use language in a non-sexist way? Why?
3. Have you heard or thought about these ideas in the past, and do you find them interesting?
4. Have you ever encountered sexist language? If so, give an example. How would a woman feel when she reads sexist language?

Stories people tell

Let's consider next the stories people tell and the ways in which they represent or reflect gender differences. As mentioned before, stories are found in all cultures. The stories we hear as children have an important effect on the way we see the world throughout our lives. I am going to repeat one so-called 'fairy tale' to you. In case you have not encountered the story of *Sleeping Beauty* before, here is a summary (there are different versions of the tale, but they all contain the basic elements of the summary below).

Sleeping Beauty

ong ago, a baby girl was born to a king and queen. The king and queen invited everyone in the land to a party to celebrate the birth of their first child. Among the guests were a number of fairies, but there was one who was overlooked when the invitations were sent out. All the fairies gave magical gifts to the baby princess, such as 'She will be beautiful' and 'She will have a beautiful singing voice'.

Then, the fairy who had not been invited arrived at the party in a towering rage, and, pointing her finger angrily at the baby's cot, declared that the princess would prick her finger on the spindle of a spinning wheel on her sixteenth birthday and die. Luckily, there was a good fairy present, who softened the malicious prophecy, and decreed that the princess would only sleep until she was kissed by her true love.

Sure enough, it happened as the fairy had said. The princess pricked her finger and fell into a deep sleep. She was rescued by her true love, a prince from a neighbouring kingdom who had overcome many obstacles (such as slaying a dragon) in order to find her. When he kissed her, she immediately awoke, declared her true love for him, and they were married and lived happily ever after.

In case you think this is 'just' a children's story, you need to look carefully at what it says about women. Like many other characters in fiction about women, the princess does almost nothing to direct her life. She only pricks her finger on the spindle of a spinning wheel (you would have thought that her parents would have told her about the evil fairy's prophecy, but girls are often protected from the dangerous realities of life) and sleeps until she is rescued by a man. How many women are like the princess, doing nothing much for themselves apart from looking beautiful, and hoping to be found or rescued by a handsome prince?

EXERCISE 3.10

1. Think about the adventure stories you have read or heard. How many of them show the male characters doing all the action, while the female characters merely sit and watch?
2. How many children's stories have you read or heard where women and girls are passive while men and boys are active?
3. How many of the childhood stories about families that you know contain women who work in kitchens, while men are active outside the home?
4. How have the stories you know influenced your idea of the appropriate roles for girls and boys, men and women?

It's all in a name

How do you address (speak to) other people? Do you use their name? What do you say if you don't know their name? Do you say 'ummm'?

In many Western cultures, we use people's surnames as a mark of politeness until we are more familiar with them and can use their first names. An extreme form of this is seen in some public schools in England, where the pupils are called 'Mr' and 'Miss'. 'Mr' is the polite title for a man, but what do you call a woman? This depends on whether she is married or not. An unmarried woman is called 'Miss', and a married woman is called 'Mrs', followed by her husband's surname. This situation, which you probably meet so often that you never think about it, is clearly unequal. Why is a man called 'Mr' whether he is married or not, while women have different titles depending on whether they are married? (Some married women are even called by their husband's first name, like 'Mrs Richard Dalloway' in Virginia Woolf's novel, *Mrs Dalloway*). The answer is that a woman's marital status makes a difference to her social role, but this is not so for a man. A married woman is seen in a different way from an unmarried one. A man keeps his essential role and value whether he is married or not. He does not lose value in the workplace when he marries; neither is he to be frowned upon if he passes a certain age without getting married. The situation is very different for women. An unmarried woman may be seen in a number of ways: if she is young, she may be seen as a 'siren' (this word derives from ancient Greek myths about beautiful mermaids whose song was so enchanting that it would lead sailors to shipwrecks in dangerous seas; nowadays it is used to mean a woman whose main interest is in attracting men sexually); if she is older than 30, people are likely to cast pitying looks at her and wonder what is 'wrong' with her if she can't attract a man to marry her. The title 'Miss' could be used as an opening for a man to make a sexual move towards her, or it could be used as a form of derision for her sad, unmarried state.

This social practice conceals a number of values. For example, hardly anyone imagines that some women might not *want* to be married and might be perfectly happy to live a single life. For these women, being 'Miss' might be exactly what they want, and they might become annoyed by people who obviously feel sorry for them. Even fewer people believe that a woman's marital status is her own private affair. One who does is Gloria Steinem, who founded the famous feminist magazine, *Ms.*, in 1972 in the United States. *Ms.*, which still appears, aimed to publish articles that were different from those usually found in 'women's magazines' and which dealt only with romance, clothes or household chores. Instead, *Ms.* publishes articles of a more intellectual and directly feminist nature. The title of the magazine is a title that women may use if they do not want their marital status to be known. 'Ms' is a way for women to gain equal titles with men and to say to the world that it does not make a difference to a woman's intellectual or physical abilities whether she is married or not. Unfortunately, though, some people think that only dangerous, radical feminists use the title 'Ms'.

EXERCISE 3.11

Write about your ideas about titles for men and women.

1. Do you think a woman should take a man's surname when she marries him? Why?
2. Do you think a man should take his wife's surname when he marries? Why?
3. Would you treat a married woman differently from an unmarried one? How? Why?
4. Would you treat a married man differently from an unmarried one? How and why?

THREE ROOM NEEDED

In this section we will focus on the idea that people want space in which to think, read and write. Sometimes this is physical space, but often it is not only physical space. People also want to find the psychological freedom to be themselves.

The ideas and exercises in this section will help you to relate the idea of space to gender, and to think about the kinds of space you do or do not have yourself.

A room of one's own

One of the ideas that has shaped people's thinking about gender issues is the concept of 'a room of one's own'. This idea comes from a lecture by the British novelist Virginia Woolf, in 1929, entitled *A Room of One's Own*. In this lecture, Woolf looked at the way women were traditionally not encouraged or enabled to write: fewer women than men were given education, and women's education was usually inferior to that of men and focused on skills such as housekeeping and hobbies. She claimed that people face material (physical) difficulties when they want to write, such as poverty and not having a quiet, private place to write where they will not be interrupted. These people lack 'a room of their own'. But men, Woolf says, are able to overcome these difficulties more easily than women, because women are often not able to be economically independent.

Woolf goes further than this, though. Some of the surprising claims and difficult questions in her essay are summarized in the following extracts:

....

… a woman must have money and a room of her own if she is to write fiction; and that, as you will see, leaves the great problem of the true nature of woman and the true nature of fiction unsolved.

Why [throughout history] did men drink wine and women water? Why was one sex so prosperous and the other so poor? What effect has poverty on fiction? What conditions are necessary for the creation of works of art? …

A very queer composite* being thus emerges [from reading literature about women]. Imaginatively she is of the highest importance; practically she is completely insignificant. She pervades* poetry from cover to cover; she is all but absent from history. She dominates the lives of kings and conquerors in fiction; in fact she was the slave of any boy whose parents forced a ring upon her finger. Some of the most inspired words, some of the most profound thoughts in literature fall from her lips; in real life she could hardly read, could scarcely spell, and was the property of her husband.

[M]aterial difficulties were formidable; but much worse were the immaterial. The indifference of the world which … men of genius have found so hard to bear was [for a woman writer] not indifference but hostility*. The world did not say to her as it said to them, Write if you choose; it makes no difference to me. The world said with a [laugh], Write? What's the good of your writing? (Adapted from: Woolf, 1929: 137)

....

* composite: made of several different parts, which may not fit together to create a unified whole

* pervades: appears throughout (texts, places, and so on)

* hostility: dislike or aggression

Many other writers have explored the idea of 'a room of one's own' in the years since Woolf wrote her lecture. The idea has been used in different ways and for different purposes. For example, Carolyn Heilbrun, an American academic and writer of detective novels, believes that women have long searched, and continue to search, for an identity 'other' than their own. Caught in the conventions of their sex, they have sought an escape from gender.

She speaks about herself and her decision to write detective novels in a way that is similar to Virginia Woolf's idea of a room of one's own:

> I believe now that I must have wanted … to create a space for myself … . I used to notice, visiting in the suburbs, that there was a room for everyone but the wife/mother, who, it was assumed, had the whole house … . If there was no space for a woman in the suburban dream house, how unlikely that there would be space in a small city apartment. So I wanted, I now guess, psychic space . … [By writing novels] I was recreating myself. (Adapted from: Heilbrun, 1988)

The two writers we have referred to are talking specifically about the problems facing women who want to write. But, of course, gender issues are not simply about women. Gender affects our ideas of ourselves and other people's ideas about us, whether we are men or women. Discrimination on the grounds of sex (whether through providing better access to education and money to one sex than the other, through treating women as inferior, or in active violence against women) affects everyone.

EXERCISE 3.12

Have you ever experienced the kinds of things that Virginia Woolf and Carolyn Heilbrun write about in the extracts that you have just read? Think about the following statements made by these two writers, and then complete the questions that follow.

⊗ 'Material difficulties were formidable; but much worse were the immaterial.'

- 'Caught in the conventions of their sex, they have sought an escape from gender.'
- 'Write? What's the good of your writing?'
- 'I wanted … to create a space for myself.'
- 'I was recreating myself.'

1. Do you face physical difficulties in your own life in finding space to read, write and study?
2. Do you also face other figurative, more abstract difficulties, such as having little time to spend on these activities or feeling that there are other demands on you that prevent you from studying, reading or writing?
3. Copy and complete the following table to explore and list your difficulties. Think about the obstacles you face when you need to find 'a room for yourself'.

The difficulties I face in my physical space	The difficulties I face in my psychological space

4. If you had 'a room of your own', what would you be able to do in it? Copy and complete the following table by listing the things that would enable you to have 'a room of your own' and how you would use it.

How I would be able to have 'a room of my own'	What I could do in 'a room of my own'

Room to write

Gcina Mhlophe is a South African storyteller, writer and actor. While she was at high school, she wrote poems and stories in Xhosa, and since moving to Johannesburg she has written and published poems and stories in English. At the beginning of her life in Johannesburg, she did much of her reading and writing in a public toilet in Johannesburg. One of the stories she wrote is called 'The Toilet'. Read this short story and think about the issues we have explored so far in this chapter. Also think about how 'The Toilet' can be seen as autobiographical writing (which we discussed in Chapter One).

'It's very important for women to write what they feel. Really, we need more writing from women. I think women understand each other better when they are alone together than when there's a man around because then there's always the possibility of pretending and that's not communication . . . . So we should come together as women and try to do some creative writing, I mean writing that will help or encourage other people who might become our fellow-writers in the future.' (Mhlophe, in Daymond, January 1996: 191)

1. What do you think about Gcina Mhlophe's ideas? Do you agree with her?
2. Do you think we need 'more writing from women'?
3. If we replaced 'women' with 'men' and 'men' with 'women' where these words appear in the paragraph, how would this change the ideas? Would you agree or disagree with these new ideas?

The Toilet

Gcina Mhlophe

Sometimes I wanted to give up and be a good girl who listened to her elders. Maybe I should have done something like teaching or nursing as my mother wished. People thought these professions were respectable, but I knew I wanted to do something different, though I was not sure what. I thought a lot about acting … My mother said that it had been a waste of good money educating me because I did not know what to do with the knowledge I had acquired. I'd come to Johannesburg for the December holidays after writing my matric exams, and then stayed on, hoping to find something to do.

My elder sister worked in Orange Grove as a domestic worker, and I stayed with her in her back room. I didn't know anybody in Jo'burg except my sister's friends whom we went to church with. The Methodist church up Fourteenth Avenue was about the only outing we had together. I was very bored and lonely.

On weekdays I was locked in my sister's room so that the Madam wouldn't see me. She was at home most of the time: painting her nails, having tea with her friends, or lying in the sun by the swimming pool. The swimming pool was very close to the room, which is why I had to keep very quiet. My sister felt bad about locking me in there, but she had no alternative. I couldn't even play the radio, so she brought me books, old magazines, and newspapers from the white people. I just read every single thing I came across: *Fair Lady*, *Woman's Weekly*, anything. But then my sister thought I was reading too much.

'What kind of wife will you make if you can't even make baby clothes, or knit yourself a jersey? I suppose you will marry an educated man like yourself, who won't mind going to bed with a book and an empty stomach.'

We would play cards at night when she knocked off, and listen to the radio, singing along softly with the songs we liked.

Then I got this temporary job in a clothing factory in town. I looked forward to meeting new people, and liked the idea of being out of that room for a change. The factory made clothes for ladies' boutiques.

The whole place was full of machines of all kinds. Some people were sewing, others were ironing with big heavy irons that pressed with a lot of steam. I had to cut all the loose threads that hang after a dress or a jacket is finished. As soon as a number of dresses in a certain style was finished, they would be sent to me and I had to count them, write the number down, and then start with the cutting of the threads. I was fascinated to discover that one person made only sleeves, another the collars, and so on until the last lady put all the pieces together, sewed on buttons, or whatever was necessary to finish.

Most people at the factory spoke Sotho, but they were nice to me – they tried to speak to me in Zulu or Xhosa, and they gave me all kinds of advice on things I didn't know. There was this girl, Gwendolene – she thought I was very stupid – she called me a bari because I always sat inside the changing room with something to read when it was time to eat my lunch, instead of going outside to meet guys. She told me it was cheaper to get myself a 'lunch boy' – somebody to buy me lunch. She told me it was wise not to sleep with him, because then I could dump him anytime I wanted to. I was very nervous about such things. I thought it was better to be a bari than to be stabbed by a city boy for his money.

The factory knocked off at four-thirty, and then I went to a park near where my sister worked. I waited there till half past six, when I could sneak into the house again without the white people seeing me. I had to leave the house before half past five in the mornings as well. That meant I had to find something to do with the time I had before I could catch the seven-thirty bus to work – about two hours. I would go to a public toilet in the park. For some reason it was never locked, so I would go in and sit on the toilet seat to read some magazine or other until the right time to catch the bus.

The first time I went into this toilet, I was on my way to the bus stop. Usually I went straight to the bus stop outside the OK Bazaars where it was well-lit, and I could see. I would wait there, reading, or just looking at the growing number of cars and buses on their way to town. On this day it was raining quite hard, so I thought I would shelter in the toilet until the rain had passed. I knocked first to see if there was anyone inside. As there was no reply, I pushed the door open and went in. It smelled a little – a dryish kind of smell, as if the toilet was not used all that often, but it was quite clean compared to many 'Non-European' toilets I knew. The floor was painted red and the walls were cream white. It did not look like it had been painted for a few years. I stood looking around, with the rain coming very hard on the zinc roof. The noise was comforting – to know I had escaped the wet – only a few of the heavy drops had got me. The plastic bag in which I carried my book and purse and neatly folded pink handkerchief was a little damp, but that was because I had used it to cover my head when I ran to the toilet. I pulled my dress down a little so that it would not get creased when I sat down. The closed lid of the toilet was going to be my seat for many mornings after that.

I was really lucky to have found that toilet because the winter was very cold. Not that it was any warmer in there, but once I'd closed the door it used to be a little less windy. Also the toilet was very small – the walls were wonderfully close to me – it felt like it was made to fit me alone. I enjoyed that kind of privacy. I did a lot of thinking while I sat on that toilet seat. I did a lot of daydreaming too – many times imagining myself in some big hall doing a really popular play with other young actors. At school, we took set books like *Buzani KuBawo* or *A Man for All Seasons* and made school plays which we toured to the other schools on weekends. I loved it very much. When I was even younger I had done little sketches taken from the Bible and on big days like Good Friday, we acted and sang happily.

I would sit there dreaming.

I was getting bored with the books I was reading – the love stories all sounded the same, and besides that I just lost interest. I started asking myself why I had not written anything since I left school. At least at school I had written some poems, or stories for the school magazine, school competitions and other magazines like *Bona* and *Inkqubela*. Our English teacher was always so encouraging. I remembered the day I showed him my first poem – I was so excited I couldn't concentrate in class for the whole day. I didn't know anything about publishing then, and I didn't ask myself if my stories were good enough. I just enjoyed writing things down when I had the time. So one Friday, after I'd started being that toilet's best customer, I bought myself a notebook in which I was hoping to write something. I didn't use it for quite a while, until one evening.

My sister had taken her usual Thursday afternoon off, and she had been delayed somewhere. I came back from work, then waited in the park for the right time to go back into the yard. The white people always had their supper at six-thirty and that was the time I used to steal my way in without disturbing them or being seen. My comings and goings had to be secret because they still didn't know I stayed there.

Then I realized that she hadn't come back, and I was scared to go out again, in case something went wrong this time. I decided to sit down in front of my sister's room, where I thought I wouldn't be noticed. I was reading a copy of *Drum* magazine and hoping that she would come back soon – before the dogs sniffed me out. For the first time I realized how stupid it was of me not to have cut myself a spare key long ago. I kept on hearing noises that sounded like the gate opening. A few times I was sure I had heard her footsteps on the concrete steps leading to the servant's quarters, but it turned out to be something or someone else.

I was trying hard to concentrate on my reading again, when I heard the two dogs playing, chasing each other nearer and nearer to where I was sitting. And then, there they were in front of me, looking as surprised as I was. For a brief moment we stared at each other, then they started to bark at me. I was sure they would tear me to pieces if I moved just one finger, so I sat very still, trying not to look at them, while my heart pounded and my mouth went dry as paper.

They barked even louder when the dogs from next door joined in, glared at me through the openings in the hedge. Then the Madam's high-pitched voice rang out above the dogs' barking.

'Ireeeeeeeene!' That's my sister's English name, which we never use. I couldn't move or answer the call – the dogs were standing right in front of me, their teeth so threateningly long. When there was no reply, she came to see what was going on.

'Oh, it's you. Hello,' She was smiling at me, chewing that gum which never left her mouth, instead of calling the dogs away from me. They had stopped barking, but they hadn't moved – they were still growling at me, waiting for her to tell them what to do.

'Please Madam, the dogs will bite me,' I pleaded, not moving my eyes from them.

'No, they won't bite you.' Then she spoke to them nicely, 'Get away now – go on,' and they went off. She was like a doll, her hair almost orange in colour, all curls round her made-up face. Her eyelashes fluttered like a doll's, her thin lips were bright red like her long nails, and she wore very high-heeled shoes. She was still smiling; I wondered if it didn't hurt after a while. When her friends came for a swim, I could always hear her forever laughing at something or other.

She scared me – I couldn't understand how she could smile like that but not want me to stay in her house.

'When did you come in? We didn't see you.'

'I've been here for some time now – my sister isn't here. I'm waiting to talk to her.'

'Oh – she's not here?' She was laughing for no reason that I could see. 'I can give her a message – you go on home – I'll tell her that you want to see her.'

Once I was outside the gate, I didn't know what to do or where to go. I walked slowly, kicking my heels. The streetlights were so very bright! Like big eyes staring at me. I wondered what the people who saw me thought I was doing, walking around at that time of the night. But then I didn't really care, because there wasn't much I could do about the situation right then. I was just thinking how things had to go wrong on that day particularly, because my sister and I were not on such good terms. Early that morning, when the alarm had gone for me to wake up, I did not jump to turn it off, so my sister got really angry with me. She had gone on about me always leaving it to ring for too long, as if it was set for her, and not for me. And when I went out to wash, I had left the door open a second too long, and that was enough to earn me another scolding.

Every morning I had to wake up straight away, roll my bedding and put it all under the bed where my sister was sleeping. I was not supposed to put on the light although it was still dark. I'd light a candle, and tiptoe my way out with a soap dish and a toothbrush. My clothes were on a hanger on a nail at the back of the door. I'd take the hanger and close the door as quietly as I could. Everything had to be ready set the night before. A washing basin full of cold water was also ready outside the door, put there because the sound of running water and the loud screech the taps made in the morning could wake the white people and they would wonder what my sister was doing up so early. I'd do everything and be off the premises by five-thirty with my shoes in my bag. I only put them on once I was safely out of the gate. And that gate made such a noise too. Many times I wished I could jump over it and save myself all that sickening careful-careful business!

Thinking about all these things took my mind away from the biting cold of the night and my wet nose, until I saw my sister walking towards me.

'Mholo, what are you doing outside in the street?' she greeted me. I quickly briefed her on what had happened.

'Oh, Yehovah! You can be so dumb sometimes! What were you doing inside in the first place? You know you should have waited for me so we could walk in together. Then I could say you were visiting or something. Now, you tell me, what am I supposed to say to them if they see you come in again? Hayi!'

She walked angrily towards the gate, with me hesitantly following her. When she opened the gate, she turned to me with an impatient whisper.

'And now why don't you come in, stupid?'

I mumbled my apologies, and followed her in. By some miracle no one seemed to have noticed us, and we quickly munched a snack of cold chicken and boiled potatoes and drank our tea, hardly on speaking terms. I just wanted to howl like a dog. I wished somebody would come and be my friend, and tell me that I was not useless, and that my sister did not hate me, and tell me that one day I would have a nice place to live … anything. It would have been really great to have someone my own age to talk to.

But also I knew that my sister was worried for me – she was scared of her employers. If they were to find out that I lived with her, they would fire her, and then we would both be walking up and down the streets. My eleven rand wages wasn't going to help us at all. I don't know how long I lay like that, unable to fall asleep, just wishing and wishing with tears running into my ears.

The next morning I woke up long before the alarm went off, but I just lay there feeling tired and depressed. If there was a way out, I would not have gone to work, but there was this other strong feeling or longing inside me. It was some kind of pain that pushed me to do everything at double speed and run to my toilet. I call it 'my' toilet because that is exactly how I felt about it. It was very rare that I ever saw anybody else go in there in the mornings. It was like they all knew I was using it, and they had to lay off or something.

When I went there, I didn't really expect to find it occupied.

I felt my spirits really lifting as I put on my shoes outside the gate. I made sure that my notebook was in my bag. In my haste I even forgot my lunchbox, but it didn't matter. I was walking faster and my feet were feeling lighter all the time. Then I noticed that the door had been painted, and that a new window pane had replaced the old broken one. I smiled to myself as I reached the door. Before long I was sitting on that toilet seat, writing a poem.

Many more mornings saw me sitting there writing. Sometimes it did not need to be a poem; I wrote anything that came into my head – in the same way I would have done if I'd had a friend to talk to. I remember some days when I felt like I was hiding something from my sister. She did not know about my toilet in the park, and she was not in the least interested in my notebook.

Then one morning I wanted to write a story about what had happened at work the day before; the supervisor screaming at me for not calling her when I'd seen the people who stole two dresses at lunch time. I had found it really funny. I had to write about it and I just hoped there were enough pages left in my notebook. It all came back to me, and I was smiling when I reached for the door, but it wouldn't open – it was locked!

I think for the first time I accepted that the toilet was not mine after all. ... Slowly I walked over to a bench nearby, watched the early spring sun come up, and wrote my story anyway.

Oosthuizen (ed.), 1987: 1–7

EXERCISE 3.13

1. How does the narrator of 'The Toilet' show her personal strength? Make a list of her actions that show that she is a strong person.
2. How do you know that she wants to be a writer?
3. How does the system of racial segregation make her life difficult? How does she overcome these difficulties?
4. How does she find 'a room of her own'?

To summarize the ideas we have explored in this section about gender and writing, write a piece in any form (such as a poem, words for a song, a paragraph, a short story or a speech) in which you explore your own ideas about the idea of being able to escape your gender and write. In order to do this, imagine expressing yourself with perfect freedom. What would you say if there were no restrictions on you?

EXERCISE 3.14

Gender is a system that creates differences between people; it is also linked to power because, very often, power is given to people because of their sex. Gender equality is not aimed at making men and women all the same: it aims to give men and women the same choices and chances in life. In a society where both sexes were equal, women would be able to *choose* to marry and have children instead of feeling forced into doing so, and men would be able to *choose* to pursue well-paid careers without feeling pressurized to provide for their families. One of the choices that women could make in such a world would be the choice to write without being laughed at or being told that 'Women can't paint; women can't write', as a male philosopher tells the painter, Lily, in Virginia Woolf's novel, *To the Lighthouse*. One way to achieve such an ideal society is to become aware of the way the system of gender difference and gender inequality works in your community.

To reinforce the ideas that you have learned in this chapter, go back to the questions at the beginning of this chapter. The last two questions read: 'How has being a girl or a boy, a man or a woman, shaped your life?' and, 'What does it mean to be a girl or a boy, a man or a woman?'

1. Taking these two questions as your starting point, interview *at least three* people in your community (the group should include at least one man and one woman, one older person and one younger one).
2. Either use a tape recorder to record their answers or write down exactly what they say in reply to the two questions.
3. Make notes of the main points that they mention.

4. Make notes about your own views and experiences of gender, either within your community or in other social groups.
5. Now write a page about what it means to be a man or a woman in your community. Your piece of writing should answer the question, 'Does gender matter in my community?'

When you write the answer to the exercise above, your writing will need to be argumentative: that is, it will need to argue for your point of view. Argumentative writing tries to convince the reader of the writer's opinion: think of the way lawyers present their cases before a court. This is done by providing evidence in support of your point of view. You need to organize your writing in such a way that you state your opinion, and then give reasons why it is valid. The evidence, or reasons, that you provide is very important. You should not rely only on your own personal experience or views. Back these up with some other supporting evidence that is factually true, such as other people's experiences. You can also refer to written texts that you have read (such as those in this chapter). In this way, you can learn to build up a convincing argument that your reader will accept.

4 Writing our Worlds: Speaking of Culture

OUR DISCUSSIONS SO far have covered a wide range of ideas, including autobiography, characterization and gender. In this chapter, our thoughts move to an area of representation that relates to those we have already thought about. It overlaps with them but also has its own particular focus. We introduce it here because you will find within it aspects of all that we have already considered. It relates to the representation of the individual, to character and point of view, and to gendered identities.

Our topic is culture. We will look at some of the meanings and uses of this term, exploring how it might usefully relate to the study of writing. In doing this, we will look at specific literary texts, to see how culture appears or functions within them. We will also think about texts that use concepts relating to culture to assert opinions and support arguments. Your explorations here will, therefore, lead you into thinking about how to read purposefully and how to express opinions in written form, such as in essays.

....

ONE THINKING ABOUT CULTURE

What is culture?

This book began with the individual. We started there in order to think about the representation of matters most immediate to each of us: ourselves and our own worlds. But individuals do not exist in isolation. We live within families, communities, societies, nations – that is, within groups of varying sizes and forms. Individuals are shaped and formed within such groups, developing within the context of shared resources and experiences. Groups come into being for a wide variety of purposes, and their functions within an individual's life are equally varied as they influence different aspects of each person's existence.

When we speak of culture, this is one of the things we have in mind: the idea of interrelatedness and influence. Culture is part of the context of being human, affecting how groups and individuals experience their lives. People form social relationships with others and distinguish themselves from those who are not part of the same grouping. Identifying with and belonging to the group becomes part of knowing how to relate to the world and to other people.

But the word 'culture' is used in widely differing senses and for many different purposes. It is not an easy term to define, as many thinkers freely admit, and often causes some confusion. 'Culture' is in fact a word that has taken on many meanings over time, with several new definitions and usages arising in recent decades when it has been used for particular intellectual purposes and in various contexts.

EXERCISE 4.1

1. What does the word 'culture' usually describe, when you use it?
2. What does it generally refer to in the media?
3. What, in your opinion, do most people mean when they talk about culture?
4. Does culture mean the same thing to everybody?
5. How many different forms of culture can you think of?
6. Often 'culture' appears in terms such as 'consumer culture', 'corporate culture', or 'pop culture'. How many other terms of this kind can you think of? What do they refer to?

Now look at the following entry from the *Oxford Advanced Learner's Dictionary*.

culture *noun*

WAY OF LIFE | **1** [U] the customs and beliefs, art, way of life and social organization of a particular country or group: *European/Islamic/American culture; working-class culture* **2** [C] a country, group, etc. with its own beliefs, etc: *The children are taught to respect different cultures; the effect of technology on traditional cultures*

ART/MUSIC/LITERATURE | **3** [U] art, music, literature etc., thought of as a group: *Venice is a beautiful city full of culture and history; popular culture* (= that is enjoyed by a lot of people); *the Minister of Culture*

BELIEFS/ATTITUDES | **4** [C, U] the beliefs and attitudes about sth that people in a particular group or organization share: *The political cultures of the United States and the United Kingdom are very different; A culture of failure exists in some schools; company culture; We are living in a consumer culture.*

The dictionary defines 'culture' in terms of how it is currently used. The definitions here all relate to how people live within groups, and to the thoughts, feelings and forms of expression of groups (or of individuals within groups).

Within some academic disciplines, the term 'culture' may take on particular, precise definitions depending on the field of study. Sociologists, for example, generally define culture as the way of life of a group, whereas some psychologists might see it as a range of constraints operating on an individual in society. In other contexts, people might refer to the culture of an organization or corporation. In this sense, the word has a similar meaning to 'ethos', the shared attitudes and values within a particular group.

In much earlier times, the meaning of 'culture' was very different from how we usually think of it today. Many hundreds of years ago it could even mean worship (deriving from an ancient Latin word source) and was widely used from the early sixteenth century onwards to refer to a society's cultivating practices. In other words, 'culture' referred to whether a society grew crops, raised animals or was nomadic.

Another sense of the word 'culture' also used to be common, but is heard less often today. In this usage, the word describes an individual whose tastes are sophisticated (someone who likes art, literature, good food and classical music might be described as 'cultured' or even as 'civilized'). In the nineteenth century, the English thinker Matthew Arnold thought of culture as 'the best that has been thought and said.' For him, knowledge lay at the heart of culture. To be knowledgeable was to be cultured. But importantly, for him, this should go hand in hand with a compassionate attitude. As he saw it, culture included a desire for excellence in learning and a commitment to living responsibly among others. Culture included both knowledge and a social dimension.

The word now most frequently suggests the fact that groups and societies in different places, and at different times, are organized differently. Such groupings have particular sets of beliefs or attitudes, and often have distinctive or characteristic ways of living and putting into practice their beliefs. But in spite of these differences, there are important similarities between societies. No culture exists free of the influence of other cultures, even when governments (such as those of North Korea or contemporary China, for example) attempt to achieve this. In the modern world, technologically-advanced countries are able to spread their influence (and products) throughout most societies, affecting the culture of those societies. It is important, therefore, to think of cultures as ever-changing entities under constant influence from other cultures. The boundaries between cultures are frequently permeable, and easily crossed. Many cultures are indeed hybrid, or mixed. They develop out of the mixing of practices, beliefs and influences that occurs when cultures meet and when the products of particular cultures are used by others. A clear example of this can be found in music, movies and television. These cultural products travel from the cultures in which they originate, and become influential in the cultures of the people who experience them. A term often heard these days, to describe this process, is 'cultural consumption'.

Think about this claim:

In the world in which most people now live, television, radio, literature, advertising, Barbie dolls, BMWs, Indian yoga, Chinese food, and myriad other cultural forms all compete for attention and inform each person's sense of identity and their response to others . ... culture has been opened up in a way that can never be closed again (despite the efforts of various 'fundamentalists'* to do so). Despite this, cultures seem to retain their own style as new influences and elements are taken up but transformed to fit new contexts. (Nuttall and Michael, 2000: 43)

* fundamentalists: those who follow strict ideas about what is correct within a given community, based on what they believe to be the most important basic values or traditions of the group

EXERCISE 4.2

1. What are the main ideas in this extract?
2. What do you think about the ideas here?
3. What examples of the mixing of cultures can you think of?
4. What do you think about the ways in which cultures influence one another, for example, through movies?
5. Frequently the mixing of cultures is a highly creative, expressive act. In linguistic terms, for example, the mingling of terms from different languages to form so-called 'slang' terms is often a site of great creativity. In a multicultural society, such as South Africa, many linguistic and cultural mixings occur. Are there contexts in which you have encountered this kind of creative mixing of words, customs and ideas?
6. What examples do you know of words that derive from other languages and cultures?
7. What do you think about the creation of slang terms by borrowing or adapting words from different languages and cultural sources?

Crossing cultural boundaries in art, writing and music seeks to cross political and social boundaries. Consider, for example, the following lyrics:

Selifikile ixesha lokusenza isigqobo sokuphila; ub' ubiziwe
yiAfrika, the same song we all sing: Akukho mali, asinamli!
As'funi mali –s'fun'ubumnandi! Akukho bumnandi …
asinamandi; the same song we all sing: Akukho mali,
asinamali! As'funi mali … .

Where are you going? Where are you coming from?
Where are you going? Are you coming from Senegal / Libya
/ Congo? / Zimbabwe? Egypt / Nigeria / Mali? Rwanda?
Uganda / Botswana / Malawi / Zanzibar? Kapa, Thekwini,
Joburg, Soweto, Ebhayi, Mowbray Kaap!

Ootata bethu kudala bekhala: the same job for thirty
years! Akukho nto ibonakalayo – except for thirty kids!
Nob' uqhub'iDatsun endala; okanye ushay' iMercedes Benz
– ub' ubiziwe yi Afrika, then we're singing the same song.

('Mowbray Kaap' by Freshlyground, 2006)

8. What is your reaction to this lyric? Why?
9. Are there other examples of cross-cultural music that you
    know of?
10. What do you think (and feel) about any of them?

Exploring culture: ordinary things

As we have seen, different uses of the term 'culture' sometimes
overlap with each other, and at other times seem to be quite
contradictory. In some contexts, the word might be used more
loosely to refer to concepts such as tradition, or various codes
of behaviour. At times, it might refer to art, or other forms of
creative and intellectual expression, especially those regarded as
excellent, important, valuable and inspiring. The values attached
to such expressions imply that culture is something prestigious
and worth aspiring towards.

Central to these differing uses is the point that culture is a
highly important feature of life lived in society or among others.
In thinking about culture, the focus often falls on how individual

identity and experience are shaped by features or practices common to a group. This means that shared practices, values, beliefs and codes shape the way of life of any nation or of groups within the nation. An important point to note is that the concept of 'culture' is often used as a way of approaching or thinking about various phenomena in society. It is a term that enables us to focus on and think about other, related ideas as well as about events, things, people and experience.

In literary studies, there are various aspects to which ideas about culture relate. In this chapter, we will look at some of these, but certainly not all, as the field is wide and often quite specialized. For our purposes in this book, the concept of culture offers intriguing ideas as part of an approach to studying language, writing and literature.

Culture may seem to be an abstract concept, but it also exists in the things we do, make and see. It is part of our environment. It exists in the ways we think and feel. It is in what we write and how we respond to what we experience; in the behaviours we value and those we reject. Similarly, it helps to shape the ideas we have about ourselves and those different from or unfamiliar to us. It affects our consciousness of our own and others' identities. Culture refers to the attitudes of groups and often, therefore, describes or displays ways of thinking or acting that characterize a group. It also influences how groups see characteristics in other groups. When others are seen as inferior in how they appear or behave, they are often regarded with prejudice. Racism is an extreme form of such prejudice. So too are the various forms of sexism, heterosexism and homophobia. A wide variety of characteristics of groups and individuals also give rise to stigma, in certain contexts. This is another extreme form of prejudice. People are stigmatized when something in their lives is seen as morally unacceptable by others: we see this daily in the lives of those living with HIV and Aids.

Thoughts on culture and character

'Personality characteristics that typify a given culture depend to some extent on traditions, the nature of the economy, and what characteristics are considered important to survival. In traditional agricultural societies, for example, group co-operation is considered essential for planting, tending, harvesting, and storing crops so responsibility, reliability, and obedience are more likely to be emphasized. In traditional hunting–gathering societies, individual ability, initiative, and bravery are deemed more important . . . . Even so, a particular society is rarely successful in fostering culturally desirable characteristics in all its members, and individual differences in personality persist despite social pressure to conform.'

(Aiken, 1999: 187)

Other illnesses and other aspects of people's lives may also give rise to stigma.

One way to understand culture is by looking at ordinary life. Raymond Williams, a leading thinker regarding the relationship between culture, writing and society, had this to say about it:

....

Culture is ordinary: that is the first fact. Every human society has its own shape, its own purposes, its own meanings. Every human society expresses these, in institutions, and in arts and learning. The making of a society is the finding of common meanings and directions ... . The growing society is there, yet also it is being made and remade in every individual mind. The making of a mind is, first, the slow learning of shapes, purposes and meanings, so that work, observation and communication are possible ... . These are the ordinary processes of human societies and human minds, and we see through them the nature of a culture: that it is always both traditional and creative; that it is both the most ordinary common meanings and the finest individual meanings ... The questions I ask about our culture are questions about our general and common purposes, yet also questions about deep personal meanings. Culture is ordinary, in every society and in every mind. (Williams, 1989: 4)

....

What do you think about the idea that culture is about the ordinary things of life, the things that make up daily life, routines and ways of thinking? Do you agree with this idea?

Read the following newspaper article to explore what is meant by the idea of culture existing in ordinary things. The writer describes a visit she undertook, as an American tourist in a foreign country, to Austria. She describes her reactions to people and places.

Understanding culture through ordinary life

by Joanna Mikulski

Friday morning we met at 8:30, prepared to explore the claustrophobic rooms of Sigmund Freud's house. The stale air … did not seem conducive to the creation of a new field of scientific study, yet the hum of the voices of the city below his second-floor window inspired a keen interest in the mechanics of life.

We left the birthplace of psychoanalysis and travelled that afternoon to the Schatzkammer, the treasury of the Habsburg monarchy. The crowns of Franz Joseph and the crib of Napoleon glimmered in soft yellow radiance. The golden, woven images of the priestly garments worn in the presence of kings and lords caused the eyes of we American students to dance. Later as I strolled through the Viennese Altstadt, my thoughts turned to the paradox of the creation of these magnificent things that tourists from around the world stand in awe before. As the Habsburg monarchs donned emerald encrusted crowns and posed as Titans*, peasants labored on their estates and grew ill in the filth of large cities. In light of the injustice surrounding their creation these honored possessions made from extraordinary wealth assume a gaudy*, tasteless aura.

* Titans: mythical, heroic figures, symbolizing power

* gaudy: very colourful and bright, over-decorated

The next day we stood in groups of seven at a table eating Greek marinated chicken wraps beside an eager salesman yelling, 'Schmeck, schmeck, schmeck!' An old woman with her belongings in a grocery bag and wearing an unraveling blue cape over a gray dress accosted us and declared us 'schwein' for eating in the midst of her hunger. Well-clothed and weight-conscious, I recognized that I walk with the grace of God among the modern world's nobility.

That evening we left our jeans at the Jugengastehaus and walked like royalty into a production of 'Mozart!', a musical with hints of 'Amadeus' and background chords played frequently on The Bear in South Bend. The rhythmic movement of the notes lingered in my head as I sat with a friend the next day in a small bakery and café a couple of blocks from the multi-cultural noise of the Vienna Altstadt. As we ate the Austrian national breakfast of a Kaiser roll and marmalade I watched a woman like my grandmother drink coffee, smoke cigarettes and chat loudly at a corner table. When we passed the café later in the afternoon she sat there still. I realized then that the key to understanding the culture of European cities and countries lies not in observation of the ornate architectural wonders with stores selling replicas of cathedrals on their ground floor, but in small journeys into the neighbourhoods in which ordinary, real people live.

Observer Newspaper, Mikulski, online, 21 April 2006

EXERCISE 4.3

1. How does the writer react to the tourist attractions she visits? Why?
2. What does she notice about the people around her?
3. What cultural clues, symbols and practices does she notice?
4. How does she feel about the two women she encounters?
5. What does she conclude about how to discover the culture of the place she is in? Why does she come to think this?

TWO WRITING, CULTURE AND TEXTS

Making meaning: cultural viewpoint

In this section, we explore one of the ways in which a society's assumptions, needs and practices influence their response to things encountered in the world. Think back to Chapter Two, and remember the importance of point of view in regard to interpretation and narrative. The point from which we look at things deeply affects how we understand them and the meanings we attribute to them.

Quite simply, we always look *from* somewhere. This idea might seem obvious. Often, though, we forget that we are situated in a particular world (or context). We forget that our understanding of things in the world is affected by where we are from. If you were to describe a society other than your own, your description would most probably be affected in some way by the differences between your world and the world you are observing and describing. There is no such thing as a description entirely free from the influence (whether conscious or unconscious) of an author's attitudes, beliefs and the society from which she or he comes. How you will describe something depends on where you come from and what you are speaking or writing about.

Bearing this in mind, read the following.

The City of Despina

by Italo Calvino

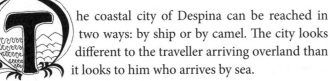he coastal city of Despina can be reached in two ways: by ship or by camel. The city looks different to the traveller arriving overland than it looks to him who arrives by sea.

When the camel-driver arriving at Despina from the desert sees, on the horizon, the buildings of Despina, the chimneys smoking, the windsocks flapping, he thinks of a ship: he knows that it is a city, but he thinks of it as a ship that will take him away from the desert. He sees the city as a ship that is about to leave harbour, the breeze already filling its sails. He thinks of all the foreign ports to which the ship might take him, of all the foreign merchandise that cranes are unloading on docks. He dreams of the chance to drink in bars in exciting places and of witnessing the fights and arguments between men from different countries. He thinks too of the possibility of meeting exotic women.

The sailor, approaching Despina from the sea, sees in the city's shape the form of a camel advancing into the desert. The camel has an embroidered saddle with a glittering fringe and is swaying gently as it moves towards oases in the middle of the desert. The sailor knows that Despina is a city, but he thinks of it as a camel with wineskins hanging from its pack and carrying bundles of wonderful food. He pictures himself as being at the front of a caravan moving away from the sea towards the shade and fresh water of an oasis filled with palm trees. He imagines the white-walled buildings of the oasis, each surrounding a courtyard in which beautiful women dance barefoot, half-hidden by veils of silk.

Each city is seen and understood differently depending on where you approach it from. The sailor and the camel-driver see, in the shape of Despina, something that will take them away from what is familiar to something new and exciting. For this reason, Despina is a border city between two deserts.

Adapted from: Calvino, 1979: 17–18

Despina is an imaginary city created by the Italian author Italo Calvino. His description of the ways in which the sailor and camel-driver see the city makes an interesting point about how we see things. We can probably never see reality just as it is. Different people see things in different ways. Any act of seeing is an interpretation: a process of giving meaning to what we see. Both the sailor and the camel-driver give the city a particular meaning. They interpret the city in different ways by seeing in it particular possibilities that define the city for them.

EXERCISE 4.4

1. How is it that the camel-driver and the sailor see different 'things' when looking at Despina?
2. The answer to this question should help us find an answer to the following: What makes us see the world in the way we do?

'Perspective' refers to the point or place from which we look at things. The sailor and camel-driver are both looking at the same thing (the city) but they see it from different spatial perspectives:

one from the sea and one from the desert. But it is not only their spatial perspectives that affect their interpretations of the city. What makes them understand the city differently is their situation. The sailor might have spent many months at sea and so interprets the city as a chance to experience things he desires and has missed while away.

Similarly, the camel-driver connects the city with the things he has missed most in the desert. They arrive at the city from different worlds (the sea and the desert) and interpret the city's appearance in terms of where they have come from and what they have experienced.

The concept of 'perspective' refers to far more than our physical location when looking at something. It suggests that the way we see things in the world relates to the place from which we look, but that 'place' is not only a physical location. 'Place' also refers to our state of mind and our expectations. In this sense, our perspective is created largely by the world in which we have grown up and in which we have learnt certain ways of seeing. These social factors combine with our individual choices to form the particular situation in which each of us lives.

In the previous chapters we considered how we live in complex contexts made up of everything that forms our world. Gender, race, occupation, social rituals, lifestyle, language, religious faith, economic class, political beliefs, educational background, family relationships and our environment all influence our perceptions. What we see and how we understand or interpret the world around us depends on both what we are looking at and the context from within which we look.

One of the most important factors that influence how we see and interpret the world is the culture (or cultures, for many people are influenced by more than one) from which we come. However, if we assume that all members of a culture think or behave in exactly the same way, our assumption would be factually inaccurate, and even racist. Nonetheless, culturally derived ideas about how to interpret what we encounter or experience frequently affect the meanings we give to things, events and behaviour.

In literary texts, such processes become visible. In an essay entitled 'Finding Culture' Robert Thornton writes about cultural studies. He makes the important point that we can think of literature as 'part and parcel with culture' and that culture is 'perceivable in literature' (in Nuttall and Michael, 2000: 42). This is what we will explore further in the rest of this chapter.

The idea that culture becomes visible in literary texts is valuable. It adds an interesting dimension to our study of texts. For instance, Edward Said, a leading intellectual in recent times, has pointed out that *Mansfield Park*, one of the novels written in the early nineteenth century by the renowned novelist, Jane Austen, reveals much about the attitudes towards colonization of the society depicted in the novel. Even though the novel does not directly mention these attitudes, the characterization of several of the protagonists suggests their attitudes towards other cultures. Likewise, as Said shows, the entire culture or way of life of the family and society represented in the book is based on the exploitation of slaves in the Caribbean plantations from which the family draws vast wealth. The relationship between the culture in Regency England, and the cultures affected by British colonialism, is an important aspect of the novel, even though the author does not focus directly on it. Texts, in ways such as this, represent, explore and are influenced by the cultural contexts in which they are written.

Since we are asking you to consider what writing reveals about culture, read the following claims about the literary form that we looked at in Chapter One:

....

The autobiographical act in South Africa, more than a literary convention, has become a cultural activity. Memoir, reminiscence, confession, testament, case history and personal journalism, all different kinds of autobiographical acts or cultural occasions in which narrators take up models of identity that have become widely available, have pervaded the culture of the 1990s and have spread into the next century. This flourishing of the autobiographical voice has emerged alongside the powerful informing context of South Africa's Truth and Reconciliation Commission, but it is also a symptom of … the post-apartheid moment in general.

Particularly since the political transition of 1994, personal disclosure has become part of … democracy itself …. Talking about their own lives, confessing, and constructing personal narratives – on the body, on the air, in music, in print – South Africans translate their selves, and their communities, into story. (Nuttall and Michael, 2000: 298–299)

EXERCISE 4.5

1. What links do the writers make between autobiography and historical events in South Africa?
2. Do you think it is true that people (in South Africa or elsewhere) are generally interested in writing about themselves?
3. Do people generally feel that their cultures 'allow' them to do so?
4. Are there things that cultures do not 'allow' people to write about?
5. Next time you visit a library or bookstore, look at the shelves for autobiography. Do you see evidence there of this widespread interest in life-writing?

Cultural identity, context and difference

You will often encounter the word 'culture' in the phrases 'cultural context' and 'cultural difference'. These phrases are based on the assumption that an individual's cultural context is relevant to the way he or she interprets the world, and that cultures differ in important ways. However, they are not evaluative claims: they should never be seen as assertions that one society is better or worse than another.

In a multi-cultural context such as South Africa there is often a tension between preserving the cultural identities of different groups (whether they are based on religion, race or language) and promoting national unity. Obviously it is essential to encourage tolerance and dialogue. But how far should society go?

Consider the following questions:

- To what extent do you think the cultural identities of different groups deserve to be protected?
- Should we attempt to throw all cultures into a 'melting pot' so that they merge into a single national – or even global – culture?
- To what extent do you feel an individual is defined by the culture of which she or he is a member?

When two or more cultures come into contact with one another we often become aware of the differences between them as well as of their similarities. One reason for this could be that when we are confronted with another culture, we become representatives of our own culture. Outside of our own culture, we are often taken as representing, in some direct sense, the entire culture of which we are members. We are, unquestionably, more aware of the fact of culture when we find ourselves at the borders of our own and other cultures.

Imagine that you have just returned from a visit to Botswana, where you have encountered Tswana culture. You visited a series of villages, saw the democratic 'kgotla' system in operation (which gives adults the right to argue in public before decisions are made by local authorities) and were impressed by the art and educational practices of the society. You decide that you wish to become a Motswana and wish to live a life as close to that of the villagers of western Botswana as possible. Assuming that you are not a Motswana or Mosotho, you would have to learn the language and learn more about the culture. Imagine that you do so, that you emigrate and find yourself in a remote village in Botswana.

EXERCISE 4.6

1. To what degree do you think you would be accepted by the local people?
2. Imagine that you are visited by people from your own earlier culture. How might they respond to the changes you have made?
3. Would you still 'feel' as if you are a member of your culture 'back home'?
4. How much of your culture would you forget?
5. Could you simply return to your own culture?

Clearly, not everyone will answer these questions in the same way. The cultural changes that the transition would demand of a Japanese student from Kyoto, for instance, would be entirely different to those demanded of a Setswana-speaking student from South Africa. If a person wanted to move from one culture to another successfully (rather than just visit it as an outsider), she or he would most probably have to:

- learn the language of the society;
- attempt to follow its social, religious and political practices;
- respect the people's beliefs; and
- accept the forms of authority in the society as valid.

Are there any dangers in speaking of 'culture' as it relates to the ways we see the world? As soon as we speak of cultures as unified and coherent, or substitute a stereotype for the complex nature of any society, we run the risk of racism. If we asserted that all individuals in a culture see things in a certain way, we would be generalizing. Most societies have considerable variations within them and we would need to bear this in mind. Individuals within a society may differ from one another more than they differ from individuals in other societies. Furthermore, no individual sees the world purely through the eyes of his or her culture. Our own unique experiences, choices, circumstances and preferences all affect the way that we see and understand our world.

EXERCISE 4.7

Think about yourself and about a friend or relative who belongs to the same culture as you, and answer these questions:

1. Do you listen to the same music?
2. Do you have the same taste in clothing?
3. Do you have the same attitude to sport?
4. Do you like the same foods and drink the same drinks?
5. Do you always agree with each other about matters of political and religious belief?
6. If you are both married, do you see the roles of husband and wife in exactly the same way?

Your answers to these questions will probably leave you with the conclusion that being from the same culture does not mean that you are exactly the same. This is true of people in all cultural groups. Why, then, do we speak of 'cultures' at all? At various points in the history of humankind, groups have come into contact with one another. At the point of meeting, individuals develop ways of understanding and describing the behaviour and attitudes of the group they encounter. Through descriptions of other cultures they are also usually defining and defending (or criticizing) their own culture. These descriptions, which we will call representations of cultures, are very important because they affect the ways in which members of different cultures behave towards one another. How they think and talk about themselves and others is frequently based on notions of cultural difference.

Because such representations are so often expressed in language (though also in film and the visual arts), we need to consider the significance of language to culture and to the process of representation. Have you ever heard someone who speaks more than one language say, 'There are words in one language that don't have exact equivalents in another language'? An example is the word 'computer' in English. In Japanese, in which there was no word to express the idea, the word sounds like 'co-poo-ta-ra', which comes from the way some pronounce the English word. In English we have a concept we refer to with the word 'weekdays'; in Italian there is no single word for this concept. Instead, it is represented by the phrase 'Lunedi a Venerdi', which literally means 'Monday to Friday'. There are also examples from South Africa, such as the Sotho 'teye' (pronounced 'ti-ya') for the English word 'tea'. The English word was, in a sense, 'Sotho-ized' or modified to fit the grammar and pronunciation of Sesotho.

Translation is a more complex process than merely looking for a word in one language that means exactly the same as a word in another. An extreme point of view concerning translation would maintain that precise translation from one language to another is not in any real sense possible. Some linguists have suggested that the structure of people's language might influence the way they see the world and name things within it. Other scholars, however, hold that culture shapes the grammar and vocabulary of a language. Whatever we might feel about this debate, the fact remains that languages may describe the world somewhat differently.

In his novel *Things Fall Apart*, the Nigerian author Chinua Achebe does not attempt to translate certain words from the Ibo language. The novel describes the Ibo society as it existed in the Niger Delta in the last years of the eighteenth century. One word that Achebe does not translate is 'osu'. In the glossary in the text, Achebe defines 'osu' as 'outcast; having been dedicated to a god, the 'osu' was taboo, and was not allowed to mix with the freeborn in any way.' The 'osu' were a group of individuals divided from Ibo society yet still members of it, who had been given by the tribe as a gift to a god. Non-'osu' (freeborn) Ibo did not associate with the 'osu': they would not converse, eat or share accommodation with the 'osu'.

The word names a cultural/religious practice of the Ibo people. The word 'osu' cannot be translated into English except through a complex description of the practice itself. An Ibo person might think of people as being either 'osu' or freeborn: the concept is part of her or his way of interpreting the people around him. When an Ibo person comes to talk to a speaker of another language, say English, he or she will have to translate the idea 'osu' into terms that an English speaker would understand.

The English words 'outcast' (*Oxford Advanced Learner's Dictionary*: 'a person who is driven away from home, friends or society, or who has no place in society') and 'taboo' ('a cultural or religious custom that forbids people to do, touch, use or talk about a certain thing: 'the taboo against incest'; 'tribal taboos'; 'Death is one of the great taboos in our culture') can be used to explain the word 'osu', but they do not express the full significance of the word in Ibo culture. The word reflects a particular belief or way of seeing the world. Its existence reflects an aspect of Ibo culture and any attempt to translate it into another language will involve representing the practice in the terms of another language.

Languages, because they name distinctive concepts, indicate that how we think about the world cannot easily be separated from the words we use to describe it. The debate about whether the language we speak determines what we think or whether we think things and then find names for them is an ongoing and interesting one. We will certainly not try to solve the problem here. But if we consider the difficulties of translation, we can draw the following conclusions.

○ There is an important connection between the language we speak and how we interpret the world.

○ Language names things and concepts and could shape how we think about the world.

○ Cross-cultural communication is a complex, but important, process to understand.

○ If we describe another culture in our own language, we are describing it in our own terms.

○ Our language reflects and creates our cultural context, because where we come from in the world affects how we speak about where we come from.

Encounters: writing and culture

We referred earlier to the idea that culture becomes perceptible or visible in literary texts. This means both that writing reveals interesting aspects of the culture it describes, and that it also reveals the cultural influences which affect what the writer writes about and how he or she writes. In order to explore this idea further in relation to identity and difference, read the following extract. It is the opening of a novel, *A Distant Shore*, by the contemporary British writer Caryl Phillips, in which the narrator exclaims:

England has changed. These days it's difficult to tell who's from here and who's not. Who belongs and who's a stranger. It's disturbing. It doesn't feel right. Three months ago, in early June, I moved out here to this new development of Stoneleigh. None of the old villagers seem comfortable with the term 'new development'. They simply call Stoneleigh the 'new houses on the hill'. After all, our houses are set on the edge of Weston, a village that is hardly going to give up its name and identity because some developer has seen a way to make a quick buck by throwing up some semi-detached bungalows, slapping a carriage lamp on the front of them and calling them 'Stoneleigh'. If anyone asks me I say I am living in Weston. Everybody does, except one or two who insist on writing their addresses as 'Stoneleigh'. The postman told me that they add 'Weston' as an afterthought, as though the former civilizes the latter. He was annoyed … He was keen that I should understand that there was nothing wrong with Weston, and once he started I could hardly get him to stop. (Phillips, 2004: 3)

....

EXERCISE 4.8

1. Strong opinions are expressed in this passage; the narrator (and others) are deeply upset. What upsets them, and why?
2. What do you notice about the way the narrator speaks about the situation?

This passage reveals much about the emotions and worldview of the narrator. As you read it, think about how she characterizes the people and the situation she is speaking about. Her personal unhappiness is apparent, but she articulates it in words that show a deep anxiety about her world. She is not just cross about something in her own life, but anxious about the society in which she lives. Her world is under threat, not simply in personal terms but in the wider sense of community and culture. It has been disrupted by development and expansion, and by changes in the community.

The narrator's words show important aspects of how differences in cultural identity affect the way a situation is interpreted. She sees the community as divided into those who belong and those who do not, labeling them dismissively as 'strangers'. Notice how the postman, conscious of a difference between the old village and the new development, is anxious to assert the superiority of the village (and its people and their ways of doing things) over the development. The village's expansion threatens people's settled ways, bringing to the surface strong feelings about the value of the old community and its way of being (its culture).

Later in the novel, the narrator has this to say:

At the top of the hill I stopped and looked back at Weston. I remember seeing it clearly, for the full moon hung heavily in the sky, as though supported by an invisible column. Bathed in the moon's bright glare, Weston looked serene and unencumbered by the problems that continued to plague the town. I'm almost embarrassed to admit it but these days whenever I go into town it's the homeless people who annoy me the most, and the frightening thing is they seem to be everywhere. There are dozens of them living beneath the underpass in boxes that used to hold fridges or big colour television sets, with their matted hair and their bottles of meths. It looks to me like they'll always be around as long as the church is happy to given them plastic cups of sweet tea and change their ulcerated bandages, without holding them accountable for anything. During the day they sit around the precincts playing the guitar like it's some kind of summer camp that they're attending. Why didn't they pay any attention at school? It's not too late to get their lives back on track. They've got their health, and they're not retarded. Well, at least not the younger ones. And they've even got some kind of talent. It's just a willful waste, that's all, and I believe most of them are doing it on purpose because they're lazy and they want sympathy, but they never get it from me. When I refuse to give them money they scream at me, and I often feel scorn when I walk past them. I didn't used to, but I do now that they've started in on me and other passers-by. A few days ago I was coming back from the hospital when I caught one of them, a filthy beast, eating out of a dustbin like a dog. I didn't say anything, but I did look at him and then he started to shout. 'You can't hurt me any more,' he said. 'You can't hurt me.' Who said I wanted to hurt him? I'm glad Dad isn't here to see what's become of his town. (Phillips, 2004: 12–13)

In this passage, we see further expressions of the anxiety that has led the narrator to feel that her place and its way of life are under threat. Her words reveal what is termed, in academic study, a process of Othering. In literary theory, the terms 'others' and 'the other' (or, in its more frequent form 'the Other'), are used to show how groups in society create an identity by defining themselves as different from other groups or cultures. Those who are different from members of the group are 'others' or, in abstract terms and symbolically, the Other. (Members of the group, those with whom one identifies, are same; those outside it are Other.) One way to understand a group's cultural identity (who the members consider themselves to be), is to identify who the group thinks it is not. The group members' ideas about how they differ from other people tells us a great deal about how they think about themselves.

One of the ways in which Othering is enacted, and the Other is designated, is by means of stereotyping. To stereotype a person or a group is to interpret their character and actions according to ideas you hold about them that are based on prejudice, generalization, or lack of knowledge. Stereotyping leads one to attribute meanings to what people say and do based on assumptions about 'the kind of person someone seems to be'. In the passage above, this process is seen in the narrator's descriptions. Many instances of stereotyping and prejudice are articulated in the narrator's words.

Frequently, fear of the Other contains elements of projection.* Here, the narrator imagines someone else to be feeling as hostile towards her as she does towards other people. This projection is unfounded, for in fact it is the other person who fears her. Similarly, as is common in processes of Othering, she uses dehumanizing terms to establish her own difference from the people she regards as utterly different from her. Calling them 'beasts,' she represents herself as superior to and inalterably different from them. She also judges them as lacking moral worth. She blames them, feeling highly judgemental and anxious about the effect of the people she regards as so alien on her own most highly prized sense of place. Notice too how the narrator's ways of seeing others and of establishing that their characteristics are so different from hers and her community's enables her to

* projection: incorrectly thinking that someone else has the thoughts or feelings, usually negative, which are in your own mind

avoid any feelings of compassion or fellowship. The prejudiced interpretations she forms make them so utterly Other that she feels no sense of sameness. This again is a marked feature of the representation of people (or cultures and groups) as Other: the absence of any sense of shared humanity, and of humaneness.

We have discussed the passages from *A Distant Shore* at some length since they bring into view, in a literary text, the processes that are frequently discussed in theoretical or philosophical texts. As you read, explore these issues yourself. Consider the ways in which characters in novels, for instance, express views that represent the values of themselves and the cultures to which they belong as being so different from those of different people. Be alert to the strategies of Othering, and think about how opinions are expressed.

Meeting others

In the following poem, think about the representation of 'self' and 'other' as expressed by the images used by the poet. It describes an encounter between people from different cultural backgrounds. As you read it, remember the points made earlier in this chapter about how culture is part of the most ordinary, day-to-day aspects of our lives – such as a chance encounter on a country road.

Rural women
by Chris Mann

Driving through hills at dusk
the bush-tips flicking the truck
I've seen their straight-backed gait
silhouetted on red-skied ridges
climbing through aloe and thorn
working their buckets of water home;
and pushing up the sun visor

I've changed gear for a corner
a wood fire drifting its aroma
with soil-scents into the cab
and heard a consonance of voices
talking of this and neighbourly that;

And clutch in have greeted a trio
stooping for water at a spring
scooping it in with small tin basins
into dark blue buckets from pools
was greeted in turn and saw
a row of guarded, polite expressions;
the flash of a smile, a woman
her arms lustrous in the gloom
kneeling up from the rock-ferns
steadying the burden on her head
a friend with a skirt of indigo
covering a gush of laughter with a hand;

And warm in a surge of feeling
have idled the engine a moment
and thought how the old romance
the tug of difference and novelty
keeps tingling man and woman
despite the deep frontiers of culture;
and nudging the truck through cattle
ebbing rich umbers down a road
the sky now smoked with mauve
have rejoiced at rural women
their presence, dimming in dusk-light,
adorned with earth-brown cloth and beads.

Mann, 1996: 46

EXERCISE 4.9

1. What does the speaker seem to be saying, in this poem, about the meeting?
2. What are the 'deep frontiers of culture'?
3. How important are they, to the speaker?
4. Think about your own experience of unfamiliar contexts, places or situations. Have you ever moved into a new work or social environment where things seemed strange or significantly different from what you were familiar with?
5. How did you feel at first?
6. How did you act?
7. What did you do to try to understand the new things you encountered?
8. Did you make any mistakes?
9. Did you adapt? How?
10. Have you met people (perhaps from another country) whose culture differs from your own?
11. What made that culture seem different from other cultures you know about?
12. How did you react to members of that culture?
13. Did you consider that culture to be equal to your own?
14. Did you want to understand more about that culture?

Alien encounters

Encounters between different groups or cultures are represented in many different literary texts and forms of writing. In the genre of science fiction, for instance, a recurring theme is that of the encounter between strangers. Such strangers are often vastly different from one another in both appearance and behaviour.

The figure of the alien appears often in science-fiction texts. Aliens (people from other planets) may look like anything at all: they may have two heads, four arms, any number of arms and legs, or they may be modelled on insects, animals, clouds or any other human phenomenon. The most common form of alien found in science fiction is the hilf, which stands for 'highly intelligent life-form'. Hilfs are comparable to humans in that they have highly developed senses and cultures, which, nevertheless, are vastly different from those of humans. When humans journey to other planets (as in the extract below) they often meet aliens, with very interesting results. The two species' reactions to each other may include fear, suspicion, curiosity, revulsion, hostility or a desire to communicate. Often there is a powerful combination of feelings when humans meet aliens. As the relationship between them unfolds, they will often learn each another's languages and begin to communicate. They may even explore how the other species does things. When this happens, we have a comparison with and a comment on Earthly inter-cultural meetings, which often contain all the feelings and behaviour patterns outlined here. This happens so often in science fiction that some critics have even speculated that aliens are a symbol for other cultures here on Earth. The way human scientists and interplanetary travellers interact with aliens is exactly the way we behave when we meet people from other cultures.

The Sparrow
by Maria Doria Russell

BACKGROUND: *A strangely assorted group of Jesuits (a sub-group of the Roman Catholic faith) have found a mysterious planet called Rakhat, whose inhabitants sing and journeyed there by spaceship. They find the weather and plants on the planet hospitable, although the plant food gives them digestive problems. The following passage describes the first meeting between the Jesuits and the inhabitants of the planet.*

There was no panic in either group. The villagers stopped a few hundred paces down the path from Emilio and unburdened themselves of the big well-made baskets, which were filled with something that was not heavy, judging from the ease with which the containers were handled, even by the smaller individuals. They were unclothed, but around their limbs and necks many wore bright ribbons, which fluttered and floated sinuously in the wind. The breeze shifted more decisively then and suddenly D.W. was aware of an exquisite scent, floral, he thought, coming from the crowd. He focused again on the openwork basketry and realized the containers were filled with white blossoms.

For a short while the two groups simply stood and looked at one another, the piping voices of juveniles* hushed by adults, murmurs and commentary falling off to silence. As the crowd quieted, D.W. took note of who spoke and who stood silent in the discussion that followed. The flankers* and point men remained on guard and aloof from the deliberations.

As D.W. took in the command structure of the group, so Anne Edwards studied the anatomy. The two species were not grotesque* to one another. They shared a general body plan: bipedal*, with forelimbs specialized for grasping and manipulation. Their faces also held a similarity in general, and the differences were not shocking or hideous to Anne; she found them beautiful, as she found many other species beautiful, here and at home. Large mobile ears, erect and carried high on the sides of the head. Gorgeous eyes, large and densely lashed, calm as camels'. The nose was convex*, broad at the tip, curving smoothly off to meet the muzzle, which projected rather more noticeably than was ever the case among humans. The mouth, lipless and broad.

There were many differences, of course. On the gross level, the most striking was that the humans were tailless, an anomaly* on their home planet as well; the vast majority of vertebrates* on Earth had tails, and Anne had never understood why apes and guinea pigs had lost them. And another human oddity stood out, here as at home: relative hairlessness. The villagers were covered with smooth dense coats of hair, lying flat to muscular bodies. They were as sleek as Siamese cats: buff-coloured with lovely dark brown markings around the eyes, like Cleopatra's kohl* and a darker shading that ran down the spine.

'They are so beautiful,' Anne breathed and she wondered, distressed, if such uniformly handsome people would find humans repulsive – flat-faced and ugly, with ridiculous patches of white and red and brown and black hair, tall and medium and short, bearded and barefaced and sexually dimorphic* to boot. We are outlandish, she thought, in the truest sense of the word …

* juveniles: young individuals of a particular species; usually used of animals

* flankers: the individuals who stood at the sides of the group

* grotesque: strange to the point of being unpleasant or offensive

* bipedal: having two legs

* convex: curving outwards

* anomaly: something unusual, an exception

* vertebrates: animals with spines in their backs

* kohl: a black powder that is placed around the eyes to make them more attractive

* dimorphic: having two different shapes

From out of the centre of the crowd an individual of middle height and indeterminate sex came forward. Anne watched, scarcely breathing, as this person separated from the group to approach them. She realized then that Marc had been making a similar biological assessment*, for as this person stepped nearer, he cried very softly, 'The eyes, Anne!' Each orbit contained a doubled iris, arranged horizontally in a figure-eight around two pupils of variable size, like the bizarre eye of the cuttlefish. This much they had seen before. It was the colour that transfixed her: a dark blue, almost violet, as luminous* as the stained glass at Chartres*.

Emilio continued to stand still, letting the person who stood before him decide what to do. At last, this individual spoke.

It was a lilting*, swooping language, full of vowels and soft buzzing consonants, fluid and melting, without any of the staccato glottal stops* and rhythmic choppiness of the language of the songs. It was, Anne decided, more beautiful, but her heart sank. It was as unlike the Singers' language as Italian was unlike Chinese. All that work, she thought, for nothing. George, who like all of them, had been trained by Emilio to recognize the Singers' language, must have been thinking the same thing. He leaned over to Anne and whispered, ' ... . On *Star Trek*, everybody spoke English!' She elbowed him but smiled to herself and took his hand, listening to the speech and tightening her grip as the speaker stopped speaking and she waited for Emilio's response.

'I don't understand,' said Emilio Sandoz in a soft clear voice, 'but I can learn if you will teach me.'

What happened next was a puzzle to all those in the Jesuit party but Sandoz. The spokesperson called a number of individuals out of the crowd, including several half-grown children, one by one. Each spoke briefly to Emilio, who met their eyes with his own calm gaze and repeated to each of them, 'I don't understand.' He was almost certain that each had spoken a different language or dialect* to him, one of which was indeed that of the Singers, and he realized that they were interpreters and that the leader was attempting to find some language they had in common. Failing in that, the adult returned to the crowd. There was a discussion that lasted a good while. Then a juvenile, much smaller than anyone who'd spoken earlier, came forward with another adult,

* assessment: a judgement that has been thought about very carefully

* luminous: giving off light

* Chartres: a town in France, famous for its beautiful cathedral

* lilting: rising and falling in a pleasant, almost musical way

* glottal stops: a speech sound made by opening and closing part of the throat

* *Star Trek*: a famous TV show about human beings exploring the rest of the universe

* dialect: a version of a language that is spoken by one group or in one area

who spoke reassuringly before gently urging the little one to approach Emilio alone.

Russell, 1996: 283–285

EXERCISE 4.10

1. What do you notice about the travellers' reactions to the inhabitants of the planet whom they meet in this encounter?
2. What do the travellers notice first about the aliens?
3. Why do you think there is so much emphasis on language in this extract?
4. From whose point of view are events seen?
5. Is the aliens' point of view expressed?
6. What emotions are felt, in this encounter, by each group?

The description of this meeting brings into view many of the characteristics that typify inter-cultural encounters. Individuals within both groups react in various ways. Assessing the potential threat of the other group, D.W. notices the things they carry, the leaders of the group, and the behaviour of individuals he regards as possible enemies. Anne Edwards focuses on the group's appearance. She makes sense of their unfamiliarity by comparing it to what she does know, naming unfamiliar features by means of comparison to familiar things. She also feels a sense of inadequacy and inferiority. Father Emilio, on the other hand, also seems aware of the insufficiency of his group's skills for this encounter. Language has failed: there is no common ground in this respect. Yet he seeks other ways to bridge the differences between them.

In the extract from *The Sparrow*, Father Emilio and his party arrive on Rakhat with the full intention of making friends with the hilfs who live there. From Earth, they have heard the inhabitants of Rakhat singing across the light-years, and admire the music. They are prepared, then, to treat the singers with admiration, friendliness and respect. They do not want to exploit them or to gain anything from visiting their planet: they only want to know more about them. This is why, when they first meet the species described above, who are called 'Runa', they are so open-minded and have such a friendly attitude. Unfortunately, though, their ignorance of cultural practices on Rakhat leads their mission to disaster. Soon after the meeting, only Father Emilio is left alive, although he is imprisoned, badly injured and in danger of losing his sanity. The rest of the book recounts what happens to bring him to such a sorry state. The solemn lesson of the text is that people should not assume that they know another culture without making thorough investigations first.

In a very different context, the following poem also explores the consequences of ignorance about others. Here, the writer seeks to inspire a sense of compassion, by speaking with respect of the cultural practices of people who had been demonized and Othered by military–political propaganda. It was written to protest against the ongoing brutality of the war fought during the 1960s and 70s in Vietnam, in which the United States played a major, and devastating, role. Written by an American poet, it shows that notions of cultural difference can at times be used to oppose the actions of powerful nations and interest groups.

The process of representation

In representing cultures, they are named (and names are not necessarily neutral or innocent). As well as being named, cultures are defined according to the specific attributes the writer thinks they have. In the course of definition – which we can think of as the process of labelling different aspects of a culture – the culture is interpreted. Interpretation means that the writer who is representing the culture gives particular meanings to aspects of the culture and its practices.

What were they like?
by Denise Levertov

Did the people of Viet Nam
Use lanterns of stone?
Did they hold ceremonies
to reverence the opening of buds?
Were they inclined to quiet laughter?
Did they use bone and ivory, jade and silver for ornament?
Had they an epic poem?
Did they distinguish between speech and singing?

Sir, their light hearts turned to stone.
It is not remembered whether in gardens
Stone lanterns illumined pleasant ways.
Perhaps they gathered once to delight in blossom,
But after the children were killed
There were no more buds.
Sir, laughter is bitter to the burned mouth.

A dream ago, perhaps. Ornament is for joy.
All the bones were charred.
It is not remembered. Remember,
Most were peasants; their life
Was in rice and bamboo.
When peaceful clouds were reflected in the paddies
And the water buffalo stepped surely along terraces,
Maybe fathers told their sons old tales.
When bombs smashed those mirrors
There was time only to scream.
There is an echo yet
Of their speech which was like a song.
It was reported their singing resembled
The flight of moths in moonlight.
Who can say? It is silent now.

Reproduced by permission of Pollinger Ltd and the proprietor
Moffett and Mphahlele (eds), 2002: 165

EXERCISE 4.11

1. What images of the way of life of the Vietnamese people appear in this poem?
2. Are there particular images in this poem that you think are interesting or effective? If so, why?
3. Who is the speaker talking to?
4. What is the speaker suggesting about the culture of the Vietnamese?
5. What does the speaker seem to feel?
6. How do you feel when you read this poem?

Discussion – and representations – of culture often occur in the context of discussions about imperialism and colonialism. Colonialism is a form of control or authority: it is the practice of one, powerful country controlling another, less powerful country. Imperialism is a similar practice, empire-building, in which a powerful country establishes control over other countries (often over a large number of territories which it has invaded or defeated in war). It also refers to situations in which powerful countries exert increasing influence over others by means of economic and cultural influence, without direct political control.

⊙ What actions or ideas do you associate with the word 'colonialism'?

⊙ How is the word 'imperialism' usually used?

Strategies for reading

Effective reading often depends on developing good strategies. When faced with reading a text for academic purposes, it is useful to survey it before reading it in detail. In other words, you read to gain a general impression of the writer's argument before examining the ideas in detail. There are two useful strategies for getting a general impression.

Firstly, you can skim. When you skim you read very quickly, deliberately leaving out parts of the text to get the main ideas. It is useful to:

⊙ look at the title and any subheadings;
⊙ look at any captions or illustrations;
⊙ look at words written in bold, italics or capitals;
⊙ quickly read the first and last paragraphs of the text, since writers often summarize their ideas in these paragraphs; and
⊙ quickly read the first sentence of each paragraph, as this will often contain the main idea of the paragraph.

Secondly, you can scan. When you scan a text, you are reading to find a particular idea or piece of information. You usually let your eyes pass quickly over the page looking for specific information without reading the whole text.

After surveying the article, the next step is to read it carefully and thoughtfully. In other words, read it in detail. This is also sometimes called the study-read phase. There are many ways of reading a text carefully. One very useful strategy is, if you come across words you do not understand, to re-read the sentence in which the word appears and then re-read the surrounding sentences. If you cannot guess the meaning in this way, look up the word in a dictionary (or in the book's glossary if there is one). If you use a dictionary, make sure that you select a meaning that fits the context.

Adapted from: START: Strategies for Academic Reading and Thinking. 1996

The following is from the transcript of a speech delivered by Edward Said, at York University in Canada, in 1993. He argues, here, from a point of view that strenuously opposes imperialism. Read the speech to see how ideas about culture overlap with ideas about imperialism. Your purpose in reading this speech is to discover what the speaker says about imperialism, colonialism and culture.

Culture and Imperialism
by Edward Said

I want to begin with an indisputable fact, namely that during the nineteenth century unprecedented power, compared to which the power of Rome, Spain, Baghdad or Constantinople in their day were far less formidable, was concentrated in Britain and France and later in other Western countries, the United States especially. This century, the nineteenth century, climaxed what has been called the 'rise of the West'. Western power allowed the imperial metropolitan centers at the end of the nineteenth century to acquire and accumulate territory and subjects on a truly astonishing scale.

… In Europe itself at the end of the nineteenth century scarcely a corner of life was untouched by the facts of empire. The economies were hungry for overseas markets, raw materials, cheap labor and profitable land. Defense and foreign policy establishments were more and more committed to the maintenance of vast tracts of distant territory and large numbers of subjugated peoples. … As I shall be using the term – and I'm not really too interested in terminological adjustments – 'imperialism' means the practice, the theory and the attitudes of a dominating metropolitan centre that rules a distant territory. 'Colonialism,' which is almost always a consequence of imperialism, is the implanting of settlements on distant territory. ... In our time direct colonialism of a kind of for example the British in India or the French in Algeria and Morocco has largely ended. Yet imperialism lingers where it often has been in a kind of general cultural sphere as well as its specific political, ideological, economic and social practices. The point I want to make is that neither imperialism nor colonialism is a simple act of accumulation and acquisition. It's not just a matter of going out there and getting a territory and sitting on it. Both of these practices are supported and perhaps even impelled by impressive cultural formations ...

... The vocabulary of classic nineteenth century imperial culture in places like England and France is plentiful with words and concepts like 'inferior' or 'subject races.' ... Out of the imperial experiences, notions about culture were clarified, reinforced, criticized or rejected.

... But there's more than that to imperialism. There was a commitment to imperialism over and above profit ... There was very little domestic resistance [in the colonizing countries] to imperial expansion during the nineteenth century, although these empires were very frequently established and maintained under adverse and even disadvantageous conditions.

... Thus I come to the present. Imperialism did not really end, did not suddenly become past once decolonization had set in motion the dismantling of the classical empires. A legacy of connections still binds countries like Algeria and India to France and Britain, respectively. A vast new population of Muslims, Africans and West Indians from former colonial territories now resides, for instance, in metropolitan Europe. Even Italy, Germany and Scandinavia today must deal with these dislocations, which are to a large degree the result of imperialism and colonialization as well as expanding European populations. Also, the end of the Cold War and of the Soviet Union has definitely changed the world map. The triumph of the United States as the last superpower suggests that a new set of force lines will structure the world. They were already beginning to be apparent in the 1960s and 1970s ...

[But,] the two general areas of agreement nearly everywhere are that personal freedom should be safeguarded and that the earth's environment should be defended against further decline. Democracy and ecology, each providing a local context and plenty of concrete combat zones, are set against a cosmic backdrop. Whether in the struggle of nationalities or in the problems of deforestation, global warming, the Aids epidemic, the interactions between individual identity embodied in minor activities like smoking or the usage of aerosol cans ...

... Lastly, no one today is purely one thing. Labels like Indian or Canadian or woman or Muslim or American are no more than starting points, which, if followed into actual experience for only a moment, are completely left behind. Imperialism consolidated the mixture of cultures and identities on a world scale. But its worst and most paradoxical gift was to allow people to believe that they were only, mainly, exclusively white or black or Western or Oriental. Just as human beings make their own history, they also make their cultures and ethnic identities. No one can deny the persisting continuities of long traditions, sustained habitations, national languages and cultural geographies. But there seems no reason except fear and prejudice to keep insisting on their separation and distinctiveness, as if that was all human life was about.

Survival, in fact, is about the connections between things ... . It is more rewarding and more difficult to think concretely and sympathetically about others than only about 'us'. But this also means not trying to rule others, not trying to classify them or put them in hierarchies, above all, not constantly to reiterate how our culture or country is number one, or not number one, for that matter. For the intellectual there's quite enough of value to do without that. Thank you.

Adapted from: Edward Said in *Zmag*, online, 23 April 2006

EXERCISE 4.12

1. Summarize the main ideas in this speech and explain how colonialism and imperialism are defined in it.
2. Also explain how the speaker thinks people should behave now, in relation to culture. What does he see as a wise attitude to one's own culture, and what is seen as potentially dangerous?

Now read the following:

What is happening in Africa? Why are signs of positive gains being overwhelmed by tragedies of sisters and brothers killing one another? Why are children being wasted and men, women and the aged turned into heaps of corpses and stragglers on refuse routes through the forests and valleys of Africa? Surely, something is wrong with our continent ... . Where now is the African philosophy, where the African culture and the African dignity on which we pride ourselves, to help us out of our present confusion? The most disturbing tragedy is the many civil wars and their effects on unarmed women, children and aged people.

The condition of the victims of war in Africa has become intolerable. That the same can be said for situations of armed conflicts in Europe, Asia and other parts of the world is, alas, no excuse for the horror that armed conflict has brought to the lives and deaths of Africans. War in Africa has caused not only physical and human damage but also moral and cultural devastation ... Africa is going through a traumatic process of regeneration and renaissance, a process of transformation. If we are not going to be lost in the 'trance' of this transformation, we must halt the ongoing deadening of moral and cultural sensitivities. [...] The roles of the state and the civil societies are important but the most important role in the recreating of African morals and cultures is that of the individual. Individuals must practice the 'modest morality of small deeds' by caring for one another, by being their brothers' and sisters' keepers. (Omotoso, 1997: 26–27)

In this piece, the writer uses the idea of culture for particular purposes. The extract comes from *Woza Africa: Music Goes to War*, which describes the efforts of a group of musicians from across Africa to pool their creative resources in a protest against armed conflict in many regions of the continent. The book is a memorial to victims of war and a call to individuals to oppose violence.

EXERCISE 4.13

1. Read the piece carefully and think about how the idea of culture is expressed. What is the writer saying about culture?
2. How do you react to the ideas in these speeches?
3. If you are interested in these ideas, find out more about them. Explore what is meant by the idea of an African renaissance and consider how the term is used in contexts such as media reports or political speeches.
4. If you were going to deliver a speech to persuade people to pay attention to something in society that you consider very important, what ideas about culture would you include?

Marketing, branding and culture

The extracts above both use the idea of culture for specific purposes relating to social and political circumstances. Another area in which notions of culture are widely used and highly significant is that of marketing and branding. A phrase widely used in many contexts is 'brand culture'. Originally used by marketing professionals to describe a process of promoting products in order to generate sales by associating particular ideas with products, and attributing specific characteristics to the consumers of those products, the idea of brand culture has spread into other contexts. This has now become one of the most frequent contexts in which we encounter the word 'culture'. The incorporation of the idea of culture into marketing is significant, because it links 'way of life' (which, as we noted earlier, is one of the basic meanings of culture) with consumerism. The term 'brand culture' makes a connection between buying products ('brands') and a group's way of life ('culture'). Often products are marketed in ways that carefully target aspects of a society's culture, by associating products with traditional values or customs. But on the other hand, marketing products by associating them with an image of how to live happy, meaningful lives – which lies at the heart of establishing a 'culture' for a brand or product – also influences the wider culture of the society being targeted. For example, a trendy, stylish lifestyle suggested by the brand culture of particular designer jeans encourages sales among those who find the idea appealing. But it also generates a sense of the value and desirability of that particular lifestyle within the wider culture of that society. It feeds ideas into that culture which may be new and often challenging to traditional customs and values.

When products are promoted across geographical boundaries, the lifestyles associated with those products are also promoted across boundaries. One consequence of this is that widely differing cultures begin to desire similar, consumer lifestyles. Local ways of life are often affected by this. A global lifestyle and culture, rather than a local culture, begins to emerge. There are many ways to view this phenomenon, which is an aspect of what is termed globalization. While it may be regarded positively as a way to promote cross-cultural commerce and communication, critics (for instance in the anti-globalization movement) oppose its effect on local culture. They often argue that it underpins a form of cultural and economic imperialism, and gives advantages to more prosperous countries and their cultures.

> Find out more about globalization and modern imperialism. Discover how these ideas are viewed – and often opposed – around the world.

Contemporary thinking about culture is also often focused on another aspect of commercial activity. This is the area of building a corporate culture and corporate identity within an organization (such as a business, financial, educational or other institution). The focus here is on describing the beliefs, goals and purposes that the organization values. The concept of 'culture' is used in this context to represent the idea that subscribing to the organization's values and aspirations is a 'way of life', and not merely an expression of desirable aims or outcomes. Similarly, managers often tell their employees to think of the business as a 'family' – with all the loyalty that this term carries with it.

In order to demonstrate and represent its culture to those who work within it and to its potential clients, the organization usually uses carefully selected symbols and images. This process of representation 'tells the story' of the organization in ways similar to those we have discussed throughout this book. In building the identity of a corporation or other organization, symbols, images and narratives are used to convey ideas (such as professionalism or excellence) by linking the ideas which they evoke with the organization. Symbols suggest meanings by 'standing for' other ideas. Careful use of symbols suggests that the organization has the values that the symbol refers to. Images are verbal or visual descriptions that create pictures in people's minds. The use of images links these mental pictures with ideas, feelings or experiences. Using them in the context of corporate culture influences how people feel about the organization or corporation.

The expressions of meaning linked with corporate culture are becoming, many would argue, increasingly significant in the way that people experience their lives. They are indeed some of the most visible examples of group identity, culture and understanding.

EXERCISE 4.14

1. Views differ regarding the value of these kinds of culture. Critics often suggest that corporate culture is a form of control, forcing people in an organization to subscribe to ideas that its leaders have chosen for them. Supporters, on the other hand, argue that it provides a supportive, empowering environment for work and that it contributes greatly to success by showing consumers what kind of organization and product they are encountering. What do you think?

2. Find out more about corporate culture. Look for other terms that use 'culture' or 'cultural' in the context of business and corporations. Try to discover what they mean, Think about the wide variety of ways in which the concept of 'culture' is currently being used.

THREE
WRITING BACK: SELF AND CULTURE

Just as writing about the culture of other people can be positive or hostile, so too can be the representation of one's own cultural background. The final extract in this chapter is drawn from a text that turns the light of inquiry onto the cultural contexts of the author. In it, we listen to the thoughts of the narrator in Phaswane Mpe's novel *Welcome to our Hillbrow*. He addresses a character named Refentše and speaks (in most of the text) to him. He presents Refentše's life as if it were a story in which he is a character. Refentše is already dead, having committed suicide. The narrator seems to encourage Refentše to scrutinize his own behaviour – and that of those he lived amongst – from a distance. In this extract the narrator is talking to Refentše about a short story he wrote once. In his life, Refentše loved Lerato, whom he called the Bone of his Heart, although he had a brief affair with Bohlale, and Lerato had an affair with Sammy. He was born in a village named Tiragalong. The narrator often addresses his thoughts to the village community as if it were a person itself.

Welcome to our Hillbrow
Phaswane Mpe

You, Refentše, had written the story of your fictitious scarecrow heroine in an attempt to grapple with these profound questions of euphemism, xenophobia, prejudice, and Aids, to which Tiragalong pretended to have answers. Your story was in English, since unlike the naïve and hopeful woman of your fiction, you knew the limitations of writing in Sepedi. But, like your heroine, you wrote your story in order to find sanctuary in the worlds of fiction that are never quite what we label them. You wrote in order to steady yourself against grief and prejudice, against the painful and complex realities of humanness.

Considering these grave questions from so many different perspectives made you think about your own transgression with

Bohlale ... You had learnt that you were as vulnerable as the drunks and womanizers that you used to criticize for their carelessness; as vulnerable as the prostitutes populating Quartz and other streets, pasted against the walls of the concrete towers of Hillbrow.

For all those reasons you would have understood, had you had time enough to reflect on things, how and why Lerato and Sammy had come to do what they did. Perhaps then, you would not have chosen to leave the face of this Earth so spectacularly. Your mother's death would not have followed yours. Nor would the Bone of your Heart have swallowed those numerous, lethal tablets that she decided to swallow after one of your enemies had threatened to inform her mother of her own contribution towards your suicide.

The enemy knew the secret, because guilty conscience had so tormented Sammy that he lost his reason. In his insanity, he had told a fragmented version of the tale of his and Lerato's betrayal of your love and trust. Tiragalong had conveniently pieced the fragments together to build up a story. It was a story with a smooth narrative current, stripped of all rough edges, devoid of any gaps that might suggest good intentions on either one's part. Some said such behaviour was only to be expected of a Johannesburg woman. Others said who could expect any better from a Lekwerekwere*. Most agreed that it was short-sighted of you to believe that any woman encountered in the city would be a good partner.

*Lekwerekwere: insulting term for a foreigner

Euphemism. Xenophobia. Prejudice. Aids. You wrote your story to think through all these issues, child of Tiragalong and Hillbrow. But your story was neither long nor sophisticated enough. You realized when it was published that it would never be sufficient. You became keenly aware that no matter what stories you might write, none of them would ever be sufficient to answer such imponderables. For to have these answers was to know the secrets of life itself. There would always be another story of love, betrayal, friendship, joy and pain to add to your narrative granary*. There would always be the need to revise, reinforce, contradict. For every new personal experience adds to our knowledge of life and living, death and dying. Every act of listening, seeing, smelling, feeling, tasting is a reconfiguring of the story of our lives.

*granary: a place where grain is stored: here, the word is used metaphorically, to suggest a storehouse for stories

... If you were still alive now, Refentše child of Hillbrow and Tiragalong, if you were still alive, all of this that you have heard seen heard about felt smelt believed disbelieved shirked embraced brewing in your consciousness would still find chilling haunting echoes in the simple words ...

Welcome to our Hillbrow ...

Adapted from: Mpe, 2001: 59–62

This novel reflects issues that relate integrally to what we have been discussing. In it, Mpe writes about the self (as represented in the figures of the narrator and Refentše) and the shifting viewpoints of that self. The novel recounts, as many novels do, the growth of an individual, from youth to a sense of adulthood – the format of the *Bildungsroman* that we discussed in Chapter Two. Yet, woven into this representation is culture. Quite clearly, deliberately and self-consciously, Refentše's life is described in relation to the many cultures of which he has been a part. The refrain the narrator uses is 'Welcome to our Hillbrow', an image (in the book) of the hybrid, mixed cultural influences that have shaped Refentše's life. He shows how the parts of the world in which he and his friends have lived all form part of the same map. Their boundaries – both geographical and emotional – blur; they cannot remain separate from one another.

But at the heart of how he understands this is a vision of how cultures define themselves on the basis of difference, rejection and often hostility. Refentše has to confront his own tendencies to think derogatorily about others, gaining insight into his own prejudices. Likewise, he becomes aware of the xenophobia (fear and dislike of foreigners) that he perceives as part and parcel of daily life in society, both in South Africa and England. This, he sees, is a form of cultural definition: those who are foreign or Other become significant as scapegoats*. Deeply troubling aspects of life (such as the Aids pandemic, or unemployment) are made understandable by attributing responsibility for them to foreigners. Migrants from other countries are judged with great hostility, blamed for spreading disease and for taking jobs from locals.

* scapegoats: those who are blamed for negative situations that they have not, in fact, caused

Tragedies and regret can be spoken about, he sees, by making sense of them according to generalizations, prejudices and stereotypes. Likewise, not talking about certain things is also a strategy for dealing with them. Euphemism (speaking about troubling things by using different, less upsetting terms) is something he places alongside fear and discrimination. Combined with rumour and gossip, it is central to society's reaction to the challenges he is writing about. He suggests that it is just as significant as hostility and discrimination. All are significant aspects of how his society responds to threatening situations.

EXERCISE 4.15

Read the passage from *Welcome to our Hillbrow* again. Consider how the speaker talks about Refentše's life; notice how he talks about the issues we have mentioned above.

1. Explain what you think the speaker means when he says, 'You wrote in order to steady yourself against grief and prejudice, against the painful and complex realities of humanness'.
2. What do you think the speaker means when he says that 'Tiragalong had conveniently pieced the fragments together to build up a story. It was a story with a smooth narrative current, stripped of all rough edges, devoid of any gaps that might suggest good intentions on either one's part'?
3. What do you think about the speaker's way of looking at his friend's life? Does it effectively show what he feels and what matters to him?
4. What do cultures avoid talking about?
5. Who does society generally blame for bad things that happen or problems that seem almost impossible to solve?

Putting pen to paper: writing your ideas

We end this book's journey through ideas about writing with practical advice about how to respond, in your own writing, to texts. In each chapter you will have encountered many questions, and will hopefully have answered some of them, whether simply in your head, or by actually writing down your ideas. Our purpose for including these questions is to allow you many opportunities to express your own opinions about what you read. One of the joys of studying literature lies, we believe, in the activity of saying what you think about the texts you are reading. The questions are all designed to guide you towards perspectives that offer new angles from which to look at texts. Each of the previous chapters also closes with advice about how to experiment with different forms of writing, such as autobiography, descriptive writing and argumentative writing.

In this, they provide a first step for writing, since they ask you to formulate ideas and opinions. In any writing, it is important to identify and decide on the main points you wish to make, before you begin to write. A useful way in which to think about these ideas is to see them as claims. When we claim something, we say that it is true, even though other people might not think so, and even though we will have to show why we think it is true. To claim something about a text you read is to say that you believe what you are saying is correct, even if others might disagree with you. However, because it might not be immediately clear why you think it is correct, and because others might have different views, you need to show why you are saying it. You need to support what you say.

The claims you make about a text are the main ideas you want to convey. You give your main ideas support by including other ideas that explain, illustrate or expand on the main ideas. These supporting ideas usually include close reference to the text you are writing about. They might also refer to other texts, including those that other people have written about the text. All the supporting ideas show why you think what you think.

In the process of deciding what supporting ideas to include, it is useful to remind yourself why you are making the claims you are making. Think about your reasons for holding the opinions you do; tell yourself why you believe your main points to be correct. When we make statements about things we are far more convincing, and confident, when we are clear in our own minds about why we are making them! Spend time, as you write, thinking about why you are writing and why you want to say what you are saying.

In formal study, such as at university, the essay is a very important means of expressing what you think. There are many ways in which to write about methods for producing good essays. One of the most important points to note is that an essay emerges from a process. It is not simply created in a flash, but is part of a process of reading, reflection, planning, and writing. It is worth remembering that the word 'essay' has roots in the concept of 'attempting'. For our purposes this is useful because it focuses us on an important characteristic of essay writing: that it is an attempt to think about and express ideas. Essays are spaces in which to try out ideas, and to try to convince other people that you have ideas they should listen to.

In the context of English studies, there are particular aspects of essay writing that are useful to recall. Writing is produced for many different purposes in various contexts (from SMS's to reports, love letters to affidavits). How you write depends on your purpose. In other subjects and disciplines, you may encounter further requirements, such as the use of subheadings, specific forms for case references, and other conventions. In English studies, subheadings are not usually required and are in fact often discouraged.

In writing about literary texts, these are some of the most important conventions. Most of them apply to other forms of writing too:

1. **When we write about literature, we generally use the present tense to refer to the events and characters in texts**. Although we talk about the events we encounter in daily life in the past tense, since we are reporting experiences, in literary essays we do not. The events described in books do not occur in the same way that events happen in real life: they are imagined. A text is, in a sense, an event with no particular time: it 'occurs' when you read it. If we used the past tense when writing about texts, it would imply that that what we say was once accurate but is no longer. (Even when fiction is written about historical characters and events, these events are presented in an imagined way. The text is not a report or history, but a fictional representation of events. We see things through the words and creative forms of a literary text.)

2. **The style of your writing needs to be fairly formal**. Writing and speaking skills are different. When we discuss books with friends and family, we use a style that is often chatty and frequently full of emotion. Many books inspire strong feelings, whether positive or negative. But there is a difference between this way of talking about texts and the style expected in essays, which needs to be objective, respectful and well-reasoned. In essays, avoid expressing opinions that can only be supported by appealing to emotions. Rather support what you say more objectively by pointing to ideas, rather than personal feelings of liking or loathing.

3. **When you write, use references to what you are discussing carefully**. There are many sets of conventions for quoting and referencing. If you are studying formally, follow the conventions prescribed by your lecturers. These are important since they allow you to write with greater ease and confidence. Quoting from texts in a clear and acceptable fashion makes your writing more effective since it shows that you have selected material to support your points diligently, and with attention to detail. Equally, choosing what to quote is important. Focus on the important aspects of any passage you wish to use, and try to focus your reader's attention on what is important in the passage. To be effective in an essay, the purpose of the quotation or reference needs to be evident to the reader. As you prepare your essay, think carefully about which quotations are relevant to your purpose, and which are not. Good persuasive or argumentative writing is not cluttered with irrelevant ideas.

   We all learn from other people, and draw on others' ideas and words when we write academically. But failure to include references for your quotations is misleading for the reader. It becomes difficult to tell what you think and what others think. When you copy the exact words and form that someone else has used to express an idea directly into your own essay, without showing that you are quoting them, you let your reader think that you made them up. In effect, you are 'stealing' those words from someone else. This is known as *plagiarism* and is not accepted when essays are assessed.

4. **Use language with care**. It is important to write as correctly as possible. Often, people feel more confident about expressing their ideas when they speak, rather than when they write, because they can use gestures and emphasis to help convey their meaning. When it comes to writing, we often write as if we were speaking. This has advantages, since it sometimes makes what we write seem more sincere, but it also has disadvantages because we neglect important grammar conventions! In an essay, ensure that you write clear, grammatically correct sentences. Check your work for errors. Avoid sentences that run on in a disjointed fashion and cover too many ideas. If you feel that you need to improve your language skills, seek help from a trustworthy source. Also, read as much as you can, since this is one of the best ways to build vocabulary, language, and writing skills.

5. **Be aware of yourself as a writer**. Quite simply, think about what you do when you write. A good way to develop your sense of what you are doing well and what you need to improve, is by keeping a writer's journal and a checklist. Use these as spaces in which to practice or develop your skills. Try things out in your journal and, in your checklist, keep a record of those aspects of your own writing that you need to pay attention to. Make a list of your own writing strengths and weaknesses. These might be areas you have identified in your own work, or they may be things that teachers and lecturers have told you about your writing. For example, if you misspell certain words, use the wrong pronouns, or forget to break up what you say into sentences of sensible length, record this in your checklist. Each time you write, check your work against it. Each time you receive feedback from lecturers, include new information in your checklist. In this way, you will be able to build up a profile of your own writing performance.

Ending our journey: Conclusion

As we have seen, people approach language and texts from many perspectives. On the basis of those perspectives and interests, they ask different questions about what they read. The four stages of our journey in this book have marked four such areas of interest in literary studies. We began by investigating 'the self' and progressed through a study of characterization to explore representations of gender and culture. These areas of interest relate to the stories we tell and the language we use in representation.

The stories we tell about who we are and who other people are, and the language in which those stories are formulated, provide a useful base for thinking about the various kinds of texts we read. We hope that the form in which we have discussed these issues here will make them accessible and interesting, and that they will help you as you explore the many ways we think and write about ourselves and about others.

Copyright acknowledgements

Press, 2005; pp. 78–9 Extract from *The Loneliness of the Long-Distance Runner* by Alan Sillitoe, Pearson Education; pp. 80–1 Extract from *Harry Potter and the Philosopher's Stone*: Copyright © J. K. Rowling 1997; pp. 82–3, 110 Extracts from *Steering the Craft: Exercises and Discussions on Story Writing for the Lone Navigator or the Mutinous Crew* by Ursula K. Le Guin, © 1998, published by the Eighth Mountain Press, Portland, Oregon 1998, Reprinted by permission of the author and publisher; pp. 86–7 'A Letter to a Son' by Charles Mungoshi, Mambo Press; pp. 91–101 'The Suit' by Can Themba, by permission of Jonathan Ball; p. 118 Dictionary entry for 'stereotype': Dictionary definitions taken from the *Oxford Advanced Learner's Dictionary*, 7th Edition © Oxford University Press, 2005; pp. 122–3 Speech from *The Book of Guys* by Garrison Keillor: Faber & Faber; p. 124 Dictionary entry for 'machismo': Dictionary definitions taken from the *Oxford Advanced Learner's Dictionary*, 7th Edition © Oxford University Press, 2005; pp. 125–7 Extract from *The Kite Runner* by Khaled Hosseini; Copyright © 2003, Used by permission of Doubleday, a division of Random House, Inc; p. 129 Dictionary entry for 'generalization': Dictionary definitions taken from the *Oxford Advanced Learner's Dictionary*, 7th Edition © Oxford University Press, 2005; pp. 137–8 'Because we're women' by Joyce Stevens: Used by permission of author; pp. 143–150 'Guidelines for non-sexist use of language' by Virginia Warren: Used by permission of author, APA (online); p. 155 Extracts from *A Room of One's Own* by Virgina Woolf; pp. 158–165 'The Toilet' by Gcina Mhlope, Reproduced by permission of the author; p. 171 Dictionary entry for 'culture': Dictionary definitions taken from the *Oxford Advanced Learner's Dictionary*, 7th Edition © Oxford University Press, 2005; p. 174 'Mowbray Kaap' by Freshlyground: Sony; p. 176 Extract from *Culture is Ordinary* by Raymond Williams, Verso; pp. 177–8 'Understanding culture through ordinary life' by Joanna Mikulski (online); pp. 179–180 Extract from *The City of Despina* by Italo Calvino: Harcourt, USA; pp. 188–190 Extracts from *A Distant Shore,* by permission of A P Watt Ltd on behalf of Caryl Phillips (author); pp. 192–3 'Rural women' by Chris Mann; pp. 195–7 Extract from *The Sparrow* by Maria Doria Russell: Random House Group; pp. 199–200 'What were they like?' by Denise Levertov: Originally published by W

W Norton, Reproduced by permission of Pollinger Limited and the proprietor; pp. 202–204 *Culture and Imperialism* by Edward Said: *Zmag* (online); p. 205 Extract from *Woza Africa: Music goes to War*: International Committee of the Red Cross; pp. 209–211 Extract from *Welcome to our Hillbrow* by Phaswane Mpe: University of Kwazulu-Natal Press.

References

Achebe, Chinua. 1958. *Things Fall Apart*, p. 150. London: Heinemann

Adey, David et al. 1986. *Companion to South African Literature*. p. 195. Johannesburg: Ad Donker Publishers

Aiken, Lewis R. 1999. *Human Differences*. pp. 1–2. New Jersey: Lawrence Erlbaum Associates

Austen, Jane. 1990. *Pride and Prejudice*. pp. 7–8. Oxford: Oxford University Press (World's Classics Series)

Bâ, Mariama. 1989. *So Long a Letter*. pp. 55–56. Oxford: Heinemann African Writers Series

Carroll, Lewis. 1998. *Alice's Adventures in Wonderland,* pp. 40–41. Oxford: Oxford University Press

Calvino, Italo. 1979. *Invisible Cities*. pp. 17–18. London: Pan Books

Cole, Estelle in Sian, G. (ed). 1994. *Gender, Sex and Sexuality*. p. 13. London: Taylor and Francis

Cummings, E. E. 1964. *73 poems*. London: Faber and Faber

Dangarembga, Tsitsi. 2001. *Nervous Conditions*. p. 1. Oxfordshire, UK: Ayebia Publishing

Dickens, Charles. 1993. *Great Expectations*. p. 2. Oxford: Heinemann (New Windmill Classics Series)

Eliot, George. 2001. *Middlemarch*. Harmondsworth: Penguin

Fitzgerald, F. Scott. 1974. *The Great Gatsby*. pp. 12–13. Harmondsworth: Penguin

Freshlyground, 2006. 'Mowbray Kaap' from *Nomvula*. South Africa: Freeground Records/Sony ATV

Heilbrun, Carolyn G. 1989. *Writing a Woman's Life*. New York: W. W. Norton & Company

Hofman, Baruch. 1985. *Character in Literature*. pp. 59–60. Ithaca and London: Cornell University Press

Hopkins, Gerard Manley. 1956. 'The Windhover' in *The Penguin Book of English Verse*. Harmondsworth: Penguin

Hosseini, Khaled. 2003. *The Kite Runner*. pp. 33–37. New York: Doubleday

Kafka, Franz. 1981. *The Metamorphosis*. New York: Bantam

Keillor, Garrison. 1993. *The Book of Guys*. pp. 12–13. New York: Penguin Books

Kimmel, Michael S. 2000. *The Gendered Society*. pp. 1–2. New York: Oxford University Press

Le Guin, Ursula K. 1998. *Steering the Craft: Exercises and Discussions on Story Writing for the Lone Navigator or the Mutinous Crew*. pp. 61–12 and p. 83. Portland, Oregon: Eighth Mountain Press

Levin, Adam. 2005. *Aidsafari*. Zebra: Cape Town

Mandela, Nelson. 1994. *Long Walk to Freedom*, pp. 317–322. Boston: Little, Brown

Mann, Chris. 1996. *South Africans: A Set of Portrait Poems*. p. 46. Pietermaritzburg: University of Natal Press

Mhlophe, Gcina, 'Men are always Women's Children' in Daymond, M. J., 'Gender and "History": 1980s South African Women's Stories in English' 191–213. *Ariel*, January 1996

Mhlophe, Gcina. 2002. *Love Child*. pp. vii–viii, pp. 1–8 and pp. 9–10. Pietermaritzburg: University of KwaZulu-Natal Press

Moffett, Helen and Mphahlele, Es'kia (eds). 2002. *Seasons Come to Pass: A Poetry Anthology for Southern African Students*. Oxford: Oxford University Press

Moggach, Deborah in Boylan, Clare (ed.). 1993. *The Agony and the Ego: the art and strategy of fiction writing explored*. London: Penguin

Morgan, Jonathan and the Bambanani Women's Group. 2005. *Long Life: Positive HIV Stories*. Cape Town: Spinifex Press and Double Storey (Juta)

Mpe, Phaswane. 2002. *Welcome to our Hillbrow*. pp. 59–62. Durban: University of KwaZulu-Natal Press

Nuttall, Sarah and Michael, Cheryl-Ann. 2000. *Senses of Culture*. p. 43 and pp. 298–299. Oxford: Oxford University Press

Omotoso, Kole, for the International Committee of the Red Cross. 1997. *Woza Africa: Music Goes to War*. pp. 26–27 and p. 82. Johannesburg: Jonathan Ball

Oosthuizen, Anne. (Ed.) 1987. *Sometimes When It Rains*. pp. 1–7. London: Pandora

Phillips, Caryl. 2004. *A Distant Shore*. p. 3 and pp. 12–13. London: Vintage

Roberts, Phil. 2000. *How Poetry Works*. p. 107. London: Penguin

Rowling, J. K. 1997. *Harry Potter and the Philosopher's Stone*. p.

7. London: Bloomsbury

Russell, Mary Doria. 1996. *The Sparrow.* pp. 283–285. London: Black Swan

Sillitoe, Alan. 1959. *The Loneliness of the Long-Distance Runner.* pp. 160–161. London: Longman Heritage of Literature Series

Smith, Roger. 'Self-Reflection and the Self' in Roy Porter (ed.) 1997. *Rewriting the Self: Histories from the Renaissance to the Present.* p. 49. London and New York: Routledge

START: Strategies for Academic Reading and Thinking. 1996. p. 25. Shuter & Shooter. Pietermaritzburg

Stevens, Joyce in Meyer, Sonia. *Herstoria*, Summer 1996, Vol. 2 No. 3

Themba, Can in Jean Marquard (ed). 1978. *A Century of South African Short Stories.* pp. 228–236. Cape Town and Johannesburg: Ad Donker

Williams, Raymond. 1989. *Resources of Hope: Culture, Democracy, Socialism.* p. 4. London: Verso

Woolf, Virginia. 1929. *A Room of One's Own.* p. 137. London: Harcourt Brace & Company

Woolf, Virginia. 2005. *Selected Works of Virginia Woolf.* p. 613. Ware: Wordsworth Editions

Internet references

APA Online: 'Guidelines for Non-Sexist Use of Language'. http://www.apa.udel.edu/apa/publications/texts/nonsexist.htl (21 April 2006)

Emory University English Department. 'Tsitsi Darangarembga'. http://www.english.emory.edu/Bahri/Dangar.html (21 April 2006)

The Free Library. 'A Treatise on Government'. http://aristotle.thefreelibrary.com/A-Treatise-on-Government (21 April 2006)

Historic Figures. 'Charles Dickens'. http://www.bbc.co.uk/history/historic_figures/dickens_charles.shtml (3 March 2006)

Mikulski in *The Observer* newspaper. http://www.nd.edu/~observer/09262000/Viewpoint/2.html (21 April 2006)

Jagne, Siga Fatima, and Parekh, Pushpa Naidu. 'Mariama Bâ 1929–1981' on *Pegasos*. http://www.kirjasto.sci.fi/mba.htm (16 March 2006)

Edward Said in *ZMag*. Extract from 'Culture and Imperialism'. http://www.zmag.org/zmag/articles/barsaid.htm (23 April 2006)

Index

A

Achebe, Chinua 187
actions 111
address, forms of 145, 152–153
'Address to the National Federation of
   Associations Convention' 122–123
A Distant Shore 188
adjectives 108–111
adverbs 108–111
African philosophy 205
Age of Reason, *see* Enlightenment period
Agha 127
Aidsafari 24–27
Aids pandemic 24–28, 211
'A Letter to a Son' 86–87
Alice's Adventures in Wonderland 17–18
alien encounters 194–198
alliteration 9
anomaly 196
anticipation 66
anti-climax 64
anti-globalization movement 207
ardent 135
argot 101
argument 90
argumentative writing 213
Aristotle 142
Arnold, Matthew 172
A Room of One's Own 154–156
arrogant 64
assessment 197
assumptions 119, 129
Austen, Jane 77–78, 182
autobiographical account 25–26
autobiographical representation 10–11
autobiographical writing 11, 158
autobiography 11, 213

B

Bâ, Mariama 65–68, 130
Bambanani Women's Group, Cape Town
   27–28
'Because we're women' 137–138
behaviour 106
   codes of 174

berating 123
Bildungsroman (novel of development) 74, 211
bipedal 196
blacking factory 62
brand culture 206
branding 206–208
Brontë, Charlotte 88
Byatt, A. S. 57–58

C

cadaverous 61
callousness 71
Calvino, Italo 179–180
Carroll, Lewis 17–18
caste system 67
Catcher in the Rye 74, 88
cathartic 99
change 73–74
character 104
   definition 58–60
   and events (plot) 106
characterization 89
characterized 67
Chartres 197
children's story 151
chrysalis 18
circulation, general 77
clues
   characters 104–105
   context and setting 103
   plot 102–103
coercion 135
collaborative form 27
colonialism 201, 202
common nouns 14
compassion 93
composite 155
condescension 61, 66
conflict 81
connotation 120
Conrad, Joseph 84
consciousness 4
consequence 71
consequent 135
contemptuous expression 18